Sexuality in adolescence

Dealing with sexuality is a crucial part of the development process of adolescence in which young people struggle to form a satisfying sense of their own identity. In *Sexuality in Adolescence* Susan Moore and Doreen Rosenthal review current work on adolescent sexual development, including data from their own studies of sexual risk-taking, and the social contexts in which young people form their sexual beliefs.

The book provides an extensive and up-to-date picture of adolescent sexuality from an international perspective. It covers such issues as the influence of family, media and other institutions on sexual behaviour, male and female constructions of sexuality, and the role of puberty in development. In addition, the authors discuss teenage pregnancy and abortion, gay and lesbian adolescence, and the behaviour of young people as sexual adventurers, exploiters and victims.

Sexuality in Adolescence provides a thorough and comprehensive text for academics and students in psychology, sociology, youth work and health education. Parents, teachers and all those who work with young people will find this book essential to understanding what adolescents are currently thinking and doing about sex, and how their values and beliefs have been shaped.

Susan Moore is Senior Lecturer in the Faculty of Education at Monash University, Australia. **Doreen Rosenthal** is Professor and Director of the Centre for the Study of Sexually Transmissible Diseases at La Trobe University, Australia.

Adolescence and Society
Series editor: John C. Coleman
The Trust for the Study of Adolescence

The general aim of the series is to make accessible to a wide readership the growing evidence relating to adolescent development. Much of this material is published in relatively inaccessible professional journals, and the goals of the books in this series will be to summarise, review and place in context current work in the field so as to interest and engage both an undergraduate and a professional audience.

The intention of the authors is to raise the profile of adolescent studies among professionals and in institutes of higher education. By publishing relatively short, readable books on interesting topics to do with youth and society, the series will make people more aware of the relevance of the subject of adolescence to a wide range of social concerns.

The books will not put forward any one theoretical viewpoint. The authors will outline the most prominent theories in the field and will include a balanced and critical assessment of each of these. Whilst some of the books may have a clinical or applied slant, the majority will concentrate on normal development.

The readership will rest primarily in two major areas: the undergraduate market, particularly in the fields of psychology, sociology and education; and the professional training market, with particular emphasis on social work, clinical and educational psychology, counselling, youth work, nursing and teacher training.

Sexuality in adolescence

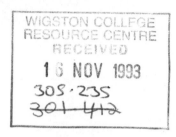
Susan Moore and Doreen Rosenthal

Routledge

London and New York

First published in 1993
by Routledge
11 New Fetter Lane, London EC4P 4EE

Simultaneously published in the USA and Canada
by Routledge
29 West 35th Street, New York, NY 10001

Typeset in Times by
LaserScript Limited, Mitcham, Surrey
Printed and bound in Great Britain by
TJ Press (Padstow) Ltd, Padstow, Cornwall

British Library Cataloguing in Publication Data

A catalogue record for this book is available from the British Library.

Library of Congress Cataloging in Publication Data

Moore, Susan M., 1945–
 Sexuality in adolescence/Susan M. Moore and Doreen A. Rosenthal.
 p. cm. – (Adolescence and society.)
 Includes bibliographical references and index.
 1. Youth–Australia–Sexual behavior. 2. Youth–Australia–Attitudes.
 3. Risk-taking (Psychology) in adolescence–Australia.
 I. Rosenthal, Doreen A., 1938– . II. Title. III. Series.
 HQ27.M635
 306.7′0853—dc20   93–9869
                                                       CIP

ISBN 0–415–07527–0 (hbk)
ISBN 0–415–07528–9 (pbk)

To Mark, Simon, and Joanna, Nic and Kristin – adolescents past, and Rebecca – adolescent present.

Contents

Acknowledgements

We would like to thank those who helped and encouraged us in writing this book. John Coleman offered us the opportunity to collect our thoughts about adolescent sexuality and consolidate them in the pages that follow. We are particularly grateful to Shirley Feldman for her critical and thoughtful reading of an earlier draft, and to Simone Buzwell, research assistant extraordinaire. Mark Goggin brought his wisdom and experience to the task of writing the chapter on gay and lesbian youth, which we think provides important insights about adolescent sexuality. Various individuals have made practical contributions to our own research into adolescent sexuality. To these people, including our academic colleagues, research assistants, and students, many thanks. The major funding for this research was provided by the Commonwealth AIDS Research Grants Committee, Australia, and we are grateful for this support.

Special thanks go to those adolescents who have talked to us and whose experiences enrich the text and have provided a framework for this book.

Finally, to our husbands, Ian and David, whose support and nurturance has made our task considerably easier, our thanks.

Introduction

WHY STUDY ADOLESCENT SEXUALITY?

It is rare to find an adult in today's society who has no questions, concerns, or conflicts about the role of sex in his or her life. How do I find the right partner? Have I chosen correctly? Are my sex drives normal? Am I sexually fulfilled? What importance do I place on monogamy? Am I at risk of sexually transmissible disease? What should I tell my children about sex? Have I struck the right balance between sexuality and other parts of my life?

Sexuality is a complex and confusing aspect of life and the way we resolve needs, desires, values, and social expectations in this area has the potential to lead to outcomes ranging from great personal satisfaction to considerable conflict and pain. Sexual questions, conflicts, and crises may begin prior to adolescence and may certainly continue after this phase of life, but there is no doubt that, for most people, adolescence is a 'critical period' in the upsurge of sexual drives, the development of sexual values, and the initiation of sexual behaviours. The advent of puberty, the power of peer group expectations, and the communication of mixed messages about sex from the adult generation make dealing with sexuality a difficult but exciting challenge for adolescents.

Parents, teachers, and all those who work or plan to work with young people in a helping or mentor role need to be aware of what is happening *now* in the adolescent generation with respect to sexual values and behaviours. We want to influence positively young people's sexuality, helping them to maximise adult sexual adjustment and life satisfaction. In this way they can find their personal solution to the question of what is the appropriate contribution of sex to the enhancement of intimate relationships. From a cautionary point of view, we also want to ensure that young people do not act in ways that curtail life's possibilities. Adolescents need the information, skills, commitment to the future and, sometimes, protection which will enable them to avoid unwanted pregnancies and sexually transmissible diseases, especially the life-threatening disease of AIDS. We need to encourage healthy and adaptive attitudes to relationships between young people. For example, the perpetration or perception of sex as an aggressive, exploitative act is an extremely undesirable outcome, from both a community and a personal point of view, and one which may be amenable to influence through work with young people and understanding of their needs.

Education about sexual values and sexual health is likely to be most effective if educators take into account the current beliefs and practices of their target audience. Sex education which stresses fear-arousing messages, punitive outcomes of experimentation, or value stances considered 'out-of-date' will fail to reach those most needing intervention, as some of the later chapters in this book will show. For example, as an AIDS prevention strategy, preaching celibacy to the already sexually active has little effect. At the other extreme, the advertising of condoms in a manner suggesting that all interesting or socially successful adolescents have multiple partners can alienate those who have made a serious commitment to a relationship in the belief (sometimes mistaken) that the relationship is safe with respect to transmission of the AIDS virus. We need to know about the different sexual subcultures of youth in order to increase our understanding of the 'sexual adolescent'. With this information, we can design appropriate sex education and informal interventions to influence values and behaviours. We can learn how better to communicate with our adolescent children about this topic. And, not the least important, we can increase our store of knowledge about this aspect of human behaviour which is not only fascinating to social scientists but to everyone.

THE IMPORTANCE OF SEXUALITY FOR ADOLESCENTS

All theories of adolescent development give sexuality a central place in negotiating the transition from child to adult. The nascent sexual urges which emerge at puberty must be blended with other aspects of teenagers' lives and channelled adaptively. It is especially important that the adolescent be able to integrate his or her sexual feelings, needs, and desires into a coherent and positive self identity, which contains, as one aspect, a sexual self. Unlike many of the activities we engage in, expression of our sexuality (for the most part) involves a relationship, no matter how limited or fleeting, with another individual. Sexual expression allows, indeed requires, a unique exposure of the self to another, an exposure which brings with it the potential for both positive and negative consequences. On the one hand there is the possibility of validating one's sense of self-worth and achieving a deeply satisfying intimate relationship. On the other hand, wrong choices can lead to destructive outcomes, to feelings of anxiety and guilt, and to a sense of unworthiness. For adolescents who are in the process of forging a satisfying and satisfactory sense of their own identity and their place in the world, dealing with these issues is a crucial part of their development.

As we shall see the task is a complex one. If we are to understand the significance of sexuality during adolescence, we need to consider how it fits into the biological, psychological, and social aspects of adolescent development. At the biological level, sexuality is the central feature, marked by the onset of puberty which signals maturation of the reproductive organs, the possibility of becoming a parent, and an increasing sex drive. With puberty, changes at the psychological level have to do with readiness for taking on adult roles, including sex and procreation. There is a shift from a primary orientation to one's family to a reliance on peers for providing guidelines for attitudes and behaviour, as well as a clarification of goals and the development of interpersonal skills and attitudes. So the adolescent learns to locate himself or herself within a network of like-minded and similar others. All of this occurs within a context of expanded cognitive skills which allow the adolescent to evaluate alternative points of view, and to recognise that many points of view, including their own, may have merit.

At a broader level, social forces shape adolescents' sexuality by establishing and re-establishing values and norms relating to sexuality, masculinity, and femininity. These expectations about 'proper', acceptable behaviour will vary as a function of many factors, including gender, culture, social class, and education. We shall deal with some of these throughout the course of this book, but one overarching influence that we need to consider is the impact of historical change in societal attitudes towards sexuality. As we shall see, twentieth-century attitudes to sexuality have undergone several swings from conservative to liberal, with consequent changes in what are considered to be acceptable outcomes for adolescent sexuality.

Griffin (1992) points to recent feminist scholarship which brings into question academic concerns over teenagers' sexual beliefs and practices. The focus on biology and heterosexuality in mainstream literature has meant that the social construction of sexuality has been largely ignored and the reality of gay and lesbian youth denied. The 'problematic' nature of adolescent sexuality is often stressed, as is its association with drug and alcohol abuse, delinquent behaviour, and other factors such as irresponsibility, poor school performance or unemployment (Brooks-Gunn and Furstenberg 1989; Ensminger 1987; Jessor and Jessor 1977). But adolescent sexuality need not be problematic. Sexual activity that is non-exploitative and safe, from the point of view of mental and physical health, may not be considered as problem behaviour, depending on one's value stance. Indeed, adolescent sexual activity can and does make a positive contribution to teenage development through increased independence, social competence, and self-esteem (Ensminger 1987). This is not to say that all teenage sexual behaviour is adaptive, healthy and moral. Clearly sexual activity can occur too early and in a context that is inappropriate. The view taken in this book is that sexuality is a normative event in adolescent development with the potential for both positive and negative consequences.

In addressing issues of adolescent sexuality, the focus has usually been on documenting sexual behaviours, usually within a biological framework. How many teenagers are sexually active? What are they doing? Are they using contraception? What is the incidence of teenage pregnancy? These are important questions and are addressed in the early chapters of this book. There is, however, an increasing awareness, resulting from concerns about HIV/AIDS and other sexually transmissible diseases, that it is not sufficient simply to describe adolescent sexual behaviour, particularly if we want to contain the spread of these diseases into this potentially 'at-risk' population. The sources of that behaviour need to be established since biological approaches to sexuality have only limited explanatory power. They do not fit with observed gender, ethnic and class differences in behaviours and beliefs. These differences point us to the need to explore the meaning of adolescents' sexual behaviour and its origins in a social world. Recognising that sexuality is socially constructed enables us to raise questions about the social context and the ways in which this channels teenagers' sexual experiences.

In the first two chapters, we deal with teenagers' sexual attitudes and practices, and with the ways in which sexuality has been theorised in adolescent development. Chapter 3 focuses on biologically determined aspects of adolescent sexuality, while Chapter 4 shifts the emphasis to a consideration of the major social influences on teenagers' sexual development and outcomes. In the next chapter, we address the ways in which social constructions of sexuality are gendered. Here we see that, in spite of current claims of gender 'equality', young boys and girls bring very different beliefs and expectations to the experience of sex. In line with our concerns that research and writing about adolescent sexuality narrowly assume its heterosexual nature, Chapter 6 describes issues around gay and lesbian adolescence. We have asked an expert in the field, Mark Goggin, to write this important chapter. Chapters 7 and 8 deal with two very different consequences of sexual risk-taking, both arising from erratic or non-existent contraceptive practice – sexually transmissible diseases, including HIV/AIDS, and unwanted or unplanned pregnancy. These consequences of sexual activity have major implications for the health and well-being of adolescents and for society at large. Chapter 9 focuses on sexual activity as problem behaviour and targets those behaviours which exploit others, such as rape and incest, or limit personal growth and development. In the last chapter, we summarise the difficulties and limitations in studying adolescent sexuality, and provide a framework in which sexuality research can be interpreted. Our conclusion draws together some themes that recur throughout the chapters and which may provide guidance for those working or living with adolescents.

1 Sexuality in the 1990s

Adolescents' behaviour and beliefs

THE TIMES THEY ARE A'CHANGING

Any understanding of today's adolescent as a sexual being must take account of the historical context. What are the changes in social norms that have occurred and what consequences do these have for expression of adolescent sexuality? Sexually, the past was a simpler place. Girls became wives and mothers and protected their virginity in order to attract a suitable husband. Boys' lives were career-oriented and they were expected to sow their sexual wild oats prior to taking on their family role of provider. Today, these goals are no longer so well defined. Ideas about 'right' and 'wrong' sexual behaviour are less rigid and boundaries between good and bad girls and boys are less clear. We know, too, that young people are delaying marriage while, at the same time, the age at which puberty begins is decreasing. This extension of the period between physical maturation and the taking up of traditional roles, together with the fact that contraception is more freely available, has led to the uncoupling of sexuality, marriage, and child-bearing. As a result, prohibitions about premarital teenage sex are less easy to enforce so that there has been a need for society to rethink its views on adolescent sexuality.

Of course, teenage and premarital sex have always been with us. What is new is the increase in the numbers of young people engaging in this behaviour in the past forty years. In particular, there has been a dramatic rise over this period in the numbers of teenage girls who are sexually active. Brooks-Gunn and Furstenberg (1989) report figures from a number of studies which reveal that there has been an increase in the number of white American 16-year-old girls having intercourse from 7 per cent in 1950 to 44 per cent in 1982. Undoubtedly this increase was due, at least partially, to the influence of the women's movement of the 1960s and 1970s and the demands for equality of sexual expression and sexual fulfilment which were advocated by members of that movement. Studies of male teenagers' sexual behaviour over this period suggest that while, historically, young boys were more sexually active than young girls, the gap between the sexes has narrowed in the past decade or so.

In a review of studies of late adolescents' sexual behaviour from 1900 to 1980, Darling *et al.* (1984) identified three periods, each characterised by different sexual standards. The earliest, which lasted until the 1940s or early 1950s was the period of the 'double standard', with sexual activity accepted for boys but prohibited for girls. During the next twenty or so years, it seemed that premarital sex was allowed for young people provided that it occurred in a love relationship that was a prelude to marriage. By the late 1960s, marriage was off the agenda for many sexually active young people of both sexes. In fact, figures reported by Hofferth (1987a) indicate that the greatest increase in teenage sexual activity occurred at this time, with a levelling off in the 1980s. Most writers explain this by the 'sexual revolution' of the 1960s and 1970s which was characterised by more permissive attitudes towards sexuality and greater concern for personal fulfilment. The trend toward later marriage may well have contributed since many believe it to be unrealistic to expect teenagers to abstain from sexual activity until marriage. So what has caused the apparent stabilisation in the rates of sexual activity among teenagers in the past ten to twenty years? Hofferth offers several suggestions including a revival of religious beliefs (long associated with lower levels of early sexual activity), fear of disease (especially in this era of AIDS and other STDs), and the effectiveness of messages about the risks of early sexual involvement. She also makes the cogent point that it would be foolish to expect that *all* teenagers would engage in premarital sex. Current estimates are that about 60 per cent of unmarried 18-year-olds are sexually active, a figure that is consistent across many Western nations, although there is variation within groups, the figure being higher for some and lower for others (Hofferth and Hayes 1987a; Rosenthal *et al.* 1990). It may be that a new, higher plateau has been reached which reflects the current impact of a number of factors which we discuss in this chapter.

PATTERNS OF SEXUAL BEHAVIOUR

Generalising about the sexual behaviour of adolescents is a dangerous procedure, given the wide range of behaviours included under this rubric, the individual differences that distinguish adolescents from each other, and the diversity of societal influences that adolescents in different subgroups experience. No less important are the differences one might expect in comparing the behaviour of 13-year-olds with that of late teenagers. With this caveat in mind, we turn to what adolescents do sexually, with whom, and when. In describing adolescents' sexual behaviour, we adopt Katchadourian's (1990) distinction between *autoerotic* behaviour – behaviour that does not rely on a partner for sexual release – and *sociosexual* behaviour, which involves another person.

Autoerotic or solitary sexual behaviour

Among these behaviours we include erotic fantasy, nocturnal emission, and masturbation. Surprisingly, there is very little research reported on any of these sexual behaviours, perhaps because they have been, and still are, regarded as very private and somewhat shameful activities. Katchadourian believes that erotic fantasy is 'by far the most common sexual activity indulged in as such or as part of other sexual behaviours', reporting that 72 per cent of teenagers in one study admitted to having erotic fantasies. He suggests that these fantasies fulfil a number of functions in the adolescent's erotic life. They are a source of pleasurable sexual arousal. They act as a substitute for the satisfaction of unattainable or inappropriate sexual needs or goals, performing a 'compensatory, wish-fulfilment function'. Finally, they provide an opportunity for adolescents to recognise their sexual needs and preferences, and to rehearse these in a way that is non-threatening for most teenagers. However, for some, erotic fantasies provoke anxieties and guilt about sexual feelings which may be perceived as perverted or forbidden. So long as sexual fantasies coexist with social sexual ties, rather than as substitutes for these, they have a positive, adaptive function.

Unlike menarche, which signals teenage girls' entry into sexual maturity, we know little about the incidence of boys' wet dreams, those disconcerting, involuntary nocturnal emissions which cause so many teenage boys embarrassment and, possibly, guilt in the morning. We know a little more about masturbation – but disturbingly little, no doubt because of the stigma traditionally attached to this practice. Although many cultures accept masturbation as a normal part of human sexuality, Western society, in the past, has maintained a strong injunction against this behaviour. Even as late as the beginning of this century, physicians, including the Surgeon General of the United States, warned that masturbation was a cause of cancer, heart disease, hysteria, impotence, and insanity. On the other side of the Pacific Ocean, in 1906, a review of a New Zealand Borstal institution (which spent considerable time examining the sexual health of the school's inmates) elicited the views of one eminent medical authority of the day. Dr William Henry Symes opined that masturbation led to imbecility and epilepsy, that 75 per cent of those addicted to this filthy habit could be 'rescued from insanity and probably death' by forcible vasectomies, and that the 'moral defectives' who remained uncured should be put on an island and flogged with the cat-o'-nine-tails. In spite of these awful dangers, many young people continued to engage, albeit surreptitiously, in this behaviour. It is not difficult to imagine the guilt, conflict, and depression caused by a seeming addiction to such a taboo and dangerous practice.

More recently, there has been a shift towards greater openness and acceptance, perhaps reflecting a more general move from a focus on sex for reproduction to sex for pleasure. That this shift is not universal is suggested by a fairly recent textbook on adolescent development in which the topic of masturbation was placed in a section entitled 'Special problems of psychosexual development' (Rogers 1981). Masturbation is the most common source of orgasm in teenagers of both sexes and the source of a boy's first ejaculation in two out of three cases (Katchadourian 1990). There is evidence of a sex difference in masturbatory practices. It seems that young girls begin to masturbate at an earlier age than boys (on average about age 12 compared with age 14) but fewer girls than boys admit to this practice. Whether girls' lower rates of reporting masturbatory behaviour reflect a real difference or simply a difference in willingness to admit to a 'stigmatised' behaviour is not known. Certainly it seems that acceptance of masturbation among boys is greater than for girls. As early as the late 1940s Kinsey and his colleagues reported that observation of peers masturbating was common for boys, prior to their own masturbatory experience. Most knowledge about masturbation among boys comes from their peer group. For girls, masturbation is a more closeted experience.

It is difficult to get accurate figures on masturbatory practices but several studies suggest that most boys and many girls engage in this behaviour. Consistent with changing and more liberal attitudes to a variety of sexual practices, Sorenson (1973) in his important study of adolescent sexuality found that younger adolescents in his sample reported that they started to masturbate at an earlier age than did the older teenagers, implying a change in cultural norms. It is perhaps significant that few recent studies of adolescent sexuality have information about this topic. But even as late as the mid-1980s, most teenagers, when asked, retained some degree of guilt about the behaviour and regarded masturbation as shameful, with fewer than one-third saying that they feel no guilt when they masturbate (Coles and Stokes 1985). Indeed, teenagers' first sexual anxiety probably revolves around the experience of masturbation.

Although self-stimulation may still cause some anxiety for teenagers, the reality is that masturbation may be both enjoyable and tension-reducing and that it does not cause physical harm. What is particularly injurious is the attitude taken toward masturbation. The severe condemnation expressed by many parents when they discover that their teenager (or small infant or toddler) is masturbating can be a disturbing drawback to the young person's psychosexual development. There is no indication that masturbation increases later sexual maladjustment. Indeed it may help inexperienced youngsters learn how to give and receive sexual pleasure, and allow for the expression of sexual feelings without entering into a relationship for which the teenager is not emotionally ready. The fantasies associated with masturbation can help the adolescent develop sexual identity and establish sexual preferences. As with many behaviours, however, excess is potentially problematic. In some cases, masturbation may reflect adjustment problems, especially when used not just as a substitute for 'real' sex when this is unavailable, but as a refuge from or replacement for satisfactory sexual relationships with peers.

Sociosexual or partnered sexual behaviour

From kissing to coitus Several studies have shown the robustness of a sequence of adolescent sexual behaviour which starts at around the age of 13 with embracing and kissing, moving through petting or fondling breasts and sex organs, and ending with intercourse. Most adolescents, especially young women, move gradually towards more intimate sexual behaviour – 'heavy' petting and intercourse – through the experience of dating and 'going steady', although cultural variations in this sequence have been described. For example, among African-American girls, sexual intercourse often precedes heavy petting. These experiences provide young people with the opportunities for sexual exploration and discovery, and for acquiring the skills in intimacy which are necessary if one is to establish a long-term partnership. It has often been suggested that premarital petting, especially to orgasm, has been used to protect girls' virginity – an important commodity in many cultures even today. In this way girls can remain technically virgins while experiencing sexual intimacy. There are, of course, other reasons for the observation that many young girls are content to restrict themselves to heavy petting without taking the next step, to sexual intercourse. Such behaviour reduces the risk of pregnancy and, perhaps more importantly, teenage girls' sexual desires may be awakened and satisfied by the direct stimulation of the clitoris which occurs during heavy petting.

The dating behaviour of teenagers has been subjected to some scrutiny and has revealed, not surprisingly, the same effects of historical context as have been shown for intercourse. In the United States, the median age when adolescents begin to date has declined over time, from about 16 years of age in the 1930s to age 13 years in the 1970s. Even as recently as the 1960s, books were still being written, advising teenagers about dating etiquette.

For example, Dr Evelyn Duvall in her book, *The Art of Dating*, gives the following advice: 'A girl who doesn't want to be too obvious in her datelessness may feign busyness [*sic*] or an intense interest in music or her family, for instance, to cover up for her lack of boyfriends.'

Timing of the first date is not as strongly related to sexual maturity as it is to age (Dornbusch *et al.* 1981) so that teenagers who mature early are no more likely to date early than are their slower maturing peers. As well as a decline in the timing of the first dating experience, rates of each precoital activity have increased among more recent cohorts while rate of petting increases with age (Chilman 1980a). There are interesting commonalities between American and Australian adolescents. McCabe and Collins (1990) investigated how the sexual desires and behaviours of Australian 16- to 17-year-old adolescents changed as the dating relationship deepened. There was a clear desire for increasing sexual intimacy from first date to going steady, although young boys wanted more intimacy than their female peers at all levels of dating. For example, on their first date, 88 per cent of boys wanted to engage in light breast petting and 41 per cent in stimulation of the girl's genitals, but only 29 per cent and 6 per cent of girls desired this experience on their first date. Boys also showed greater acceleration in their desire for intimacy as they progressed through the dating stages. For example, desire for intercourse progressed for girls from 2 per cent at the first date to 8 percent on going steady. Comparable figures for boys were 12 and 45 per cent. The reported behaviour of boys and girls showed similar differences between the sexes although these diminish as the relationship deepens, so that by the time young people are going steady there appears to be mutuality of behaviours with boys and girls engaging in similar activities. A similar progression in behaviour among American teenagers was reported by Roche (1986).

This study also revealed that adolescents are least permissive when asked about their beliefs of what is proper or appropriate sexual activity in dating, are somewhat more permissive when it comes to their own behaviour, and most permissive when asked to report what they believe other teenagers are doing. These last two findings confirm an early study in Australia by Collins (1974) which found that teenagers overestimated the sexual experience of their peers. The danger of this sort of belief is that, in an attempt to conform to a false norm about peer sexual activity, teenagers may feel obliged to engage in behaviours which they neither desire nor feel ready for.

As might be expected, there is a strong relationship between dating experiences and teenage sexual attitudes and behaviours. Those teenagers who have steady or regular partners are more likely to have premarital sex than are casual daters. Early dating experience seems to be associated with more permissive attitudes to premarital sex as well as to early sexual experience. For example, in one study (Miller *et al.* 1986), 82 per cent of teenagers who had begun dating at age 12 had experienced intercourse by late adolescence. For those who started dating at age 14, this figure dropped to 56 per cent, and 17 per cent for those whose dating experiences began at age 16.

Just how many teenagers are virgins and how many are sexually experienced? We have seen that there has been a substantial increase in teenage sexual activity in the past few decades. In a major study of 2000 British 15- to 19-year-olds interviewed in the early 1960s, Schofield (1968) found that only 20 per cent of boys and 12 per cent of girls had had sexual intercourse. Ten years later, over 50 per cent of 1500 teenagers aged 16 to 19 years reported that they were non-virgins (Farrell 1978). In two national surveys of young American women, Zelnik *et al.* (1981) found that in 1971 30 per cent of 15- to 19-year-old women had had premarital sexual intercourse, a figure rising to 41 per cent in 1976. Most studies in the late 1970s, across a number of Western countries, suggest that by the end of high school about 35 per cent of teenagers are non-virgins. By the mid 1980s, at age 18, 67 per cent of boys and 44 per cent of girls are no longer virgins (Hofferth and Hayes 1987a). These figures are similar to those available for our own study of Australian adolescents (Rosenthal *et al.* 1990), although we found substantial differences among cultural subgroups in the rates of sexual activity.

The trend toward first experience of sex or sexual 'debut' at younger ages is true of most Western countries (Goldman and Goldman 1988). In Sweden, the age of initiation into sex dropped from an average of 19 years to 16 years in the past four decades. In the United States, there has been a similar shift, with a dramatic rise in the proportion of younger girls – especially whites – experiencing sex during the 1970s (Hofferth and Hayes 1987a). A similar trend is apparent in Australia where, in 1981–2, 40 per cent of 17-year-olds were sexually experienced (Australian Institute of Family Studies 1981–2) but by 1988, 60 per cent reported that they were non-virgins at that age (Goldman and Goldman 1988). A slightly higher figure of 63 per cent is reported for a sample of 17-year-old British adolescents, with 40 per cent reporting their first sexual intercourse at 15 years of age or younger – 9 per cent at 13 years or earlier (Ford and Morgan 1989). The Goldmans found that during the period between 14 and 19 years of age, 80 per cent of their respondents had their first experience of sexual intercourse, while 8 per cent of young boys and girls reported the transition from virgin to non-virgin between 10 and 13 years of age.

Just as the numbers of teenagers engaging in sex have increased, at least until recently, and their age of initiation is declining, so too are they becoming more sexually adventurous. Young people are engaging in a wider variety of sexual behaviours than before and with more partners. The practice of oral sex is now widespread among adolescents and there seems to have been a shift in formerly negative attitudes to less traditional sexual practices. Thirty-three per cent of British adolescents reported that they would engage in oral sex outside a steady relationship, while 21 per cent were willing to do so within a steady relationship (Ford and Morgan 1989). Among 18-year-olds surveyed by the authors, 46 per cent of boys and 28 per cent of girls had engaged in oral sex with casual partners. Corresponding figures for regular or steady partners were 56 per cent and 58 per cent respectively. In a younger sample of 16-year-olds, the figures were even higher, reaching 100 per cent for homeless young boys, with casual and regular partners. Katchadourian (1990) reports that among senior high school students 50 per cent of males and 41 per cent of females engage in cunnilingus and 44 per cent of males and 32 per cent of females engage in fellatio. The incidence of anal sex in our two Australian samples was surprisingly high for some groups. Although anal sex was relatively uncommon among our 18-year-olds, 25 per cent of our 16-year-old homeless boys and girls reported that they engaged in this practice with casual or regular partners (or both). Unprotected anal intercourse is reported by more than 20 per cent of heterosexual teenage girls attending clinics in New York and San Francisco (Moscicki *et al.* 1988).

We need to be cautious in accepting too readily the evidence for an increase in sexual activity and variety. Attitudes to sexuality are more liberal than in previous decades so that the teenagers of today may be more willing to admit to these behaviours than their predecessors. Nevertheless, the generality of these findings across studies in different countries, using different samples and different information-gathering strategies suggests that real changes have occurred.

As well as focusing on specific activities, other studies have investigated patterns of sexual relationships. Sorenson (1973) identified two patterns of sexual behaviour among the teenagers that he studied. The first, serial monogamists, described a group who had experienced short-term, sequential relationships which were monogamous – a pattern which describes the sexual activity of many in our teenage sample (Rosenthal *et al.* 1991). The second group, the sexual adventurers (mostly boys), were – as the label suggests – sexually active with a variety of partners to whom they were not faithful. Again, this is a pattern which we found among some of our adolescents, although less commonly than the first.

THE SEXUAL CONTEXT

Studies that investigate the age of sexual debut rarely tell us much about the context in which this significant event occurs. Is early sexual debut related to regular and frequent subsequent sexual activity? Who are the partners of these young people? Is initiation of sexual activity voluntary? Is it a pleasurable experience or one fraught with negative emotions? It seems that having had intercourse once (and at an early age) does not necessarily mean that the young person maintains a high level of sexual activity. For some young adolescents, sexual intercourse is sporadic and rare, often a one-off experience. However, once the transition to non-virgin is made, subsequent acts of intercourse are likely to follow quite quickly. In 1982, only 5 per cent of American teenagers who had ever had intercourse had it once only. Two-thirds had intercourse a second time within three months of their first experience. Ford and Morgan's British teenagers were equally active and, of their 16- to 18-year-olds, 44 per cent reported that their last act of sexual intercourse occurred within the past seven days. But having ever had sex does not mean that a teenager is currently sexually active. Nine per cent of Ford and Morgan's non-virgin teenagers had not had intercourse during the previous year.

As might be expected, frequency of intercourse is related to the nature of the relationship with one's partner – the more committed the relationship (going steady), the more frequent the sexual activity. Young girls tend to engage in fewer acts of intercourse with 'casual' partners than do boys, and are more likely to report that sexual activity occurs with regular or steady partners. Of course, it is possible that these young girls are avoiding the socially unacceptable role – at least for women – of taking part in 'one-night-stands' by deluding themselves that the relationship with a new partner will last and is one characterised by love and commitment. Certainly, boys seem to be more willing than girls to engage in uncommitted sex. In one recently reported study, four times as many male than female college students reported having sex with a stranger more than twice in the previous year. For high schoolers, the gender difference was equally marked.

Young women whose sexual experiences begin early report that their partners are older – on average about three years – than themselves while teenage boys report their partners to be the same age as themselves or slightly younger (Schofield 1968). An interesting study of a representative group of young Danish late adolescents who reported on the age of their first sexual partner (Wielandt *et al.* 1989) initially confirmed the usual gender differences in partner age but subsequent analyses cast doubt on the validity of this commonly accepted pattern. The researchers were able to cross-check reports of partner age by comparing the self-reported age with the partner-reported age of sexual debut for couples who were both engaging in sex for the first time. Assuming that self-reported age is correct, it was evident that young women perceived their partner to be older than he actually was, especially so among the youngest (16-year-old) girls. This report bias was not evident for boys. Wielandt and her colleagues suggest that the systematic misreporting of the age of their male partners may be due to 'wishful thinking for an older first sexual partner', in line with societal expectations.

If we turn to the quality of adolescents' first experience of sexual intercourse it seems that, for many young people, their first act of coitus is not a pleasurable one. Bettelheim captures something of the flavour of the experience, at least for an earlier generation of teenagers.

> American middle-class youth learns about sex in the back seat of a car, or during a slightly drunken party, or because there was nothing better to do to kill boredom. . . . The first sexual experience often leaves in-effaceable impressions, marred by a total lack of experience on either side. Both partners feeling anxious and insecure, neither one can offer encouragement to the other, nor can they take comfort from the accomplished sex act, since they cannot be sure they did it well.
>
> (Bettelheim 1962)

Lette and Carey's (1979) fictional 'surfie chick', eager to be initiated into the mysteries of sex, provides a more graphic account of the experience.

> Bruce was still trying to screw me. We both took off our clothes. I could see this great, hulking, looming thing in the darkness, with blonde hair and glasses. Then there was a hand on my breast. Knead. Knead. Knead. . . . I didn't know how he got an erection. I didn't even know what an erection was. There was just this hard mysterious thing zooming towards me as Bruce mounted and shoved it in. Well, he tried to shove it in. He tried and tried and tried to shove it in. For half an hour he tried. . . . It just wouldn't work. What a marvellous sensation! Being split up the middle! . . . I waited in agony to pass out. He gave up.
>
> (Lette and Carey 1979: 40–41)

For a substantial minority of young people, the initiation of sex is not voluntary (an issue that we deal with more fully in a later chapter). Nevertheless, for most girls (and somewhat fewer boys) the act occurs in the context of an affectionate relationship. In spite of this, emotional reactions to the event vary. McCabe and Collins (1990) report a study conducted in the early 1970s which revealed that only half the girls enjoyed the experience, while 40 per cent had negative reactions such as guilt, anxiety about pregnancy, or fear of discovery. Boys, on the other hand, felt quite differently about their first experience of sex, claiming feelings of excitement and satisfaction. It might be expected that these attitudes would have changed as ideas of sexual liberalism took hold. In fact, more recent research confirms the ambivalent emotional outcomes of teenagers' sexual debut. On the whole, though, even if their first coital experience is unrewarding, particularly for girls, many teenagers find subsequent sexual intercourse to be a positive experience.

TEENAGERS' ATTITUDES TO SEX

How do these young people feel about premarital sex and the apparent liberalisation in society's attitudes to teenage sex? And what is the relationship between attitudes and sexual behaviour? Are liberal attitudes associated with promiscuous sexual behaviour? Prior to the 'sexual revolution' of the 1960s, there were strong gender differences in attitudes to premarital sex. For young girls, sex was equated with love, and was only acceptable in a love relationship. Adolescent boys, on the other hand, were more likely to hold permissive attitudes and be favourably disposed to casual sexual adventures. This double standard extended to virginal status at marriage. Most young boys, while wanting to be sexually experienced themselves, required their wives to be virgins at marriage. There was considerable social support for this double standard, the most prevalent view being that girls 'set the standard' for sexual behaviour and that boys have the right to 'get what they can'. Post 1960s, attitudes as well as behaviours changed. The work of Yankelovich (1974) clearly demonstrated a change in teenagers' moral norms around the issue of sex. He reported an increasing consensus that abortion, homosexuality, and premarital sex are not morally wrong. Later studies have substantiated these findings. As Coleman (1980) reports, young people today consider sexuality and sexual behaviour to be a matter of private rather than public morality. Most adolescents express liberal attitudes to premarital sex, although favouring a view that premarital sex is acceptable in the context of a relationship that is long-term, monogamous, and committed.

Indeed, the prevailing sexual climate today has been characterised as one where sexual promiscuity and exploitation are rejected in favour of an ideology of 'permissiveness with affection' (Reiss 1967). Steinberg (1985) has suggested that this view has been responsible for a decline in the popularity of the double standard that allowed men, but not women, to engage in premarital sex. There is, however, clear evidence from a recent study of Australian teenagers (Moore and Rosenthal 1992b) that the double standard is alive and well, although unpopular, especially with girls. At least half of the young people in our sample expressed a sexual ideology that reflected a belief that the sexual standards for boys were different from those for girls, a point made by Lees (1986) in her study of English teenage girls. Girls were equally as likely as boys to hold this view, most compellingly articulated in response to questions like 'How do you feel about girls/boys who engage in one-night-stands?'

> I would think she is too easy, not a slut but I would say she doesn't feel anything. [*Boys?*] It doesn't really bother me. It's different. People say we should be equal and the same, but the fact is it is not. For a man to have many sexual partners is okay but for a girl to have many sexual partners, she is considered pretty low and a guy is considered what a man, a stud. He has had some experience, he is great.
>
> (16-year-old girl)

Boys were more likely to be described favourably as 'studs' and girls unfavourably as 'sluts' if they engaged in casual sexual behaviour. This fits well with Lees' claim that, unlike boys who are not judged simply in terms of their sexual activity (which in any case is likely to enhance their reputation), the social standing of girls is defined by their sexual reputation.

These issues are taken up in a later chapter; the point here is that while there has been a considerable increase in the extent of teenage sexual activity, the changes in attitudes are neither as substantial nor as clearcut as might be expected if we use behaviour as an indicator of attitudes. Some confirmation of this comes from an American study in which changes in sexual guilt – self-mediated punishment for violating standards of proper sexual conduct – were monitored over time (Gerrard 1987). Although there was no decrease in the sexual guilt expressed by the different cohorts of young women over a five-year period, there was a substantial increase in sexual activity. Gerrard's explanation of this apparent anomaly is that the level of sexual guilt necessary to inhibit sexual activity in 1973 was no longer sufficient to achieve this five years later.

DETERMINANTS OF SEXUAL BEHAVIOUR

If sexual attitudes are imperfect predictors of adolescent sexual activity, what other factors help us understand adolescents' sexuality? This issue provides a major focus for the remainder of this book. We shall deal with the most important biological, psychological, and sociological influences on sexual behaviour in later chapters. These include the impact of puberty as well as factors such as family and peer influences, and the role of cultural norms. For the present, we describe briefly some sociocultural antecedents of teenage sexual activity to which we do not return at a later stage.

It has been suggested that sociocultural factors determine how adolescent sexuality is expressed through the cultural context which pervades the adolescent's daily life. Social institutions such as the family and religion exert their influence in three ways. They provide the norms for acceptable sexual behaviour; individuals in powerful roles in these institutions use norms as the basis for informal controls; and, finally, there are often formal rules which constrain sexual behaviour through fear of institutional sanctions. In fact, religion – actually, extent of religious belief, rather than affiliation with a religion – is strongly related to teenage sexual behaviour. Young people who are observant of religious customs and teaching are more likely to refrain from premarital sex than their less religious peers. Those teenagers who are members of fundamentalist religions are less likely to engage in premarital sex than members of other denominations. There is an interesting question here as to whether there is a direct influence of religion on sexual behaviour or whether the two are part of a general conservatism among some teenagers. A recent study suggests that the effect operates in two directions. More religious adolescents are less likely to engage in sexual intercourse, and adolescents who have started their sexual activity early are likely to become less interested in religion.

One of the most powerful influences on adolescents' sexual experience is race. Large black-white differences are regularly reported in the United States. African-American boys and girls become sexually active earlier than white adolescents and, at every age, more African-Americans than whites are having intercourse (Hofferth and Hayes 1987a). The reasons for this racial difference are complex. Some writers believe that the socioeconomic differences between blacks and whites account for the racial disparity in sexual behaviour; others take a cultural norms approach, arguing that there are significant differences in the acceptability of early sexual experience. Hofferth and Hayes suggest that the two explanations are not mutually exclusive, pointing to the likelihood, for example, of long-term poverty leading to different outlooks on marriage and child-bearing which affect attitudes to early sexual activity. In fact, a recent survey has shown that differences between black and white adolescents persist, even when a variety of social class and other social disadvantage indicators are taken into account. One factor that appeared to be important was the racial composition of the schools attended by these African-American teenagers. There was a higher proportion of sexually experienced African-Americans in segregated schools than in racially diverse schools. Among blacks and whites at these latter schools, there were only small differences in the likelihood of being sexually active. As Hofferth and Hayes point out, to some extent school segregation is a surrogate for socioeconomic status among African-Americans and reflects the pervasive nature of their social disadvantage.

Social class has been frequently implicated as a key factor in studies of teenage sexual behaviour even when race is not the focus. Living in poverty is associated with early sexual activity, possibly through the impact of poor life satisfaction and even poorer prospects. While many teenagers aspire to good jobs and adequate incomes, with all the security that these imply, the reality is that many are trapped in a cycle of poverty. Small wonder that the perceived lack of options and desirable alternatives for the future lead some young people to increased sexual activity as a way of achieving immediate, if short-lived, pleasure. The nature of the inner-city environment may be another reason for the association between poverty and early sexual activity. Living in an environment characterised by poor and crowded housing and serious social disorganisation, teenagers are often exposed to many forms of deviant behaviour, as well as to sex, at a very young age. Hofferth and Hayes suggest that in these environments there is a street culture which valorises male virility, as expressed in a variety of sexual exploits. Certainly the finding that rural youth, usually part of a close-knit homogeneous culture, are less sexually experienced than their urban peers supports the potentially malign influence on teenage sexual behaviour of crowded inner-city living.

There is clear evidence for the impact of cultural norms when we look at several Australian studies. Consistent with conservative cultural expectations about sex, which make premarital sex an unacceptable activity for the Chinese, we found that a high proportion of young Chinese-Australian teenagers were virgins, whereas their Anglo-Celtic counterparts reported relatively high levels of sexual experience, in keeping with the more liberal views about premarital sex that exist within that culture (Rosenthal *et al.* 1990). These findings are similar to the behaviours reported by Khoo (1985), who also found that more liberal attitudes were expressed by Australians of English descent than by Southern Europeans or Asians. Of particular interest in our study was the relatively high level of sexual activity of boys of Greek descent, and the extremely low rates of premarital sex reported by the Greek girls. Both the high rate for boys and the disparity between the sexes can be explained by the greater sexual freedom given to boys in the Greek culture, and the strong emphasis on chastity for girls. We found similar attitudes among younger Greek-Australian teenagers, especially in matters of chastity and fidelity.

> It is important for a girl to be a virgin on her wedding day. Because [if you were not a virgin] when you did get married and you tried to walk down the aisle wearing white, God would strike you down. In front of everyone!
>
> (Greek-Australian girl)

> [Virginity] is something you should take care of, something special. I think it symbolises that you are clean and that there is nothing dirty

about you . . . . You should keep it for your future husband even though he may have slept around.

(Greek-Australian girl)

A final influence to which we briefly allude here is that of education. It seems that higher levels of educational achievement and clear educational goals are related to lower rates of premarital sex for both boys and girls. The association between educational outcomes and sexual behaviour is mediated by a number of factors, including those discussed above. The achieving student is likely to come from a relatively well-to-do family, to place a high value on achievement, to be more goal-oriented, and able to plan for the future. All these characteristics may lead to a low likelihood of sexual involvement at an early age (Jessor and Jessor 1975). Perhaps involvement in a sexual relationship distracts young girls from their studies and, conversely, involvement in studies makes teenage girls less interested in a sexual relationship (or less interesting to boys). It is likely that non-achieving schoolgirls have a more difficult time than their male peers, who have an alternate route to high school success via sports, and whose academic failure may be cushioned by sports success. In these circumstances, one possible consequence of school failure for girls is an attempt to seek confirmation of themselves as worthy individuals through a love-sex relationship.

We have by no means exhausted the sociocultural factors which are associated with early sexual teenage activity, nor have we attempted here anything more than a brief description and a limited explanation of the effects of these factors. Later chapters will place these and other influences in the context of the adolescent's struggle to develop a sense of his or her sexual identity. For now we turn to one other aspect of sexual behaviour which is a source of particular concern, in the light of the increases in activity that have been reported.

RESPONSIBLE SEX? USING CONTRACEPTION

The increased sexual activity among teenagers has led to concerns about young women's heightened risk of unwanted pregnancies and, more recently, the dangers of sexually transmissible diseases (STDs), especially the frightening and lethal disease of AIDS. We might expect, in the light of these threats to adolescents' well-being and sexual health, that young people would have adopted contraceptive methods – and particularly condoms – with great alacrity. What do the figures on contraceptive use show? Alarmingly, whether we take as a measure contraceptive use at first intercourse, or the extent to which contraceptives are ever used, there is evidence that many adolescents are ignoring sexual health messages.

Although there was a considerable increase in adolescents' acceptance of condoms during the 1980s, with condom use doubling for boys and girls during that period, there is still room for improvement. In all studies of contraceptive use at initiation of sex, between one-third and two-thirds of adolescents report using no contraception, a figure that is higher for African-Americans than whites, boys than girls, and older than younger teenagers. Even in the late 1980s, one study of American teenagers showed that four in ten unmarried males aged 17–19 used no method of contraception or only ineffective methods at first intercourse (Sonenstein *et al.* 1989). Studies of sexual initiation up to the early 1980s indicated that male methods of contraception seem to be favoured by all teenagers, a choice that declines with on-going sexual activity. Poor contraceptive use at the time of sexual debut may be partly explained by the unplanned nature of that event. Although subsequent sexual activity is often unplanned, the incidence of planned acts of intercourse warrant rather more evidence of responsible contraception than appears to be the case.

Contraceptive use by sexually active teenagers is alarmingly irregular or non-existent, a consistent finding in Western countries. In Canada, Meikle *et al.* (1985) found that only 34 per cent of their high school students used contraception every time they had sex, while 27 per cent never did so, figures which are replicated in several authoritative studies of American teenagers in the 1970s (Morrison 1985) and of Australian teenagers even more recently (McCabe and Collins 1990; Rosenthal *et al.* 1990). It seems that with greater sexual experience, the responsibility for contraception falls on the young woman. The favoured on-going method is the contraceptive pill (used by 58 per cent of Australian teenagers in one large study and from one-half to two-thirds in several United States studies reviewed by Chilman (1980a)), while condoms – at least in the 1970s – fell somewhat out of favour. Given the current focus on the dangers of HIV transmission, as well as other STDs, it is likely that the popularity of condoms as a long-term contraceptive and disease precaution may increase. Indeed, data from both the United States and Australia suggest that such an increase has occurred in the past few years.

A number of studies have drawn attention to problems arising from the inconsistent contraceptive behaviour of male teenagers, their apparent lack of concern about contraception, and the tendency for some young girls to rely on the 'contraceptive vigilance' of their partners. Why are so many young people, especially males, resistant to contraception? When effective methods of contraception are readily available and the dangers of unprotected sex, both in terms of unwanted pregnancies and of potentially lethal or at least debilitating disease are known to teenagers, why are they so cavalier in their use of this technology?

SHOWERS IN RAINCOATS?

There are a number of reasons for contraceptive risk-taking among adolescents. They may be ignorant about the need for contraception, they may not know how to use contraceptives, or they may be lacking in the skills necessary to go about the often embarrassing or difficult process of gaining access to contraceptive advice and devices. Even with the appropriate knowledge and skills, teenagers may not like the idea of using contraception or, at best, feel ambivalent about this 'intrusion' into their sexual life. Finally, of course, there may be overwhelming structural barriers to contraceptive use. If access to contraception is difficult, either physically or psychologically, or if the cost of contraception is beyond the reach of the adolescent then it is likely that, even with the best intentions, contraceptive use will be minimal or absent.

Another factor which makes decisions about contraception difficult is the often sporadic nature of adolescent sexual activity. Unlike most adult sexual behaviour, teenagers' forays into sexual intercourse are likely to be inconsistent and marked by long 'droughts' with no activity. This makes the choice of contraceptive difficult, with 'female' options such as the pill or IUD non-optimal, and the condom a more logical option. But, as we shall see, there are barriers to making this apparently reasonable choice. Of course, an added difficulty is that some contraceptives are effective for just that purpose, avoiding pregnancy, but ineffective in disease prevention. Concerns about sexually transmissible diseases add further complexity to the decision about which contraceptive to use.

One way of understanding contraceptive behaviour in the light of the many possible barriers to contraceptive use is to turn the problem on its head. What factors must be present for adequate contraceptive behaviour to occur? Urberg (1982), drawing from the problem-solving literature, suggests that there are five major steps in the process. First, the individual must recognise that pregnancy (or disease) is a likely outcome of unprotected sex. Next, he or she must be motivated to do something about this. This step involves the belief that one needs to, and can do, something effective, as well as the belief that the possible outcome is undesirable. Third, the individual must be able to generate possible solutions to the problem; fourth, these solutions must be evaluated and one chosen; and finally, the chosen solution must be implemented. Each of these steps in the decision-making process is a necessary but not sufficient condition for effective contraceptive use.

How knowledgeable are adolescents about their bodies and the reproductive process, and about the relationship between sexual activity and disease? What evidence is there that this knowledge has an impact on adolescents' use of contraceptives? The answer to the first question is encouraging. Many studies have shown that most teenagers, even young ones, have some understanding of conception and how their bodies work, they know that a girl can become pregnant if she has intercourse, and the older teenagers are reasonably well-informed about contraception. Sexually transmissible diseases present a different picture. With the exception of HIV/AIDS, teenagers have surprisingly little knowledge of these diseases, or of their methods of transmission and ways of avoiding infection. In one recent study conducted by the authors, more than 50 per cent of a group of Australian university students (mostly young women) had never heard of chlamydia and more than one-quarter had not heard of gonorrhoea. As we shall see in a later chapter, concern about the AIDS epidemic and its potential threat to the well-being of young, sexually active people has led to high levels of knowledge about the importance of 'safe sex' and the role of condoms in minimising the risk of HIV infection.

For those young people who lack the appropriate knowledge, the solution may appear simple. Contraceptive use can be increased by remedying adolescent ignorance. But even when adolescents seem to have adequate knowledge it is clear that effective contraception does not always follow. There is considerable evidence that adolescents do not always have high levels of motivation to contracept. One characteristic that has been attributed to adolescents is the 'personal fable' – a belief that nothing bad or undesirable (including pregnancy or sexually transmitted disease) will happen to them. This perceived invulnerability to nasty events has been well documented in the case of pregnancy (Urberg 1982) and STDs (Moore and Rosenthal 1991a), and is associated with an increase in sexual risk-taking. Another important motivating force is the sense of control that one has over life events. Some adolescents express fatalistic attitudes, feeling powerless and unable to change the course of life's events. If teenagers feel that becoming pregnant or getting an STD is out of their control, they are unlikely to be motivated to go to the necessary effort to use contraceptives. Somewhat related to this is the idea of self-efficacy, or confidence in dealing with contraception. For those teenagers who have little confidence in their ability to purchase condoms or go to the doctor for a prescription for the pill, contraception looms as an almost insurmountable hurdle to negotiate. Even in this enlightened age when condoms are advertised widely as an important precautionary device for avoiding AIDS, and are readily available in vending machines, almost half of our teenage respondents, both boys and girls, reported low levels of confidence in dealing with these matters. Such difficulties are likely to lead to avoidance of contraception, putting it in the 'too hard' basket.

Among those teenagers for whom contraception is a perceived option, attitudes vary. For some, using contraception is inconsistent with a view that sex is, or should be, spontaneous and unpremeditated. It is perhaps surprising that, in one study, young men were found to be more accepting of condoms than young women (Moore and Rosenthal 1991b). For girls, even in today's more enlightened climate, there is a high psychological cost in acknowledging that they are prepared for casual sex (as might be assumed by the practice of ongoing contraception, such as taking the pill, or carrying around a condom 'in case'). Other young people find contraception to be 'messy' or 'unnatural'. Still others say that it interferes with the enjoyment of sex. One familiar complaint from boys is that using condoms is like having 'showers in raincoats'.

> They are necessary, but I think they are disgusting things – quite awful.
> (16-year-old boy)

> I personally hate the things, they are uncomfortable. They can be fun but it is just a hassle. You start getting into it and you have to stop and put them on. It is less exciting because you have to start all over again.
> (16-year-old boy)

> They're alright but I don't really like them. I know they are useful but they say it is like wearing a raincoat and is not enjoyable.
> (16-year-old girl)

Most negative attitudes are directed towards male contraceptive methods, an unfortunate view since condoms are an optimal method of contraception among teenagers, certainly at first intercourse. While some enlightened boys today accept that the possible price for not using condoms is too high, for others, the benefits do not outweigh the costs. There has been some empirical support for this 'cost-benefit' analysis (Pleck *et al.* 1991), with young boys' condom use or non-use apparently dependent on a mix of factors. For example, if they believed that it was the male's responsibility to prevent pregnancy, young boys were more likely to use condoms. If they believed that their partner was on the pill, or that pleasure would be reduced, condom use was inhibited.

Even if a teenager wants to use contraception, that decision usually has to be negotiated with the sexual partner except in those cases where the female has made the decision to use the pill or other long-term devices such as an IUD. Here it is essential that the couple have the social skills which will enable open communication of their wishes and needs. Studies of teenage communication about sexuality and contraception reveal that many teenagers fail to discuss these important issues during a sexual encounter. Girls are particularly diffident about initiating contraception discussions, their lack of assertiveness leaving them vulnerable when their partner is resistant to the use of contraceptives. There is some evidence that girls are expected by boys to take the responsibility for contraception (Moore and Rosenthal 1991b), an expectation which may be unrealistic when considered in the context of the difficulties girls face in asserting their sexual needs. Even when both partners have the best of intentions, there can be failure to contracept. Many of our teenagers reported non-use of condoms during a specific sexual encounter, in spite of their previous intention to have 'safe' sex.

What is going on here? With increased exposure to messages about contraception, particularly condoms, in the media and through sexual health programmes in schools, and with increasingly easy access to contraceptives, at point of sale and through family planning clinics, we might expect to see most teenagers acting responsibly in their contraceptive behaviour. Yet this is not the case. Why? Everything we know tells us that much of teenage sex is unplanned and that explanations of teenage sexual behaviour do not fit easily into rational decision-making or problem-solving models of the sort proposed by Urberg. At best these give an idealised and partial explanation of the behaviour in question. What needs to be taken into account is the situationally determined and urgent nature of adolescent sex. What sort of relationship does the teenager have with his or her partner? Is it a 'long-standing' sexual relationship or a casual 'one-night-stand'? Do alcohol or drugs play a part in the encounter? How sexually aroused are the partners? To what extent are they able to control their sexual urges in the absence of contraception? All these questions and many more need to be asked and answered before we can understand why adolescents fail to take adequate precautions against pregnancy or disease.

A CONTEXTUAL FRAMEWORK

Adolescent sexuality is subject to a complex web of influences, including the physical and psychological characteristics of the individual, the historical period, and the ecological setting. The decisions that young people make about their sexuality, the behaviours they engage in, the values and attitudes that they hold – all these are shaped by the particular context in which the adolescent lives his or her life. At any given time, choices about sexual behaviour will reflect the different physical, social, and economic environments in which adolescents live, and their personal qualities and life histories. Given the diversity of experiences that young people draw on, consciously or unconsciously, in determining their sexual behaviours, it is not surprising that we find a remarkable heterogeneity in those behaviours.

Because the choices made by adolescents flow on and affect their sexual well-being as adults, we need to understand the inconsistencies as well as the consistencies in young people's sexual behaviour, the commonalities as well as the differences, and the rational as well as the non-rational bases for that behaviour. Adolescents must make important decisions about sexuality which will reverberate throughout their lives. In this chapter, we have considered several of those decisions: the decision whether or not to initiate sexual behaviour and, if they are sexually active, whether or not to use contraception; the decision about the timing and nature of relationships, and acceptable sexual practices. All these decisions are made in the context of what the adolescent feels is right and proper for him or her to endorse. For some adolescents, there is little difficulty in making these decisions. For others, the choices are hard to evaluate. We let two of our 16-year-old girls speak for themselves on the issue of premarital sex.

> I think I am a pretty modern girl. I don't believe that you actually have to be married [to have sex]. But you can't do it with anyone. It has to be someone you really love and trust. Someone you have been seeing for a really long time.

> You shouldn't have to wait until you get married to have sex, because people don't get married until they are about twenty-five or something, and you can't be married to the same guy all your life and only have sex with him. You have got to have sex with a few different people.

2 Sexuality and adolescent development

Theoretical perspectives

Coping with sexuality has been regarded by some theorists as one of life's essential developmental tasks. In this chapter, we examine theoretical perspectives on the role of young people's emerging sexual behaviours, feelings, and attitudes in their overall development. Before this, we consider the general and often-discussed question of whether developing sexuality is, of necessity, a stressful and conflict-ridden experience.

DEVELOPING SEXUALITY: STORM AND STRESS?

G. Stanley Hall (1940) regarded adolescence as a time of storm and stress in which conflict and confusion inevitably accompany awakening sexual impulses, bodily changes, and an increased awareness of self and society. Many theorists have continued to emphasise the conflict-driven nature of this stage of life, taking the view, implicitly or explicitly, that coping with biological drives is a stressful but necessary accompaniment of adult adjustment (see, for example, Freud 1969; Gallatin 1975; Havighurst 1951, 1953, 1964). On the other hand, cross-cultural studies have suggested that the level of conflict and stress experienced by adolescents can vary greatly, at least in part as a function of the prevailing cultural norms about sexual expression (Mead 1939, 1950). Although there has been recent criticism of the validity of Mead's data-gathering techniques, so that her conclusions about the relatively stress-free coming of age of Samoan youth must now be considered questionable (Freeman 1983), other writers on Western youth (for example, Douvan and Adelson 1966; Offer *et al.* 1981) have also downplayed the conflictual aspects of adolescence. This research, though, rarely examines the internal conflicts surrounding bodily changes, sexual maturation, and sexual initiation so questions about the likelihood of puberty-related stress must still be addressed.

The view encapsulated by the writings of Lapsley *et al.* (1985) is that stresses and conflicts are undoubtedly experienced by many adolescents, but that these are largely unrelated to the biological changes of puberty. Lapsley and his colleagues view adolescence as a relatively recent cultural invention, produced by economic and social conditions which prolong childhood – ostensibly for the benefit of the individual. Examples of these conditions include the enactment of child labour laws, a minimum school leaving age, and laws designed to protect children from sexual exploitation. While these may have been implemented to allow adolescents to achieve adult status in a gradual manner – seemingly an advantage in our complex world – these social changes place adolescents in the stressful state of 'status deprivation'. Adolescence is best defined not by the transition to new roles, but by the exclusion from old roles. Adolescents must put away childish beliefs and behaviours but they may not yet begin an autonomous lifestyle. Theorists who adopt this 'inventionist' view (Bakan 1971; Demos and Demos 1969; Lapsley *et al.* 1985; Lapsley and Rice 1988) cite historical material to argue that the phenomenon of a prolonged adolescence is not a developmental necessity arising out of biological stresses, but a cultural imposition which causes tensions of its own. The implication of their writings is that the conflicts accompanying sexual maturation may be greatly exaggerated as a result of social norms.

Another perspective which emphasises the cultural definition of sexual stress comes from English writers who use discourse analysis as their conceptual tool, such as Hollway (1984) and Lees (1989). These writers argue that the kind of language we use in discussing sexual matters sets a framework for the way we think about sex, a framework which may be more powerful and pervasive in producing stress and conflict than biological drives.

In evaluating the place of sexuality in human development, it is obvious that we cannot ignore the role of biology. However, personal, historical and cultural perceptions of the meanings of sexual maturation and sexual expression are bound to influence the manner in which adolescents cope with these challenges, and the stresses and conflicts they experience in so doing. The theoretical approaches that follow vary in the extent to which they emphasise nature over nurture, but each makes an important contribution to our understanding of adolescent sexual development.

FOCUS ON NATURE

The psychosexual theorists

The major theorists writing about adolescence from a psychosexual perspective, Sigmund Freud, Anna Freud, and Peter Blos, attached great significance to the impact of sexual drives on the psychological functioning of the person. All three viewed the onset of adolescence as a difficult time psychologically because of the increased strength of these drives. This occurs concurrently with the adolescent's developing physical capacities to actually carry out sexual wishes and fantasies – which may come into conflict with social and internalised taboos.

Sigmund Freud

Freud (1924, 1935, 1950, 1953) postulated that all behaviours, thoughts and feelings are motivated by *drives* and these drives are, in turn, closely related to biological functioning. The mechanisms of these drives are often not available to conscious scrutiny. Thus, Freud hypothesised the existence of the *unconscious,* a set of thoughts, wishes, feelings, and motives which have strong influences on behaviour but which are not amenable to introspection, except under unusual circumstances. Freud assumed two drives, one arising from the sexual and erotic component of human nature (termed libido), and another aggressive or destructive one, although in some formulations Freud suggested the existence of only the former. Psychosexual development involves the transformation of libido to specific body parts or zones, with excessive tension arising in these zones if relief mechanisms cannot be found.

Increasingly with maturation, mental (often unconscious) rather than physical strategies must be found for the release of tension. These strategies include fantasies, or defense mechanisms such as the sublimation of sexual desire into other activities like productive or creative work and the denial of sexuality through repression (often accompanied by an ascetic lifestyle). Another strategy is through the projection of sexual fantasies onto other people so that they may be rejected (as with the censor) or responded to (as in the individual who fantasises about others' sexual overtures). According to Freud, personality is structured to allow for the relief of tension in ways which are (normally) socially acceptable and consistent with an individual's conscious and unconscious values and attitudes.

The critical role of sexuality in personality development has been described by Freud in terms of psychosexual stages, each focusing on different bodily functions. The infant gains gratification through oral stimulation. Babies use their mouths to explore the environment, to express tension and to experience pleasure. In the second year of life, the anus becomes the most sexualised part of the body. As children gain control of their sphincter muscles and musculature in general, they learn ways to take control of their world. This can lead to conflict with parents who seek to socialise the child whose will (or ego) is beginning to exert itself. At the phallic stage, from about 3 to 7 years, children become more aware of their genitals and seek sexual satisfaction through an immature version of adult sexuality, called by Freud the Oedipal conflict (for boys) and the Electra conflict (for girls). These conflicts involve children feeling strong attraction to mother, then (for girls) to the opposite-sex parent, and rivalry and hostility toward the same-sex parent. These attractions and hostilities are so emotionally disturbing to the child that they are repressed into the unconscious, through a process involving identification with the same-sex parent. Identification heralds the beginnings of sex role development and the formation of the superego, in which the values and ideals of the family and society (as perceived by the child) are incorporated into a 'conscience' and an 'ideal self'. At this point the child learns to understand rules and the difference between right and wrong. When the Oedipal or Electra conflicts are resolved through this identification, the child moves into the latency period, and sexual drives are relatively quiescent.

Identification with the same-sex parent is viewed as somehow more satisfying and complete for the male. He is able, through this identification, to reduce his fear of castration by the father (through the mechanism of 'identification with the aggressor'). The boy knows that he will gain father's approval by becoming like him, and is secure in the (unconscious) knowledge that he will one day attain the desired sexual consummation with mother, or at least someone just like her. This last achievement is denied to a girl because she does not have a penis herself and, what is more, she has become aware of this lack (penis envy). However, because she has no castration fears like the boy (since she has already been castrated in fantasy), the motive for identification with the desired parent is less strong and identification is weaker. The implication of this is that superego strength is also weaker and the female is relegated to a potentially less moral state than the male.

After latency comes puberty, with its hormonal changes, which leads to a reawakening of sexual energies and the dawning of the adult, genital stage of development. At puberty, all the earlier conflicts and desires resurface and must be dealt with by the maturing ego. For example, the male adolescent is now physically able to act out his Oedipal fantasies, but the constraints of society and of his own superego do not permit this consummation to proceed. At an unconscious level, adolescents must learn ways to rechannel these sexual energies toward peers and away from parents. The irrational behaviours which often ensue can lead to a good deal of family conflict. At a conscious level, adolescents must learn the social skills necessary to begin peer relationships which will eventually lead to fully functioning adult sexuality. The way adolescents learn to deal with their burgeoning sexual feelings will be influenced by the way earlier unconscious conflicts were handled.

Freud believed that the psychological conflicts experienced by adolescents and adults arise from failure to satisfy or to express specific wishes during childhood. At any of the childhood stages, sexualised impulses may be so frustrated (or so overwhelmingly gratified) that the person continues to seek gratification of those wishes at later life stages – either to make up for inadequate earlier satisfaction or to recapture a 'lost paradise'. This is termed fixation. So, for example, anxiety about sexuality in adolescence may lead to a return to oral gratifications, such as binge eating, or to anal concerns expressed as rebelliousness or extreme untidiness. During adolescence, the strength of these fixations and the ability to sublimate and channel sexual drives in acceptable ways will jointly crystallise into the adolescent's life orientation. This life orientation will include, as one of its most important components, the individual's unique pattern of sexual adjustment.

Much feminist writing from the 1960s to the present has centred on criticism of Freud's formulation of the Oedipal mechanism, with its implication of women's moral inferiority, and the 'anatomy is destiny' approach to sex roles. Archer and Lloyd (1982) have summarised such critiques in their text on sex differences and Chilman, too, is sceptical about the psychoanalytic approach to female sexual development. She comments:

> Freud won indignant reactions from today's liberated women through his 'penis envy' theory. According to Freud, females resent their gender because they feel that their genital equipment is inferior to that of the male. The little girl, upon seeing the male penis, feels cheated and thereafter longs to have one too. . . . Upon reflection, it seems more likely that the little girl would envy her mother's sexual equipment than her father's. The adult female body, with its breasts and voluptuous curves, is a long way from the small girl's relatively simple body.
>
> (Chilman 1980a: 52)

Research and clinical insights into childhood sexual abuse have also brought into question Freud's ideas about the Oedipal conflict as representing the child's secret fantasies about sexual closeness with a parent. The Freudian interpretation that clients' 'memories' of child-adult rape were simply wish-fulfilling fantasies seems unlikely in the light of recent data about the high incidence of childhood sexual abuse and its aftermath of repression and other symptomatology, issues that will be discussed in more detail in a later chapter.

Finally, the Freudian emphasis on the importance of vaginal, as opposed to clitoral, orgasm as an indicator of maturity and adjustment in women has also been criticised. It took a long history of sexologists from Havelock Ellis through Kinsey to Masters and Johnson to put the myth of the vaginal orgasm to rest, establishing the clitoris as the most important sex organ for women. Thus activities such as female masturbation and cunnilingus could be viewed as aspects of mature female sexuality rather than retarded development, and sexual satisfaction for women an appropriate goal for sex, rather than only 'other-oriented' goals, such as reproduction or partner satisfaction. The resentment felt by many feminist writers toward psychoanalytic approaches has arisen because psychoanalysts have misunderstood, or interpreted in a phallocentric or male-oriented way, a number of aspects of women's sexual experience. In spite of this legitimate questioning of Freud's understanding of female sexuality, we should recognise the insights that Freud has offered about human behaviour and sexuality. Nevertheless, these insights must be continually checked against research findings and against people's own interpretations of their sexual experiences.

Anna Freud

Like her father, Anna Freud believed that libido, or sexual energy, was a vital factor in the course of development. Unlike her father, Anna Freud focused on adolescent development, arguing that all behaviour is influenced by the course of sexual maturation and that sexual development in adolescence occurs in an atmosphere of unconscious, if not conscious, turbulence. Because the hormonal upsurge of puberty leads to an increase in sex drives and this in turn leads to a reawakening and necessary reworking of all the infantile unconscious conflicts, there can be no emotionally painless initiation into adolescence. In fact, one of Anna Freud's most influential articles is entitled 'Adolescence as a developmental disturbance' (1969).

Defence mechanisms, or the ego's unconscious strategies for handling anxiety, are the key to understanding adolescent adjustment. If new defences against the upsurge of sexual drives do not come into play, the adolescent may be overwhelmed by instinctual forces, becoming overly impulsive, unable to tolerate frustration, and concerned only with short-term self-gratification. The ego may defend rigidly against these sexual drives with massive repression, leading to an individual who denies the legitimacy of his or her sexual feelings. A more common response to these instinctual forces is a kind of stop–start coping, which is marked by the alternation of contradictory behaviours. The adolescent can be loving and affectionate at one moment, angry and aggressive the next. Depression alternates with spontaneous *joie de vivre*, self-centredness with selflessness, submissive behaviour with rebelliousness, dependence with independence. Such changes show that the defences being put into play are only temporarily successful. However, with maturity, more stable defences and more acceptable outlets for sexual drives develop.

Anna Freud describes two defences she sees as common examples of adolescent coping mechanisms. The first of these is asceticism – the ego's inability to allow any pleasurable activity in case the temptation to 'over-indulge' becomes too great and the instinctual floodgates open (to mix a metaphor). Adolescents who use this defence may take on severe regimens such as dieting, studying, or training for sport in a manner that seems more obsessive than healthy. The second is intellectualisation – a preoccupation with abstractions as the ego attempts to gain control of instinctual impulses through seemingly rational means. These means are described as 'seemingly' rational because, while high-minded beliefs may be expounded, the adolescent does not necessarily carry out these expressed ideals in interactions with family and friends, and rarely welcomes this being pointed out!

Peter Blos

Perhaps the most influential adolescent theorist using a psychoanalytic framework, Blos (1962, 1988) describes adolescence as the second individuation process. The first step in the journey toward definition of selfhood occurs at the end of the second year of life, when the child experiences the power of his/her developing sense of control and ability to move away from mother. Adolescent individuation is about learning to sever some of the emotional ties with parents – the recognition that emotional and sexual needs must be met from outside the family. According to Blos, this process has a sense of urgency emanating from the strength of drives, but it is also accompanied by feelings of isolation, loneliness and confusion, so that conflict and swings of emotion are inevitable concomitants. Adolescent friendships can be particularly intense, as the withdrawal of affective bonds from family members frees up psychic energy to be re-invested in new relationships. Romanticism and falling in love are common as there is a need for these new relationships to replace the intensity of family ties and the feelings of loss which ensue. It is as if teenage romantic love occurs as a rebound from the lost and taboo relationships with family.

To cope with this second individuation process, Blos believes that the adolescent must experience some degree of ego regression. He or she becomes preoccupied with the drives, impulses, wishes, and fantasies that were characteristic of earlier developmental stages. Regression, or 'being childish', allows for the release of a certain amount of psychic energy which the adolescent can channel in new directions, and so gradually develop new coping mechanisms. Like all psychoanalytic theorists, Blos views the physical changes of puberty and the development of mature sexuality as inevitably tied up with conflict and as underlying psychological adjustment at a more pervasive level. He states:

> Not only is it true that adolescents of both sexes are deeply affected by the physical changes taking place in their own bodies – but on a more subtle and unconscious plane, the process of pubescence affects the development of their interests, their social behaviour and the quality of their affective life.
>
> (Blos 1962: 5)

Each of these theorists paints a picture of adolescence as a period in which high levels of unconscious conflict must, perforce, spill over into consciousness. Sexuality is viewed as the basis for this turbulence. Resolution of conflicts is dependent on the development of good coping mechanisms which, in turn, depend on childhood experiences and the adequacy with which earlier conflicts are resolved. Adult maturity and adjustment, in general as well as in the sexual domain, depend heavily on the successful course of adolescence and the young person's ability to learn new coping strategies and to modify childhood defences. 'Successful' outcomes for men and women are hypothesised to be different, as adjustment is measured in terms of taking on traditionally defined masculine or feminine roles. This view is held by Erik Erikson, another major writer on adolescent development. Although Erikson could be categorised as a psychosexual theorist, we have considered him separately, because of his emphasis on the potential of environmental factors to alter and shape the course of life adjustment, over and above biological factors.

Erik Erikson: psychosocial theory

Erikson's theory (1959, 1963, 1968), although taking some account of the social context, still adopts the position that 'anatomy is destiny'. Great importance is attributed to the role of puberty, the upsurge of sex drives, and the differences in psychological development of the sexes. However, Erikson does place greater emphasis than the psychosexual theorists on the cultural factors that mediate the level of conflict associated with drive processes. Erikson postulates that psychological development proceeds through a series of stages across the life-span, each stage characterised by a major crisis or conflict to be worked through and resolved. Resolution of these crises involves attaining a mature and workable balance between opposing forces or tendencies, for example the balance between one's need for others and the need to be autonomous. Successful resolution of new crises will depend in part on the resolution of earlier crises, in part on the strength of drives, and in part on the presence of appropriate social supports. The ideal environment for maximising attainment of a mature stage resolution can take many forms, and at each stage the vital features will be different. So, for example, whereas the infant is best served by an intense relationship with a parent figure, teenagers will, in the normal course of events, be able to work though the crises associated with adolescence more satisfactorily if parent figures can loosen the reins.

As well as the major crisis being acted out, at each life stage there is a reworking on a different plane of earlier conflicts, together with an immature grappling with conflicts yet to attain ascendancy. Along with the theorists discussed earlier, Erikson argues that at adolescence earlier conflicts must be dealt with again and, at the same time, later ones are foreshadowed.

For Erikson, establishing a sense of identity is the major task of adolescence. By identity, he means a coherent sense of self, based on a commitment to present and future roles, ideology, and values regarding future relationships. Ego identity develops out of a gradual integration of all identifications, so that adolescents who move satisfactorily through this stage have an inner confidence about who they are and where they are going. The opposite is identity diffusion, the inability to co-ordinate past identifications with new roles, the inability to find a niche in life, and the confusion and alienation which accompanies this state. One important aspect of identity formation is learning to be comfortable with one's body and sexuality. Others involve choice of occupation, establishing values, and finding a role in relation to one's friends and family which is not at odds with other aspects of the self. Erikson argues that sexuality is an important aspect of identity formation for both sexes. By this he means coping with the bodily changes of puberty and coming to terms with one's new 'sexualised' body, developing a sexual ideology, and consolidating one's sex role and sexual orientation. However, it is only at the next stage, that of 'intimacy versus isolation', that true heterosexual intimacy is established. This is marked by compromise, sharing of goals, and 'the experience of the climactic mutuality of orgasm'.

Adolescent falling in love and sexual experimentation is described as contributing to the quest for self-definition, rather than an indicator of true intimacy.

> To a considerable extent, adolescent love is an attempt to arrive at a definition of one's identity by projecting one's diffused self-image on another and by seeing it thus reflected and gradually clarified. That is why so much young love is conversation.

(Erikson 1968: 132)

Erikson cautions against pressure on young people to make permanent commitments too early in life, when an adequate sense of personal identity has not been established. When the young person's potential for exploration has been closed off too soon, Erikson argues, the relationships formed can be mistaken for truly intimate ones.

Much is made of the different forms which identity development ought to take for boys and girls. Erikson claims (1968) that identity formation for boys centres largely around career and ideology issues, whereas for girls the emphasis is on interpersonal matters. In defining these differences, Erikson was heavily influenced by the 'biological inevitability' stance of Freud and by biological differences between the sexes. Male genitalia – external and 'thrusting' – provide the unconscious metaphor for successful development as a man. This involves forging a place in the world, mastery of the environment, concern with externals or 'outer space', and a focus on separateness and individuality. For women, the appropriate direction for development is nurturance of the 'inner space' and development as a person through connectedness and relational experience.

There is certainly evidence, up to the 1980s, in support of different developmental orientations for male and female teenagers (Archer 1985; Douvan and Adelson 1966). However, many critics have pointed out that this state of affairs is by no means universal and is as likely to be based on the different socialisation of girls and boys as on biological differences between the sexes (see especially the work of Carol Gilligan, 1982). In an extension of the gender 'difference' hypothesis to aspects of body image, Lerner and Spanier (1980) found little support for the speculation that teenage boys' emphasis on mastery of the external world would lead them to be more concerned with bodily effectiveness, while girls' emphasis on inner space would predispose them toward concerns about attractiveness, not effectiveness.

While the debate still exists about gender differences in the path to identity formation, we might ask whether the differentiation of identity styles for the sexes is healthy for individuals or for the community, and whether recent changes in young women's roles in society might lead to a diminution of these differences. A further point at issue relates to Erikson's insistence that successful maturation results from a developmental sequence in which identity develops prior to resolution of the intimacy–isolation conflict. Support for Erikson's position came from early studies such as Orlofsky *et al.* (1973). They found greater capacity for intimate relationships among young people with more fully formed identities. They labelled as 'pseudo-intimate' those with immature identity development who described a particular relationship as central to their lives. These relationships did not appear to be characterised by a high degree of mutuality and were likely to be one-sided and based on overcoming personal deficit ('I am nothing without him').

Following a review of studies which support the claim that identity precedes intimacy, Adams (1991) suggests that the pathway through these stages of development may take different directions for different individuals. Some young people stress the importance of their interpersonal skills in working through both stages; for others the interpersonal skills lag behind as individuality develops through mastery and autonomy. These different pathways may not necessarily be linked with gender *per se*, but with sex role orientation. This, in turn, is linked with the kind of socialisation one has experienced. Those with a more 'feminine' sex role orientation (whether boys or girls), for whom the nurturant and interpersonal aspects of existence have been stressed, will incorporate more fully these features as part of identity development. Those with a more masculine orientation, for whom socialisation has stressed individual achievement, will move through the identity and intimacy stages of development in ways which appear to be less overlapping. The issue of sexual adjustment is one which clearly involves both self-understanding and the ability to relate sensitively to others, so that in Erikson's terms, successful identity and intimacy achievement are important, whatever their mode or pathway of development.

Marcia (1966, 1976) took Erikson's ideas about identity development further and formulated a sequence of four developmental stages or statuses, based on exploration and commitment. We can relate these stages to the development of adolescent sexuality in the following ways. At the first level, *identity diffusion*, the adolescent has not thought deeply, if at all, about sexuality and sexual values, and is not struggling to make any decisions or commitments. Adolescents at the *identity foreclosure* stage have committed themselves to some decisions without experiencing any crisis or questioning. The decisions are often parentally determined or chosen because of fashion or peer group pressure. In the area of sexuality an example of foreclosure would be accepting without question parental sexual values, or undertaking an arranged marriage. Another kind of foreclosed identity occurs when adolescents make hasty decisions or put themselves in difficult-to-reverse situations which lead to a limitation of life options, such as early pregnancy.

According to Marcia, adolescents at the stage of *identity moratorium* are searching for clearer directions and beliefs. They may have ideas about where they are headed, but more thinking and questioning needs to occur before commitment is made. This is a time of experimentation and learning. It can be conflict ridden, as adolescents question parental beliefs and try out all kinds of value and behavioural options in the search for a sense of self.

In the sexual domain, these teenagers could be avoiding the pressure to go steady by trying to play the field. On the other hand, they may experiment with an intimate relationship but in a situation which is unlikely to lead to permanent commitment. There could be experimentation with different styles of relating to the opposite sex, with different sexual values, and with different sexual orientations. It is important that teenagers at this stage do not become labelled and thus typecast into permanent life patterns which are not in their best interests, such a delinquent, drug addict, or 'slut'. The moratorium stage serves the important function of giving the adolescent time to make life choices in this complex world. To make those choices requires finding out about and testing some of the available options.

In the final stage, *identity achievement*, which occurs late in adolescence, options have been explored and considered choices made about career, ideology, personal relationships, and sexuality. In fact, we appear, at present, to be experiencing the phenomenon of delayed identity achievement, in which adolescents engage in longer periods of experimentation before commitments to career and marriage, partnership or family are made. There is a world-wide trend against marrying young and child-bearing is being delayed quite commonly until late twenties, early thirties, or even later, as women work to become established in careers and couples work to obtain material comfort before beginning a family (McDonald 1991).

Despite the worries they can cause parents, these delays are probably adaptive, given the complexity of the modern world and the extent to which coping skills must be learned. Today's young people must be prepared to change careers during their lives, and to deal with interpersonal and sexual stresses (such as the risk of AIDS) that their parents did not have to face. Although delaying identity achievement may have an adaptive function, it also presents potential difficulties. These may arise from the high expectations put on marriage and partnership by young people who have a well-established sense of self and are reluctant to make the compromises required – in Erikson's terms – for an intimate relationship. We need to know more about the relationships between identity development and sexual adjustment among older adolescents and young adults, both in the narrow sense of the achievement of sexual satisfaction and, more broadly, the sense of being able to develop and sustain intimate relationships.

Criticisms of Erikson's model of adolescent development largely concern the separate development hypothesised for boys and girls, and his assumption of heterosexuality as the universal goal of mature sexuality. Another attack comes from writers such as Chilman (1980a), who questions the universality and importance of identity development. Chilman suggests that issues of identity are paramount only for adolescents from affluent, middle-class groups whose cultural values support individuality, and for adolescents in these groups who are highly intelligent and have the freedom and opportunities to choose the directions their lives will take. It certainly may be the case that aspects of identity formation such as career choice are not relevant to all adolescents. But learning to cope with sexuality and to place sexuality within the context of one's self-identity is an essential task for all adolescents.

SEXUALITY AND THE SOCIAL CONTEXT

Lerner and Spanier's sexual socialisation model

These theorists have provided a 'job description' for the sexual develop-ment of adolescents, describing a series of sexual tasks as important achievements at this stage.

> Sexual socialisation is the process of becoming sexual, of taking on a gender identity, learning sex roles, understanding sexual behaviour, and generally acquiring the knowledge, skills and dispositions that allow a person to function sexually in a given culture.
>
> (Lerner and Spanier 1980: 289)

Sexuality develops through a life-long process of sexual socialisation as conscious and unconscious attitudes form and alter through childhood, adolescence, middle, and old age. These shifting attitudes, together with changing physical desires and capacities, form the basis for new behaviours. Sexual socialisation reaches an important phase in adoles-cence, as hormonal balances change, genitals develop to their adult form, bodily functions alter, and new feelings are experienced. These changes occur at the same time as other important social and psychological develop-ments. The task for the adolescent is to integrate the physical, social and emotional aspects of sexuality with other developmental domains. While this difficult task is unlikely to be accomplished by the end of adolescence, if ever, each teenager will take steps in this direction and the progress he or she makes will influence future adjustment and life-course, both sexually and in other aspects of life.

Lerner and Spanier (1980) argue that the following aspects of development together comprise the process of 'sexual socialisation': (a) development of a sex-object preference, (b) development of gender iden-tity, (c) development of sex roles, (d) acquiring sexual skills, knowledge and values, and (e) development of dispositions to act in sexual contexts. The first of these, based on both biological-hereditary and social-psychological factors, involves the choice of which sex will become the focus of sexual interest. Most people are heterosexual, a small but significant proportion of the population are homosexual, and for some, the focus of sexual interest will shift at various points through the life-span.

The development of gender identity or the identification of oneself as male or female is a task of sexual socialisation usually completed early in life, except in rare cases. The social definition of a child at birth customarily follows the anatomical sex of the child and gender identity is formed over the next few years as the child is reinforced by others in that sexual designation (see, for example, Money and Ehrhardt 1972). At the same time, children develop an understanding that their sex is an unchanging feature, and that, for example, girls cannot grow up to be 'daddies'. They also learn, in both direct and subtle ways, to behave according to conventional expectations about appropriate behaviour for their sex.

In rare cases there are discrepancies between the person's designated sex and their internal feelings and self-definition, or mistakes in the original designation which do not become obvious until gender identity is entrenched. Gender identity becomes a crisis issue for such individuals, who may wish to cross-dress, live as the opposite sex, or have sex-change operations. While such situations are uncommon, more frequent among teenagers may be feelings of rejection of perceived aspects of their gender identity. For example a boy may feel uncomfortable about behaving in 'macho' ways expected of him, or a girl may feel embarrassed by external signs of her gender (such as breast development), or reject perceived female sex role expectations to be flirtatious or to act 'dumb' in the presence of boys. This aspect of gender identity overlaps with Lerner and Spanier's third component of sexual socialisation, the development of sex roles.

Sex role development means learning how to be psychologically masculine or feminine. Traditional sex roles for females encompass such traits as nurturance, emotionality, warmth, expressiveness, co-operation, and dependency, while the corresponding traits for males are independence, assertion, self-sufficiency, competitiveness, and instrumental effectiveness. Earlier conceptions of sex roles assumed that the mature, adjusted course of development involved taking on traditional roles (Broverman *et al.* 1970; McCandless 1970), and psychoanalytic models still contain elements of this view (as we have seen in our discussion of Erikson's work). Arguments about the relationship between adjustment and sex roles were stimulated by Bem's (1974) conception of psychological masculinity and femininity as independent dimensions, rather than the two ends of a bi-polar continuum. Bem (1975) argued that more adjusted individuals in today's complex society needed to be able to access both their masculine and feminine sides – to be both expressive and instrumental or 'androgynous' – depending on the situation. Other research suggests a 'masculinity' model of adjustment, linking masculine qualities with adjustment and self-esteem (Antill and Cunningham 1980; Feather 1985; Jones *et al.* 1978). Although Cunningham (1990) concludes that masculinity benefits the adjustment and self-esteem of young girls these benefits are less clear for young boys and in the area of developing sexual relationships, there is evidence that androgyny is advantageous (McCabe 1984; McCabe and Collins 1979).

Development of sex roles occurs partly – or perhaps completely – via the socialisation process which encourages and rewards some behaviours and attitudes while discouraging and punishing others. Because of this, in societies with strong gender stereotyping, sex roles will align markedly with designated sex. In societies with less rigidly defined gender roles (such as our own), the boundaries between traditional and non-traditional will be blurred, and more traits will be viewed as unrelated to gender. The actual processes by which this happens are not well understood. By adolescence, however, we know that much of what constitutes one's sex role has already been learned, but there is still more to learn. There are also decisions still to be made, such as the appropriate role to take in relating to the opposite sex. We examine the links between sexual behaviour, sex role, and sex role stereotyping in detail in Chapter 5.

The next important aspect of sexual socialisation in Lerner and Spanier's model, and one of particular relevance to adolescent development, is the acquisition of sexual skills, knowledge, and values. Young people are vitally interested in sex and are open to new information, while at the same time questioning values and experimenting with behaviour. Parents and formal channels such as school are important sources of learning about sexuality, but much of this occurs within the peer group context. The ways in which these social influences operate are taken up in Chapter 4. What is apparent, though, is that teenagers acquire many myths about sex and learn inappropriate behaviours and values, as well as appropriate skills and positive, safe and life-enhancing values.

In exploring the development of sexual behavioural patterns, Lerner and Spanier point out that teenagers with similar attitudes, knowledge and sexual skills may behave quite differently in similar sexual situations. They suggest that the final aspect of sexual socialisation is the development of predispositions to act in certain ways in sexual contexts. Predispositions may relate to social factors, the particular relationship of the moment, or the teenager's past experience. For example, teenage girls are less likely to take precautions against sexually transmissible diseases if they interpret their current relationship as 'steady'. Under the influence of alcohol, adolescents may feel more confident about experimenting sexually, or engaging in sexual experiences that they would avoid in a more rational state.

The sexual socialisation model is important because it integrates many aspects of sexuality in order to describe the fully functioning sexual person, giving prominence to the role of learning and experience in sexual development. In this way, the model provides a counter to the heavily biological stances of the psychoanalytic theorists. We turn now to a model of sexuality which emphasises the social, contextual aspects of development, but embeds the development of adolescent sexuality within broader developmental issues.

Adolescent sexuality as a developmental task

While not presenting his views as a formal theory, Robert Selverstone (1989) has some interesting ideas about how the development of sexuality contributes to overall healthy development at adolescence.

> Healthy adolescent sexual behaviour is just one aspect of overall healthy adolescent development. The key question about what constitutes healthy adolescent sexuality is not so much the extent of conformity to traditional demands for abstinence, but the extent to which adolescent sexual behaviour fosters or impedes the development of healthy self esteem, and concomitant mastery of a teenager's developmental tasks. Such behaviour should be respectful and not exploitative of others, and it should not endanger the physical or mental health of the participants.
>
> (Selverstone 1989: 1)

Sclverstone regards sexual behaviour as one of the key ways, in modern society, for adolescents to 'de-satellise' or begin, emotionally, to leave the family orbit and move toward independence. Successful moves toward the gradual attainment of adult sexuality will heighten feelings of self-esteem and perceived competence to cope. They will also contribute to the attainment of the four developmental tasks which Selverstone views as relevant to today's youth. These tasks are identity, connectedness, power, and hope/joy.

There is agreement with Erikson that identity achievement is the central task for adolescence, such that the young person comes to view himself or herself as an independent being with a direction in life and a sense of uniqueness and self-worth. Experiencing oneself as a sexual being, making decisions about sexuality, and learning to relate in a sexual way can contribute to that sense of identity.

Connectedness with others is important in adolescence because emotional distancing from family can be a lonely and daunting process. Yet this is a necessary part of growing up and adolescents have the opportunity to forge new relationships and emotional ties with their peer group. Teenagers can learn about themselves by talking and interacting with peers. They can receive emotional support to help cope with all the changes and new experiences occurring during this period of life, and they can learn the give and take of intimate relationships with non-family members. To be part of a group, to be connected with others, is seen by Selverstone as an important task of adolescence. The connected adolescent will learn the norms and mores of sexual interaction more readily, and will be cushioned from some of the disappointments and set-backs which accompany the moves to sexual maturity. Conversely, the ability to handle relationships and sexuality will contribute to a sense of being part of a group.

According to Selverstone, the process of maturity also depends on achieving a sense of power and control over one's life. This comes from mastery, from being free enough to try new things and experience success at self-initiated tasks. Feeling good about one's bodily appearance and effectiveness, and about one's ability to relate to others, can contribute to that power.

Finally, Selverstone underscores the importance for adolescents of a sense of optimism about the future, which arises from success in the preceding tasks. The hopefulness, confidence in the future, and spontaneous joy of youth is what will spur on young people to move through the rough patches ahead in the path to maturity. Sexuality as a source of joy should not be underestimated – sexual feelings can act as a positive motivator and a source of life energy.

Of course, while all of these tasks can contribute to successful sexual development, their unsuccessful resolution can affect and be affected by experiences in the sexual domain. Adolescents can use sex indiscriminately in an attempt to bolster popularity and self-esteem, a strategy which is not always successful. For example, Orr *et al.* (1989) found a link between early sexual initiation and poor self-esteem for girls, a finding in accord with Selverstone's case material which suggested that loss of virginity prior to 15 years for girls is often regretted or feels premature. Sex can be used to gain power over others (see Chapter 9), or can become the inappropriate focus of identity formation, for example the person who feels they are defined by their level of sexual attractiveness. Selverstone suggests that sexual involvement is one of the ways we learn to feel lovable, but that inappropriate involvement and sexual risk-taking can be counter-productive in the quest toward self-definition and personal integration.

BLENDING NATURE AND NURTURE

The biosocial model of adolescent sexual behaviour

Edward Smith (1989) has built on the work of Udry and his colleagues (Udry 1979; Udry *et al.* 1985; Udry *et al.* 1986) to produce a model of adolescent sexual behaviour which delineates biological and psychological influences and their interactions. He limits his emphasis to the prediction of various aspects of sexual behaviour, such as age of initiation of intercourse, frequency of sexual activity, number of partners, contraceptive practices and the like. Unlike theorists discussed earlier, Smith does not emphasise the interrelationships between sexual development and general adjustment although, because those interrelationships are likely to be strong, his model has implications for those who counsel young people and deliver sex education.

While psychosexual theories of behaviour take account of biological influences in a general way only, Smith's biosocial model considers specific, potentially measurable biological aspects of adolescence and uses these to predict sexual behaviour. As well, he postulates a range of social processes which encourage or discourage sexual involvement, modify the form in which sexual behaviour is expressed, and define appropriate sexual partners. Hormonal changes during adolescence are viewed as having both a direct effect on libido (or sexual motivation) and an indirect effect on sexual involvement by changing the adolescent's physical appearance. In this way, external 'signposts' indicate that sexual maturity is beginning, while at the same time producing variations in perceived attractiveness. The attractiveness of particular physical characteristics – such as large breasts and soft skin for a woman, and a muscular build for a male – may have evolutionary significance, as they relate to correlates of good reproductive and nurturing capacities (Savin-Williams and Weisfield 1989).

As we have already seen, there are various cultural, as well as biological, sources of influence on sexual behaviour. These sources of social influence act together to affect the adolescents' attitudes toward sexual involvement and behavioural norms, as well as providing – or not providing – opportunities for sexual interaction. The social and biological forces interact in complex ways. For example, a young person who appears sexually mature and has physical features designated attractive by the prevailing culture may experience more social pressures to act in sexual ways than a late developing youth or one who is perceived to be unattractive. Peers and potential sexual partners of sexually mature youths may encourage sexual involvement. Praise, popularity and self-esteem may accrue from engaging in sex. On the other hand, parents may be wary of the sexual potential of early maturing teenagers and may offer many sanctions against sex. All of this will be mediated by the young person's own sexual desires and the attitudes and values developed prior to puberty. In Chapter 3, we discuss research studies in which sexual behaviour is associated with both hormonal changes and social influences (such as best friend's sexual experience). The way these factors interact differs for boys and girls, with evidence that the latter are more susceptible to the social, and males to the biological, influences (Udry 1988).

SOCIOCULTURAL INTERPRETATIONS OF SEXUALITY

Various writers have described the sexual behaviours typical of different cultures (for example, Reiss 1967) and attempted to account for these behavioural differences through analysis of prevailing cultural norms. Some of these norms are explicit and open, with clear guidelines about their enactment. One example of this relates to laws about the age of consent. Other norms are expressed by group members but not necessarily adhered to. For example, in our society we may openly deplore sexual violence yet much of this behaviour occurs without censure, particularly in a domestic context. There are also instances of conflict between the mores and norms of subgroups within a particular society. While an older generation may value sexual restraint and deplore permissiveness, the younger generation may hold a different view, valuing experimentation and sexual liberalism. As one 15-year-old Italian-Australian girl says,

> My parents were engaged to each other when they were really really young, about 12 or 13. Sex before marriage – no way! It is just the things they believe in, and they put it across to you . . . you just know that is the way you are supposed to act. I don't think I will be like my parents. I will try hard *not* to be like them.

And, as we shall see in Chapter 5, sexual norms and mores are regarded differently by boys and girls, men and women. To confuse the matter further, many social norms and values are implicit and not articulated well or even at all. As a result, it may not be possible for many to express clearly what the rule is or why it exists, although the consequences of non-adherence may be severe. An analysis of appropriate courting behaviour in our society provides a good example of this issue. What is meant by 'coming on too strong', for example, and how is it that some individuals can get away with certain sexual overtures while others would be rejected if they engaged in similar behaviours? When is a woman too sexy and when is she not sexy enough? When is it appropriate for a female to take the initiative in courting behaviour?

The analysis of a society's sexual norms is important in understanding the sexual behaviours of individuals. It is a difficult task for those looking at their society from within because of the problems of being objective about one's own situation but also because, from within, we may not always see the wood for the trees. Miner (1956) made this point beautifully in a paper entitled 'Body ritual among the Nacimera', in which he described the strange habits of a tribe of North Americans who undertake, among other bodily rituals, daily rites associated with the mouth. If these rites are not performed it is believed by these people that teeth will fall out, gums bleed, and friends and lovers reject them. The practices consist of inserting bundles of stiff hairs into the mouth, along with magical powders, then moving the bundles around in formalised gestures, at least twice, sometimes more often, per day. To look at the cleaning of teeth in this way certainly sheds a different light on its practice. Other descriptions of cultural practices of the 'Nacimera' (American backwards) become both fascinating and amusing as they are isolated and examined from a sociocultural perspective. A similar description of the sexual practices of Western nations from the outside would be equally enlightening. Indeed, this is what sociologists have tried to do in a number of different ways.

Gagnon and Simon (1973) use the term 'sexual scripts' to describe the stereotypic and ritualised ways in which we behave sexually and the social prescriptions for this behaviour. These scripts refer to what we do sexually – for example, how courting will take place. They also, to some extent, programme our desires. For example, scripts provide guidelines as to who will be judged as attractive and desirable within a particular culture. Gagnon and Simon argue that men and women are socialised to follow different sexual scripts and that much of what has been interpreted as a function of a biological sex drive is, in fact, culturally determined. A number of other writers have attempted to fill out the detail of what constitutes adolescent sexual scripts through analysis of social interactions (Libby 1976), adolescent literature, myths and stories (McRobbie 1991; Walkerdine 1984), and the way people talk about sex and relationships (Lees 1989; Hollway 1984). This last form of research has become known as discourse analysis, with discourses conceptualised as systems of understanding which are adopted by individuals in order to interpret their worlds. These systems of understanding are reflected in the ways we talk about sex and relationships. In Chapter 5 we focus on the different sexual scripts adopted by young teenagers and describe some discourses which represent male–female interactions in Western society.

LETTING TEENAGERS SPEAK

The preceding discussion has focused on psychologists' and sociologists' views of adolescent sexuality and its developmental unfolding and consequences. But teenagers themselves have their own theories of sex and how it impinges on their lives. They express, more or less coherently, both a diversity and a similarity of views on these subjects. It is our strong belief that any theory which attempts to explain human behaviour must take into account the experiences and attitudes of its target population – in all their variety as well as consistency. To illustrate this point, we conclude this chapter with the voices of young people aged 15 to 18 years from a range of backgrounds, who were asked what they thought about one particular aspect of their sexual lives, namely virginity.

> It's traditional I know. If you're a virgin it means holding yourself back for that one person you're going to marry. When you walk down the aisle with that white dress – and it has to be white – you're that conscious if you've clouded it at all. So you'll be pure. I know that is really old fashioned, but that's how I think it should be.

> For a guy [virginity is] bad. It shows he is weak and can't get it off with a woman and that sort of thing.

> I don't think it exists anymore. People usually end up losing their virginity before they are married anyway. So I don't believe in it.

> It is something that you should not take lightly – it is pretty serious. You have to be pretty serious about someone to have sex for the first time.

> I think virginity is a good thing. I don't think you have to prove yourself to people by losing your virginity. I would love to have my virginity back again. The thrill of having sex for the first time and waiting so long would make it so much better. I know a lot of girls who are virgins, and I respect them for that.

> [I] don't know – it is good, but people might pick on you.

> It is just that you are the only one who has made love to her, and if someone else has, and you come along and get married to her, then you come across that person that she has made love with – well, there would still be that bond and you would feel uncomfortable with her.

> A girl should be a virgin, but for a guy it doesn't matter.

Clearly, there is no single sexual culture among adolescents. For example, across the teenage years, young people's sexual worlds are very different, attesting to the degree of change occurring over this age span. But we are on equally shaky ground if we try to generalise across the sexes, or ethnic groups, or socioeconomic status, or possibly even interest groups such as stamp collectors and football fans. The words of our teenagers serve to illustrate some of this variation, which provides a challenge for theory makers and those working with young people.

We have not attempted, in this chapter, to describe and evaluate every theory that deals with adolescent sexuality. Rather, we have been selective, showing the range of approaches applied to the psychology of adolescent sex. Research which is summarised in subsequent chapters is usually influenced or motivated by aspects of these models presented, although the researcher may not always be explicit about the assumptions with which she or he is working. Theories and models provide us with new insights and new ways of looking at behaviour. They help us to forge conceptual links between the plethora of data available on teenagers' sexual behaviour, attitudes, knowledge, and beliefs. They enable us to understand the antecedents of adolescent sexuality and its expression among the youth of today. Theories can also help in predicting adult sexual outcomes. They link sexuality with other aspects of adjustment and coping skills. What is important is that we view these theoretical approaches not as static, but as developing frameworks which can eventually lead to better integration of research data, case material, common sense, and personal experience.

3   Biological aspects of sexual development

Adolescent sexuality is inextricably tied up with the events of puberty, in which the adolescent's body develops its adult shape and reproductive functioning and the hormonal changes affect sex drives in complex ways. Although biological development does not tell us everything about how and why we behave sexually, understanding of these processes is vital if the whole picture of sexual development is to emerge. In this chapter we describe the biology of sexual development, together with research on the relationships between biology and psychological variables, especially those related to sexual expression and sexual confidence.

IN THE BEGINNING . . .

Puberty's onset marks the beginning of adult sexual development, a process for which biological preparations have been occurring since conception. The single cell which begins life, and arises from the combination of mother's egg and father's sperm, contains twenty-three pairs of chromosomes. One pair of chromosomes holds the determinants of genetic sex. This pair is either XX, denoting a female, or XY, denoting a male. Each of these genetic configurations provides a blueprint for sexual development of the male or female type but, particularly in the case of the male, does not guarantee this development. Certain conditions in the physiological environment of the uterus must prevail. After birth, although the die is usually cast in a biological sense, conditions of the psychological environment and their interactions with biological features of the individual can influence the ways in which maleness and femaleness are manifest. This influence extends, eventually, to how puberty is coped with and how adult sexuality takes shape. Some of the details of these complex interactions, which are by no means fully understood, will be discussed in this chapter.

For the first six weeks of life, the human embryo is sexually undifferentiated. Then, in the normal course of events, males develop testicles and, somewhat later, females develop ovaries. These structures, termed gonads, produce hormones which direct the development of male and female internal and external sex organs. Hormone secretion and balance is controlled by the reproductive endocrine system, involving complex interactions between the brain, the pituitary gland (a small organ at the base of the brain which receives signals from the brain and releases hormones into the bloodstream), and the gonads. Both male and female reproductive systems produce androgen (the masculinising hormone) and oestrogen (the feminising hormone), but it is the concentration and balance of these hormones throughout life which determine male or female morphology and, to some extent, behaviour. In utero, testicles produce enough androgen to dominate the oestrogen in the male, while ovaries produce enough oestrogen to dominate the androgen in the female.

In rare cases when the male embryo does not produce sufficient androgens, or there are problems within the reproductive endocrine system relating to androgen sensitivity, the result is a girl-child, in spite of the XY chromosomes. The studies by Money and his associates (Money 1968; Money and Ehrhardt 1972; Money *et al.* 1955) of sexual abnormalities at birth and in childhood led to the conclusion that 'Unless there is sufficient push in the male direction, the fetus will take the female turn at any subsequent fork (of embryonic development). Whether there is a female push or not, nature's first choice is to make Eve' (Money and Tucker 1975: 73).

Abnormalities in the oestrogen production of the female fetus are usually overcome by the oestrogens of the mother, so that female development does not need an 'extra hormonal push' (Chilman 1980a). Cases have occurred, however, in which females have received prenatally an oversupply of androgens because of drugs inappropriately prescribed to the mothers. In these cases, some girls were born with masculinised genitalia but their internal reproductive systems were unaffected. Although these girls underwent corrective surgery for abnormalities, and grew up to have a clear sense of female identity, they tended to behave as 'tomboys' in comparison with a matched control group of girls who had not been susceptible to these androgenising effects (Money and Ehrhardt 1972).

It has been postulated that hormonal differences between males and females produce differences not only in physiological structures, but in brain structure and function (Bardwick 1971; Moir and Jessel 1989). Bardwick concluded on the basis of some animal studies that brain differences arise in the prenatal and early infancy stages of life as a result of the effects of the sex hormones on the central nervous system. Male and female brains are predisposed to differentially perceive and respond to stimuli, according to this view, which has been expressed in popular form by Moir and Jessel (1989) in their book *Brainsex*. Thus, the basis for many behaviours attributed solely to differential socialising of the sexes (Maccoby and Jacklin 1974) has been re-attributed to biology. Like all nature–nurture controversies, the 'truth' is difficult to tease out and the attempt to do so is perhaps not even sensible as biological and social forces are so intertwined. Clearly, biological differences affect the way individuals respond to environmental stimuli. Equally clearly, environment can modify biology. Discussions about the origins of sex differences in behaviour and personality are often more motivated by political than scientific concerns. This may be due to an awareness that an over-emphasis on biological explanations can be interpreted – incorrectly – as somehow implying the validity of rigid and unchanging sex role stereotyping.

It is difficult to summarise all of sexual development prior to puberty. Everything that happens to every individual child, in a physiological, a psychological, and a social sense, is relevant. By puberty, much is set in developmental terms. However, there is considerable potential for flexibility and both adaptive and maladaptive change, as at any point in life. Although puberty does not inevitably change amenable children into rebellious, confused, stress-ridden and sex-crazed adolescents, it has particular power as a life-influencing event because of the extent of change which occurs to the individual in a relatively short time-span. Teenagers experience change in physical appearance, strength and power, change in feelings, change in others' expectations, change in social pressures, and potentially, change in ways of thinking about the world and about themselves.

ABOUT 10 OR 12 YEARS LATER . . .

The word puberty means 'to be covered in fine hair' and is derived from the Latin *pubescere* meaning 'to grow hairy or mossy'. The bodily changes associated with this phenomenon begin when part of the brain, the hypothalamus, signals the pituitary gland to release hormones called gonadotrophins into the bloodstream. These hormones, the release of which precedes noticeable bodily changes by about a year, stimulate increased production of oestrogen and androgen by the ovaries in the girl and the testes in the boy. The ovaries increase their production of oestrogen sixfold in the girl's body, and the testes produce twenty times the amount of the androgen, testosterone, in the boy's body. As we have said, both sexes have male and female hormones circulating in the bloodstream, but the balance is different. During adolescence, a boy's androgen level becomes 20 to 60 per cent higher than that of a girl, while her oestrogen level becomes 20 to 30 per cent higher than his (Nielsen 1991).

What triggers off the signal from the hypothalamus to the pituitary to begin the release of gonadotrophins is largely unknown. It is obviously not age alone, as puberty begins at different times for different people although most adolescents begin within the age range of 9 to 16. Precocious or delayed puberty is usually related to disease, the effects of drugs, or engaging in practices inimical to physical health, such as excessive dieting. The average age at onset of puberty has shown a trend toward earlier occurrence – the secular trend – which cuts across geographic and ethnic lines. Some recent research, however, suggests that this trend has slowed in the last twenty or so years (Brooks-Gunn and Reiter 1990). The decline in the age of puberty is thought to be due to improvements in nutrition and living conditions and has been linked with diet and weight in early infancy and late childhood (Liestol 1982). Frisch and Revelle (1970) present the controversial hypothesis that attainment of a critical body weight and a related change in metabolic rate triggers off the decrease in hypothalamic sensitivity to sex hormones which in turn leads to pituitary activation. They cite as evidence the mean weight of girls at menarche (about 47 kg) which has not changed over the past 125 years even though the age at which this weight is achieved has declined (Newman and Newman 1986).

THE CHANGES . . .

Bodily alterations at puberty include the growth spurt which is accompanied by changes in strength and body proportion, development of the primary sex characteristics (the external genitalia and internal organs which control their functioning), and of the secondary sex characteristics. These last are features which distinguish males and females but are not directly connected with reproduction, such as facial hair in males, breast development in females, and pubic hair for both sexes. Each of these changes will be briefly described in this section. Detailed descriptions are available from Marshall and Tanner (1969, 1970).

At adolescence, the final phase of physical growth occurs, resulting in adult stature and physical sexual maturity. About one year after pubertal hormonal activity has been initiated, the adolescent growth spurt begins. This leads to an average increase in height for girls of 19.6 cm and for boys of 21.1 cm, although there is great individual variation. The growth spurt begins for girls any time between 9.5 years and 15 years, with the average age at about 10.5 years. The peak year of growth occurs at 12 years and the growth spurt is usually completed by age 14. For boys, the growth spurt starts later on average – between 10.5 and 16 years – with the average age of commencement being 12.5, peak at age 14, and spurt completion at 16 (Tanner 1970). The average duration of the growth spurt is 2.8 years for both sexes (Faust 1977).

Growth in height is dramatic during this period. Much of this is in trunk length and the long bones of the legs, contributing to the stereotype of the gangly adolescent (Katchadourian 1977). Because of the delay in onset of the growth spurt among boys, 12-year-old girls are on average taller than boys, but this is reversed for all subsequent ages. Weight gains occur also, largely due to increases in muscle and fat, with increases in muscle size contributing to increased strength. Power, athletic skill, and endurance all increase progressively and rapidly through adolescence with most boys surpassing most girls on these dimensions. Bodily proportions also alter. Children begin puberty with shoulders slightly broader than hips. For girls, the shoulder width/hip width ratio decreases throughout puberty while for boys this ratio increases (Newman and Newman 1986).

Sexual maturation for girls includes the growth of pubic and axillary hair, breast development, and menarche (the onset of menstruation). This occurs usually between 10 and 16 years with a mean age for American and British populations of around 12.5 years (Faust 1977; Marshall and Tanner 1969; Tanner 1966). The menstrual cycle introduces a pattern of hormonal variations associated with ovulation, building up of the uterine lining in preparation for fertilisation, and the shedding of this lining via the menstrual period. Oestrogen and progesterone levels rise and fall in association with these events. The uterus, vagina, vulva, clitoris and other internal structures undergo growth and development so that the teenage girl has a functional reproductive system about twelve to eighteen months after the first menstrual period and is physically capable of bearing children.

Sexual maturation for boys involves increased growth of the testes, scrotum and penis, pubic, bodily and facial hair development, and maturation of the internal prostate gland and the seminal vesicles. The first ejaculation of seminal fluid is likely to occur about two years after the beginning of pubic hair growth – either as a spontaneous emission or the result of masturbation. The number and mobility of sperm present in the seminal fluid increases throughout puberty with a corresponding increase in fertility. Other changes include an increase in the size of the larynx, leading to the voice changing to a deeper register and, for boys and girls alike, growth of the sweat glands with accompanying increases in body odour, and enlargement of the pores on facial skin. This last change, accompanied by hormonal changes, leads to the increased likelihood of acne.

It would be surprising if these momentous changes came and went without impact. The alterations to appearance, sexualisation of the body, increasing hormone concentrations and their effects on mood and libido, uneven growth rates, and inevitable comparisons with one's peers must all be coped with and incorporated into a new, adult body image. Mood swings, embarrassment and self-consciousness are common at this age. Physical awkwardness often results from growth asynchronies. Arms that are 15 cm longer than they were a year ago are apt to knock things over. Teenagers often appear to others as 'all arms and legs'. Other potential embarrassments for the self-conscious teenager include body odours and acne. Many young people worry whether their growth patterns are normal. The peer group can be relentless in its pressure for conformity so being, or even feeling, different in terms of body shape or fitness can be stressful. The effects of pubertal change on body image, the role of perceived attractiveness in adjustment to bodily changes, and the effects of early and late puberty are discussed in more detail in a later section of this chapter.

ADOLESCENTS: SLAVES TO THEIR HORMONES?

Recent research shows us that young people are not mere slaves to hormonal changes, but there is no doubt that these changes can have complex emotional and behavioural effects. The strength of these depends in part on the social context in which the adolescent finds himself or herself. Buchanan *et al.* (1992) argue that there are four types of hormone-behaviour associations. The first is that increasing or decreasing concentrations of hormones (within the normal range) affect moods or behaviours. Buchanan *et al.* give the example that among adult humans, oestrogen is associated with more positive moods and its lack with depression and negative affect, mainly in women. Among adolescent girls, higher levels of oestrogen have also been shown to relate to more positive mood (Eccles *et al.* 1988). On the negative side, higher androstenedione has been associated with lower energy, and higher testosterone with lower frustration tolerance, in adolescent boys (Nottelmann *et al.* 1985; Olweus 1986). In fact, across a number of studies, oestrogen rises have been associated with positive affect, and testosterone rises with increased aggression.

A second type of hormone effect postulated by Buchanan is the adjustment required when hormone levels deviate from the levels to which the individual is accustomed, an effect often related to developmental change. For example, while adult women may be used to the effects of hormone level variations accompanying the menstrual cycle, early-adolescent girls may be highly responsive to these. As an illustration of this, Brooks-Gunn and Warren (1989) found that although oestrogen is generally associated with higher activation and feelings of well-being in animals and adult humans, for girls at an early stage of puberty, high oestrogen predicts depression and lowered impulse control. Susman and Nottelmann have also shown that high concentrations of certain hormones *for one's age* are associated with negative moods (Nottelmann *et al.* 1985, 1987; Susman *et al.* 1985). Thus the important determiners of mood are not necessarily hormone levels or even their fluctuations *per se*, but the deviations in concentration from what the adolescent is used to.

A third kind of effect comes about through hormone 'irregularity' or fluctuations in hormone surges which do not follow a standard pattern. Cyclical patterns of hormone activity such as those experienced during the menstrual cycle can occur with unpredictable irregularity during early adolescence when these cycles are establishing themselves. Some evidence that this irregularity affects mood comes from studies of adult women for whom atypical patterns of hormone change have been linked to negative mood and behavioural symptoms (Coppen and Kessel 1963; Dennerstein *et al.* 1984). Buchanan and her colleagues have at present found only limited links between hormone variability (or irregularity) and mood swings in adolescence but this is an area in which there has as yet been little systematic research.

Finally, there are possibilities for complex interactions between hormone levels, moods, behaviours, and other biological and social variables. These include an individual's sensitivity to the various hormones, his or her predisposition toward the behaviour of interest, or contextual factors such as strong social sanctions against certain behaviours. For example, level of circulating testosterone in boys is a significant predictor of sexual arousal, coital activity, masturbation, thinking about sex, and future intentions with respect to sexual activity (Udry 1988; Udry *et al.* 1985). For girls, the adrenal androgens – including testosterone – predict non-coital sexual activity (such as fantasy and masturbation), and arousal. But prediction of actual sexual intercourse depends on social conditions such as best friend's sexual activity, the girl's participation in sports, or the presence of father in the home (Udry 1988). It seems that the behavioural concomitants of testosterone for girls are modified by the social forces surrounding the expression of female sexuality, including the influence of significant others.

The ways in which hormone effects in adolescence are conceptualised by Buchanan underscores the importance of studying the relationships between biological variables and behaviour within both a biological and a social context. The biological context refers to the interaction which any hormone change will have with all the other bodily systems, and the relationship of this change to normal patterns of variation and to age and developmental norms. The social context refers to the individual's attitudes, habits, beliefs and past behaviours together with the expectations and norms of significant others, and how this moderates or accentuates the effects of hormones. Among teenagers, these contexts are in a state of rapid change so that while we know that hormone levels affect behaviour, the details of these effects are likely to vary greatly between individuals and even within the one individual over time.

HOW DO I LOOK?

Tuesday September 8th

Lousy stinking school on Thursday. I tried my old uniform on but I have outgrown it so badly that my father is being forced to buy me a new one tomorrow. He is going up the wall but I can't help it if my body is in a growth period can I? I am only five centimetres shorter than Pandora now. My thing remains static at twelve centimetres.

Friday February 26th

My thing is now thirteen centimetres long when it is extended. When it is contracted it is hardly worth measuring. My general physique is improving. I think the back-stretching exercises are paying off. I used to be the sort of boy who had sand kicked in his face, now I'm the sort of boy who watches somebody else have it kicked in their face.

(Townsend 1982)

One of the most compelling examples of the biological-social nexus comes from teenagers' concerns about their bodies. Psychologists have commonly addressed this by examining adolescents' feelings about their body image and the consequences of physical attractiveness. Most teenage boys and men say that they want to be taller, more muscular and heavier. Many, if not most, teenage girls dislike their bodies, seeing themselves as fat or overweight when in fact they are either average or below average weight for their age and height. A study of nearly 6,000 adolescents between 12 and 17 years of age showed that 70 per cent of the girls wanted to be thinner. The most popular girls were the most concerned about being thin (Duncan *et al.* 1985). Moreover, Dummer's (1987) study of 1000 competitive swimmers whose bodies were fit and trim showed that the teenage girls were more dissatisfied with their bodies than the boys and wanted, more than any other change, to lose weight. Edgar (1974) questioned over 1000 Australian high school students and found that the majority were dissatisfied with some aspect of their body or personality, including concerns about hair, acne, weight, muscles, and figure. Girls are generally more dissatisfied with their bodies than boys and this dissatisfaction affects their overall self confidence to a greater extent. For example, in Clifford's (1971) study, when adolescents were asked to rate the item, 'myself', among a list of aspects of body satisfaction, boys rated this most highly while girls rated as twentieth this overall evaluation of the bodily self.

These attitudes do not develop in isolation. Schonfeld (1969) showed that family attitudes were important to the adolescent's acceptance of his or her own body. Maladaptive family patterns led to adolescents feeling insecure about their bodies and conflicted about aspects of sexuality and bodily functioning. Among these families were those that overstressed 'the body beautiful' and overreacted to slight deviations and even normal development. These families tended to make a big fuss about pubic hair or the appearance of a pimple. A second maladaptive pattern occurred among parents who projected their own anxieties about bodies and sexuality onto their children. In these families, for example, sexual motives which were not present were imputed to their children. A third family environment was one in which parents communicated anxieties about their children not growing quickly enough or, in some cases, growing up too quickly and becoming too independent.

While many studies have been concerned with the body image in adolescents, few have asked teenagers about their responses to their developing genitals. Is this a source of conflict, pride, or anxiety? Does it pass relatively unnoticed? Attitudes to genitals will begin to develop in childhood and be influenced by family attitudes, such as beliefs about modesty, cleanliness, and sexuality. How do these attitudes affect young people's responses to the changes in their primary and secondary sex characteristics? From early infancy, parental ways of touching the child, holding him or her, expressing approval or disapproval, and reacting to children's activities in relation to bathing, handling of genitals, toilet training, and masturbation help to shape the child's body image and beliefs about the 'goodness' and 'badness' or 'cleanness' and 'dirtiness' of various bodily parts. Children in our society are socialised to believe that some bodily parts, notably the genitals, are not the subject of polite conversation nor are they to be viewed or touched publicly. Thus many a two-year-old touching his or her genitals is told sharply to 'stop doing that', a command which must be confusing and anxiety-arousing given that the act was probably a pleasurable one. Within this social framework, it would not be surprising if genital growth was a source of adolescent anxiety. The fictional Adrian Mole, quoted above, kept a graph of the size of his 'thing' (penis) on his bedroom wall and his diary expresses mixtures of pride, mortification, misery and joy about his developing body and sexuality.

There is no doubt that how we look affects how people treat us and young people are particularly vulnerable to the pressures to meet culturally prescribed standards of beauty because of their desire to belong. Lerner *et al.* (1976) found female college students' self-esteem more strongly related

to their perceptions of physical attractiveness than to physical effectiveness, that is, fitness and strength. For boys, while self-esteem was
somewhat more related to effectiveness than attractiveness, the two ratings
were highly correlated. This suggests that the judgments boys make about
how good-looking they are are strongly linked with judgments about how
fit they feel. Peterson (1989) suggests that one of the most important
prerequisites for boys feeling attractive is the need to shave. She quotes the
study by Tobin-Richards *et al.* (1983) which concludes that this development is more important to young boys' satisfaction with their appearances
than other physical criteria such as an athletic physique.

The same study indicated that the two factors contributing most
strongly to girls' bodily acceptance were breast development and
weight. Weight was seen as more important to girls than to boys in terms
of satisfaction with physique. As most girls valued thinness, those more
advanced in their puberty (and so heavier) were less satisfied.
Prepubertal girls were also more satisfied with their less pronounced
facial features and small hands and feet. However the counterbalancing
effect which helped more pubertally advanced girls feel better about
their bodies was breast development, which was valued because of its
appeal to males. It appears that an 'ideal' female shape for the current
generation is that of 'child-woman', in which mature breast development is superimposed on the prepubertal body. Never mind that this is
virtually an impossible shape for most women to achieve.

Fashion has increased the stresses on adolescent females with respect to
body image and one of the outcomes has been a preoccupation with weight
and an upsurge of the syndromes of anorexia nervosa and bulimia. The
former is an obsessional and often unrealistic desire for thinness
accompanied by excessive dieting to the point of starvation, while the latter
refers to regular eating binges followed by purging by self-induced
vomiting or laxatives. An illustration of this preoccupation comes from a
study by Boocock and Trethewie (1981) of 65 high school girls who were
neither anorexic nor obese. These researchers modified a closed circuit
television so that the girl could project her subjective body image of front
and side-on width by adjusting a dial which could stretch or shrink the
picture up to 25 per cent wider or narrower than the girl's actual size. In line
with earlier research (Dwyer and Mayer 1968–9) it was shown that a
substantial proportion of girls who were underweight in terms of standard
age/height norms had a vision of themselves as fat and responded to this by
dieting. By contrast, some of the overweight girls were unaware that they
had a problem. There is obviously a need to encourage young people to be
more realistic about bodily size and shape through education about the
contribution of pubertal development to normal weight gain, the

importance of a healthy diet, and the distorting influences of fashion and media on beliefs about beauty. This is a tall order given that adults are often similarly preoccupied with appearance and weight and do not provide particularly convincing role models (Wolf 1991).

Social factors alone may not be sufficient to account for the occurrence of eating disorders like anorexia (Casper 1989). A psychoanalytic inter-pretation of this disease is that it represents an unconscious flight from sexual maturity through a return to a child-like body state and, usually, the cessation of menstruation when weight reduces to a certain level (Kessler 1966). Minuchin *et al.* (1978), on the other hand, view anorexia as a way of coping with overcontrolling parents. Anorexics sometimes come from families that have high demands for achievement and conformity. Unable to meet these standards, they may feel unable to control their own lives. By limiting food intake, anorexics gain a sense of self-control, as well as control over others through resisting attempts to make them eat. Other explanations centre around physiological factors such as abnormal hypo-thalamic activity or psychological factors such as the desire for attention or individuality (Brumberg 1988; Garfinkel and Garner 1982). Along with bulimia, anorexia and milder eating disorders are most common among females in adolescence and early adulthood. These body image disturbances are likely to relate to developing sexuality and have effects on relationships between the sexes but in ways which have not yet been explored through systematic research.

SOONER OR LATER: THE TIMING OF PUBERTY

The timing of puberty and the psychological effects of this biological event have been widely researched. Unfortunately, comparison between studies is often difficult because different measures are used to assess pubertal status (for example bone age, age of menarche, development of secondary sexual characteristics) and the use of different standards in the definition of early and late maturers (Brooks-Gunn and Reiter 1990). Results of these studies also depend on the comparison groups used, so that larger differences are found when early and late maturers are compared, than when early or late developers are compared with those maturing within the average or normal time span.

There is scant evidence that the biological factors associated with timing of puberty lead directly to psychological outcomes (Petersen and Taylor 1980). Rather, it is more likely that biological changes affect psychological events both through personal perceptions of these events and through the meanings ascribed to them by family, peers, and society. Such mediating variables might be feelings about growing up, conflict with parents or peers, cultural fashions with regard to body shape, and social norms concerning sexuality.

Early maturing boys have advantages over their late maturing counterparts in self assurance, poise, confidence, relaxation, and popularity – in fact in a range of social, emotional and academic performance characteristics (Mussen and Jones 1957; Peskin 1967). Because of their more manly appearance, early developers are more likely to be chosen as leaders, to be popular with peers, and to be given responsibility by adults. These are all situations that are likely to increase feelings of self-worth and self-esteem. On the other hand, late developing boys are at a disadvantage in many areas of behaviour and adjustment during adolescence. They are shorter and less strong which means they are less likely to be successful at competitive sport or in winning the admiration of girls, both activities valued highly by the peer group. The advantage enjoyed by early maturers was demonstrated by Mussen and Jones (1957) who found significant differences in the self-evaluations of early and late maturing boys. Late maturers completing projective tests such as the Thematic Apperception Test and the Rorschach Test consistently interpreted the central figures in these ambiguous stimuli as foolish or weak individuals, unable to solve problems without assistance, and scorned by others. Themes expressed by early maturers were centred around potency and positive self-attributions.

Some of these effects have been shown to persist into adulthood (Ames 1957; Jones 1965; Peskin 1973) although Brooks-Gunn and Reiter (1990) suggest that later in life the popular, early maturing boys may be at a disadvantage. The attributes which increased their prestige during adolescence may presage rigid, sex-stereotyped attributes in middle age rather than more flexible, adaptive characteristics. Ames (1957) found that although early maturers had a more active social life in adulthood, late maturers appeared to enjoy the best relationships with their wives and children. To gain popularity with girls, late maturing boys may have to rely on developing their sensitivity and interpersonal communication skills, characteristics which will hold them in good stead in later intimate relationships

In contrast to boys, early maturing does not appear to advantage adolescent girls. These physically mature girls have poorer body images than late maturers (Blyth *et al.* 1985; Duncan *et al.* 1985) and are more likely to experience eating disorders (Brooks-Gunn and Warren 1985). This may be due to their relatively heavier weight in early puberty, a 'problem' which persists throughout life together with shorter stature. Emotional health may be poorer, with early maturers who experience stress at home more likely to suffer from depression (Paikoff *et al.* 1991). Difficulties seem to extend to school performance. In their longitudinal study, Simmons *et al.* (1983) showed that, at ages 11 to 13, late maturing girls were doing exceptionally well at school while early maturers received lower marks and had more disciplinary problems than average or late maturers. By age 16, early maturers were dating more and considered themselves more popular with the opposite sex than average and late maturers but there were no differences between groups in same-sex popularity. Simmons *et al.* do not interpret early maturing girls' popularity with boys in a positive light, regarding it as often accompanied by lowered self-esteem and a lack of emotional readiness. Data presented in a later chapter about early sexual initiation support this conclusion. Peterson (1989) interprets the school achievement differences between the groups as related to differences in opposite sex interest and responses to the stresses of puberty. She suggests that early maturers may be distracted from their studies by a precocious interest in boys. Alternatively, their poorer achievement may relate to the stresses which accompany a body developing at a faster rate than the capacity to deal with emotions. Another possibility is that late maturing girls compensate for their lack of popularity with boys by concentrating on school work. What is of interest here are the links being made between sexual development and many other aspects of life with precocity, delay, and asynchronies in this area affecting other aspects of adolescent development such as school work and popularity.

Not all research shows negative consequences for early maturing girls. Peskin (1973) found that by the age of 30, women who had reached menarche early were more responsible, self-directed, and objective in their thinking than their late maturing peers. They were more poised in social situations, and more psychologically flexible. Like the late maturing boys, these girls who had faced the stresses of being out of step with their peers may have developed coping mechanisms which were conducive to later adjustment.

To sum up, the research conclusions are that, in the short term at least, late maturing is more stressful for boys and early maturing more stressful for girls, although the lessons learned from coping with that stress may contribute to adjustment in later life. Why the difference between the sexes? Given that girls mature earlier than boys on average, it is the early maturing girls and the late maturing boys who are most out of step with their peers, most outside of the normative period for pubertal growth and development (Brooks-Gunn *et al.* 1985). Extremely early maturing boys or extremely late maturing girls would be similarly stressed according to this framework and, in fact, there is evidence that this is the case (Frisk *et al.* 1966; Jaquish and Savin-Williams 1981).

An important caution in the interpretation of studies of early and late maturers is that effects are by no means universal, vary greatly between individuals, and are affected by the social context in which puberty occurs. For example, early maturation predicted leadership skills among working-class but not middle-class boys (Clausen 1975). Clausen also found that early maturation was associated with high self confidence in middle-class girls but lack of confidence in working-class girls. Another example is the finding by Blyth *et al.* (1985) of a relationship between timing of puberty effects and type of school attended. Teenagers' preparation for puberty, the cultural expectations associated with this event, the 'protection' offered by society for those who mature early in body but not emotionally, and the opportunities for enhancing self-esteem given to those who are later maturing than their peers – all these factors and many others will influence the nature and timing of the effects of puberty.

MENSTRUATION: CURSE, COMFORT OR JUST INCONVENIENT?

> When I discovered it . . . [my mother] told me to come with her, and we went in to the living room to tell my father. She just looked at me and then at him and said, 'Well, your little girl is a young lady now!' My dad gave me a hug and congratulated me and I felt grown up and proud that I was a lady at last.
>
> (Shipman 1971: 331)

> I had no information whatsoever, no hint that anything was going to happen to me. . . . I thought I was on the point of death from internal hemorrhage. . . . What did my highly educated mother do? She read me a furious lecture about what a bad, evil, immoral thing I was to start menstruating at the age of eleven! So young and so vile! Even after thirty years I can feel the shock of hearing her condemm me for 'doing' something I had no idea occurred.
>
> (Weideger 1976: 169)

The psychoanalytic literature has tended to characterise first menstruation as anxiety-arousing and distressing (e.g. Deutsch 1944). The psychoanalyst Benedek is quoted in Bardwick (1971) as viewing menstruation to be the forerunner of 'the pain of defloration and the injuries that will be felt in childbirth' (Bardwick 1971: 50). Some support for this view of menstruation is found in a study by Shainess (1961) who found that women who had no preparation for their first period experienced fantasies of being cut or damaged. As Bardwick points out, negative feelings towards menstruation and the menstruating woman are expressed in all cultures. Menstruating women are also often perceived as unclean or taboo. Holding positive views of one's body is not made easy in the face of subtle or overt social messages that there is something dirty or unacceptable about this natural bodily function. Although tampon manufacturers have worked hard at sanitising the image of periods by tasteful advertisements of their wares, the social meaning of menstruation in modern Western society is still unclear. The association between blood and injury or illness has to be put aside by young women if menstruation is to be accepted as part of healthy, normal functioning. Menstruating girls must also come to terms with the hassles of periods which include, for some, discomfort and mood swings.

Menstruation, marking as it does the beginning of 'womanhood', may be perceived as having great psychological as well as physical significance by girls and their parents. All the social meanings of being a woman are activated, such as ideas about sexiness, reproductive capacity, 'availability', and pressures toward stereotyping. Parents may feel ambivalent or negative about their child growing up, and being potentially sexually vulnerable. Given this confusion of potential responses, it would be surprising if some stresses did not ensue from achievement of this milestone in sexual maturation.

Earlier literature on menstruation suggested a high frequency of negative reactions, but conclusions were often based on retrospective reports of clinical adult samples (Brooks-Gunn 1984; Grief and Ulman 1982). Negative experiences have been associated with lack of preparedness for first menses (Brooks-Gunn and Reiter 1990). It is interesting that the number of women who report being unprepared increases dramatically with the age cohort. Today's young women are far better prepared than their mothers and grandmothers and are likely to have had extensive discussions about this topic with their mothers and girlfriends (Brooks-Gunn and Ruble 1982). But there is still embarrassment and a sense of privacy associated with menstruation, reflecting ambivalent or negative social attitudes. Girls almost never discuss menstruation with boys or their fathers, and even among girlfriends, they remain reluctant to discuss the topic immediately after they have their first period (Brooks-Gunn and Ruble 1979). One study revealed that only one-quarter tell anyone other than their mothers when they reach menarche although later on there may be a sharing with friends of tales of symptoms and discomforts (Brooks-Gunn *et al.* 1986).

Perhaps as a result of better preparedness and less socially restrictive attitudes toward matters bodily and sexual – but also possibly because of improved health and fitness – young women in the 1980s and 1990s are far less likely to express extremely negative responses to menstruation than were the women of earlier generations. When Brooks-Gunn and her colleagues interviewed girls within two or three months of their first period, about 20 per cent reported only positive responses, and about 20 per cent reported negative ones. The remainder felt unsure or expressed mixed emotions. About two-thirds were somewhat frightened or upset although the intensity of these feelings was mild (Ruble and Brooks-Gunn 1982). These researchers reject the notion of menstruation as a developmental crisis, viewing it as a challenge to self-definition, an event to be incorporated in the developing self-concept. Girls who successfully meet this challenge and define their menstrual experience within a relatively positive framework will be those who have been best prepared, who do not reach puberty at a much earlier age than their peers, and who receive their information about menstruation from positively valued sources.

WET DREAMS: DOES ANYBODY OUT THERE CARE?

Our knowledge of the psychological meaning of this sign that fertility is developing in boys is far less detailed than our knowledge of the effects of menstruation. First ejaculations may be a source of guilt in boys if they are associated with masturbation (Garbarino 1985) although the severe social condemnation of masturbation and its presumption as the cause of various health problems is largely a thing of the past as we have seen earlier. Gaddis and Brooks-Gunn (1985) interviewed a small sample of adolescent boys about their emotional reactions to first ejaculation and found that two-thirds of the sample felt a little frightened by the experience although most had positive responses. Unlike girls, who had mostly discussed their first menstruation quite extensively with their mothers, none of the boys had discussed ejaculation with their peers and only one had mentioned the event to his father. Furthermore, the boys were extremely reluctant to engage in such discussions. Another issue of interest in the sexual maturation of boys is the problems and difficulties they have in controlling erections – well documented in folklore but not in research. Such events may be embarrassing and humiliating (Garbarino 1985) or coped with readily via joking and humour. We do not really know how most young boys feel about untimely or unexpected erections. Further research on the psychological meaning of sexual maturation in adolescent boys is important but difficult to carry out because boys are embarrassed to talk about sexual topics in a serious way (Brooks-Gunn and Reiter 1990; Moore *et al.* 1991).

SEXUAL INITIATION

What is the link between pubertal development and the initiation of sexual behaviour? The answer to this question is extremely complex because, although we are affected by our hormones, we are also strongly influenced by the social lens through which we view sex. Consideration of cultures with very different sexual mores from our own highlights this point. Marshall and Suggs (1971) have described the sexual behaviours of the inhabitants of Inis Beag (a small island off the coast of Ireland) and of Mangaia, an island in the South Pacific. The first of these is a sexually restrictive culture, in which it is reported that a number of sexual activities common to Western developed nations are unknown (such as French kissing and hand stimulation of the genitals), sex education is rare, nudity is considered disgusting, and intercourse bad for the health. Premarital sex in this society is unknown, yet puberty occurs as it does among all human beings. The physiological changes which accompany puberty do not lead inevitably to sexual experimentation, presumably because hormonally-related events are not interpreted in a way which allows for this to happen. In contrast, the Mangaian adolescent is instructed in awareness of his or her genitals, trained in the arts of love-making by older women, and encouraged to have many sexual experiences with a number of partners before settling down with a marriage partner. Puberty is considered a milestone in development and sexual behaviour is socially sanctioned to occur subsequently.

There is, nevertheless, in Western society, a clear association between the signs of pubertal development and the initiation of adolescent sexual activity (Udry 1979; Westney *et al.* 1983; Zelnik *et al.* 1981). After puberty, more and more young people gain sexual experience, usually outside of marriage, as we have seen in Chapter 1. The relationship between onset of puberty and sexual debut varies between subcultures and social groups, however. For example, in the United States, African-Americans become sexually active earlier than Caucasians (Bauman and Udry 1981; Newcomer and Udry 1983). The average time between onset of puberty and first intercourse has also varied across the last two or three decades, with greater approval accorded to premarital sex in the last twenty or thirty years together with an earlier age of sexual initiation (Kantner and Zelnik 1972; Zelnik and Kantner 1977, 1980). Sexual experience sometimes occurs prior to puberty although more commonly among boys than girls (Weber *et al.* 1989). Among the delinquent at-risk adolescents who comprised this sample, boys described their sexual initiations for the most part as normal, expected and enjoyable. The girls who had experienced prepubertal intercourse usually reported it as sexual abuse. Weber *et al.* suggest that prepubertal sexual events may be more common than once realised, not only among delinquents but among non-delinquents sharing a similar cultural and social background. Hofferth and Hayes (1987a) have also pointed out an increasing frequency of prepubertal intercourse among certain groups of adolescent boys, suggesting once again that social pressures and norms can override the effects of hormones.

A very interesting study by Smith *et al.* (1985) illustrates the complex interaction between biology and social forces in relation to sexual initiation, and the different pattern of this interaction for boys and girls. White adolescents aged 12 to 15 years were asked about their own sexual behaviour and that of their friends. Close friends' responses were able to be identified through an anonymous coding system. Respondents were also asked to rate themselves on different aspects of pubertal development. For boys, these were related to androgen-associated changes such as voice deepening and for girls, to oestrogen-based changes (such as breast development and menarche) and androgen-related developments like bodily hair. Boys and girls were both asked to match their pubertal development stage to Tanner's (1962) drawings depicting stages of genital development. In this way sexual behaviour could be linked to both puberty stage and peer influence. For boys, hormonally related changes and best friend's sexual behaviour were both positively associated with their level of sexual involvement. For girls, the results were more complex. They suggested that androgen levels, as measured by pubic hair stage (and reflecting level of sex drive), and oestrogen levels (representing outward signs of sexual maturity) have separate positive influences on sexual behaviour. Best friend's sexual behaviour was also influential. Interactions between these predictors were such that at low levels of androgen development (low sex drive), a young girl was less likely to become sexually involved whatever her friends were doing, while at higher levels of sex drive, friends' behaviour became a positive influence. The extent to which the girl looks sexually developed will also influence sexual involvement, presumably by acting as a signal to potential partners that she is sexually mature.

Udry *et al.* (1985) have interpreted the results of this and other studies to mean that social influences on sexual behaviour are stronger for girls than for boys. Such studies point to the need to understand simultaneously the roles of both biological maturation and social norms on the initiation of sexual intercourse and the engaging in other sexual behaviours such as fantasy and masturbation. While this chapter has reviewed the role of puberty in sexual development and sexual behaviour, in the next chapter we delineate some relevant social forces. The complex interaction between culture and biology must not, however, be overlooked.

4   Social influences on adolescent sexuality

In olden days a glimpse of stocking was looked on as something shocking, now, Heaven knows, anything goes . . . .

The words of the old Cole Porter song suggest that it is not only at this stage of history that we have worried about declining sexual standards and loose morals. The song also makes it clear that what is sexually appropriate or inappropriate changes in accordance with the atmosphere of the times. In this chapter we examine the effects of some of the social influences on adolescents' thinking about sex, what they do, and when they do it. These social factors shape and interact with biology. We learn how to interpret and act out our sexual feelings on the basis of the social attitudes we extract from our cultural contexts. These attitudes are initially formed at home, so that parental models and teachings are important. But, increasingly, as children get older they are influenced by the contexts provided by the peer group and the wider social arena. We discuss the nature of these proximal, family and peer influences, and those more distal aspects of the social milieu which impinge upon sexual behaviour and attitudes.

PROXIMAL SOCIAL INFLUENCES

Parents

Education in sex hygiene is needed to establish better standards. . . . The present unfortunate position, where so many gain their first misinformation about sex from some precocious youngster and the furtiveness and indecency which surrounds the whole matter, should be forestalled. Parents may do much by answering truthfully the justifiable curiosity of the young child. The glib lies or stern reproofs, so often employed, are stupid and futile. The later instruction is deferred, the more difficult it is for parents to share the confidences of their young adolescents. Just when they might most help their growing boys and girls, who are just entering a new world of sex, their help is not sought.

(Sutton 1944: 558)

The psychological literature assures us of the profound influence that parents have on the lives of their children. Parents are regarded as the primary socialisers of their children, with influence over a variety of beliefs and behaviours. When we turn to the domain of sexuality, we are dealing with an area of human functioning that has long been surrounded by guilt, mystery, and controversy. For some parents, nakedness in the home is shameful, for others, an acceptable natural event. For some parents, sex is a joyful expression of love, for others an uncomfortable and sometimes unpleasant activity. How do parents translate their own feelings about sexuality into messages that they give their children? What influence do parents have on the sexual beliefs and behaviours of young people and how are these influences manifested?

Parents can influence adolescent sexual behaviour through four different avenues according to Thornton and Camburn (1987). Firstly, parental attitudes regarding adolescent sexual behaviours may influence adolescent attitudes. Second, the marital and child-bearing behaviour of parents, including experiences with divorce, remarriage, living arrangements, and apparent behaviours toward the opposite sex may provide and support role models for young people. Third, the religious environment of the home may affect adolescent attitudes to sex and likely experiences of sexual guilt. Finally, the educational and work experience of the parents may influence attitudes and present opportunities for sexual experience while the parents are away from home. Most research concerns the first two of these – mores and modelling. The third will be considered in a later section on the influence of religion more generally.

Parents often find initiating and sustaining discussions about sexuality with their teenagers extremely difficult. They feel that they lack knowledge, are embarrassed by the topic, and often have misperceptions about their adolescent's behaviour. For example, asked about parents' responsibility for AIDS education for their teenagers, one parent in a recent study responded:

> I like to think parents should be, but it is my experience that it is a very difficult thing for far too many parents and kids to discuss. Also, many parents prefer to believe their kids are virgins or could not accept their kids might have a homosexual experience. As for drugs!!

(Collis 1991)

Not surprisingly, expressed parental approval of adolescent sexual activity is relatively low, especially for daughters. Darling and Hicks (1982) characterised the major parental communications about sex as reflecting these sentiments: 'Pregnancy before marriage can lead to terrible things'; 'No nice person has sex before marriage'; 'Petting can too easily lead to intercourse'; and – the one positive message – 'Sex is a good way of expressing your love for someone'. In their study, they found that both sons and daughters heard more of the cautionary messages than the positive one, but the difference was greater for females. Although sexual discussion was rare in our study of late adolescents (Moore and Rosenthal 1991c), it was much more common between mothers and daughters than between either parent and their sons. In spite of the lack of overt communication about sex, sons were far more likely than daughters to perceive liberal parental attitudes to sex.

Moore *et al.* (1986) investigated the assertion that parental communication and monitoring would discourage premarital sexual activity. They found this not to be the case among their 15- and 16-year-olds, with one exception. Parents who held traditional attitudes to sex and had communicated these to their daughters were the only group whose attitudes had apparently influenced their children's sexual behaviour. In this case, their daughters were less likely to have had intercourse. There is evidence of the socialisation process putting a brake on female sexuality, with parents' rare discussions about sex with their children consisting for the most part of warnings to their daughters. The poet, Anne Sexton, writes to her 16-year-old daughter:

> The right thing, the nice thing the kindtoyourself [*sic*] thing is to wait until it will be something special, not just fumbling on the grass or on a couch or in a car. . . . I really think it's better to wait until you're older and readier to handle it.
>
> (Payne 1983: 36)

The possibility that there are many misperceptions and miscommunications between parents and their adolescent children about sex is difficult to ignore. Collis (1991) asked parents of 16-year-old teenagers for estimates about the level of sexual activity among 16-year-olds generally, and received answers reflecting current norms. The same parents, asked their beliefs about their own teenager's sexual activities, were far more conservative in their estimates. In other words, parents found it hard to believe that their own children might have experienced intercourse, even though they recognised that similarly aged teenagers were often sexually active. Moreover, parents held more optimistic beliefs than adolescents' teachers about adolescent condom use, knowledge, and parent–child communication, and stronger beliefs in parental influence. The data from studies such as those of Moore *et al.* (1986) and Collis (1991) suggest that parents may be seeing what they would like to see, rather than what is.

Katchadourian (1990) suggests that such misperceptions may arise from the incest taboo. Discussions about sex are a form of sexual interaction and, in the family context, these discussions are often embarrassing, even when both parents and adolescents have liberal attitudes and are comfortable about talking with peers about sexual matters. Furthermore, there may be some adaptive function in parents 'turning a blind eye' (even unconsciously) to adolescent sexual experimentation. Experimentation is one way in today's society for young people to gain a sense of independence from parents, to begin the process of growing up and taking on adult roles. Given that economic independence for teenagers is becoming less possible, the move to independence through sexuality may have healthy elements. Of course it has its risks as well. The concerned parent needs to tread the fine line between respecting an adolescent's privacy and providing information and a values framework so that the teenager can make sensible and well. informed decisions about sexual behaviour.

It is of interest, then, that adult behaviour, of various sorts, has more influence on teenage sexual behaviour than adult talk.

> If your parents are divorced or separated, and your mum or dad brings home different people on weekends and each night of the week and stuff, you sort of think that [having sex] is no big deal. It is not special or anything like that. But if your parents are married and stuff like that, you sort of see it as a big deal and should only share it if you love the person.
> (16-year-old girl)

For example, nonvirginity in youths has been associated with non-authoritative parenting (Hill 1987; Kandel 1990), permissiveness, and lack of parental support (Inazu and Fox 1980; Jessor and Jessor 1977). There is a strong relationship between a mother's own sexual experience as a teenager and that of her own adolescent daughter (Newcomer and Udry 1983). Girls from single-parent families are more likely to become sexually active at an earlier age than those who grow up in two-parent families (Inazu and Fox 1980; Newcomer and Udry 1983; Zelnik *et al.* 1981). The mechanisms underlying these associations are not clearly understood, however. They may be a function of role modelling, or they may reflect a lack of parental supervision, or they may, in some way, relate to paternal absence.

Studies which relate the initiation of early sexual activity to lack of family closeness and lack of parental support suggest that adolescents who seek independence early due to unsatisfactory family relationships regard sex as part of the expression of that independence. On the other hand, it is entirely possible that the causal chain operates in the opposite way. Thus, an adolescent's sexual behaviour may lead to a withdrawal of closeness within a family. Feldman and Brown (1992) investigated the possibility that parents influence their children's sexual expression indirectly, via the socialisation of coping strategies and personality traits. They showed that learned restraint – incorporating the ability to delay gratification, inhibit aggression, exercise impulse control, be considerate of others, and act responsibly – was a factor which mediated between family interaction patterns and adolescent sexual expression for boys. Family environment measures taken when the boys were in grade 6 (aged 10 to 12) predicted with 70 per cent accuracy those boys who would be virgins or non-virgins four years later. Low-restraint boys were characterised by less supportive families, rejecting fathers, indulgent parents, *and* a greater number of sexual partners at mid-adolescence. Although more research is needed in this area (for example, to investigate the role of restraint for girls), it is clear that the influence which parents have over their adolescents in the sexual domain is more likely to be indirect than a result of direct communications.

Udry and his colleagues also point out that parents influence their children's sexuality through genetic inheritance, as well as through their socialising techniques. Parents provide genes which affect appearance, which influences attractiveness, which, in turn, influences opportunities for sexual encounters. Further, there is a genetic aspect to early puberty, and this is associated with earlier sexual experiences, especially for boys. These interactions between biology and socialisation need to be considered in teasing out the complex ways in which parents influence their children's sexual development and behaviour.

Peers

While peer influence has little impact, relative to that of parents, on young children, there is a shift at adolescence, with peers becoming more important in forming teenagers' beliefs and regulating their behaviour. Peer influence and pressure is often cited as one of the most influential factors affecting adolescent sexual decisions although there is little research on the extent of this influence and how it is exerted (Hofferth and Hayes 1987a). Presumably, peer influence can operate in a number of ways. Teenagers can obtain information about sex from their friends, which may serve to guide decision-making about sex. This information is, of course, not always accurate, as reflected in long-standing teenage myths about fertility such as 'You can't get pregnant the first time you have sex'. Second, adolescents can accept peer attitudes about sexuality. These can be implicitly reflected in peer behaviour, which the teenager may use as a model for his or her own behaviour, or they can be actively proselytised through discussion, questioning, teasing, dares, shaming, and the like (Lewis and Lewis 1984). The strong desire of many young people to be like their admired age-mates and part of a group can lead them to engage in the sexual behaviours, and express the sexual attitudes, that they perceive as characteristic of a particular 'hero' or group. It is well to remember that these peer influences are not always negative, as friends and adolescent groups may express and model healthy as well as unhealthy sexual attitudes and behaviours. This issue receives scant attention in current research, where the emphasis seems often to address only adult disapproval of peer influence on adolescent sexuality.

Research about sources of sex information for adolescents shows overwhelmingly that peers are a major influence in this area, with parents playing a minor role in the sex education of their children (Davis and Harris 1982; Libby and Carlson 1973; Miller 1976; Shipman 1968; Thornburg 1981). In our survey of undergraduate students aged 17 to 20 years (Moore and Rosenthal 1991c), we found that 69 per cent of sexually active young people felt they could discuss any concerns they had about sex with their friends, while only 33 and 15 per cent respectively felt this way about discussing sexual problems with mother or father. Similarly, 61 per cent agreed that a good deal of their sex education came from friends, with few crediting either parent with providing sex education. Among these late adolescents, 73 per cent had talked about 'many aspects' of contraception with peers, but only 37 per cent had done so with mothers and 15 per cent with fathers. However, although discussion and information-sharing about sexual matters was common among age-mates, it was interesting to note that practical assistance from peers in matters of arranging contraception or encouraging safer sexual practices was rare. Only 22 per cent said that peers had 'helped me arrange for contraception, for example, been to the doctor with me'. Even fewer (17 per cent) said that friends had 'helped me arrange for AIDS precautions, for example, buying condoms'. Parental involvement was even less common. For example, only 5 per cent of fathers had helped their sexually active children arrange for contraception or protection.

It seems that peers and friends take an active role in each other's sex education, but the role of these non-sexual partners is largely confined to talk. While it is certainly important for the young person who is establishing values and rehearsing for adult sexuality to have the sympathetic ear and counsel of friends, the sex education provided from this source is limited and often not supplemented by other sources. On its own, this can be a case of 'the blind leading the blind', with incomplete and wrong information being disseminated and, as is shown by our study, with vital elements like the establishment of non-risky sexual behaviours neglected.

In addition to the transmission of knowledge, peer influence works through the transmission of attitudes. Fishbein and Ajzen (1975), in their theory of reasoned action, argued that the perceived attitudes and values of significant others (normative beliefs) have an important effect in shaping an individual's intention to engage in a particular action and, ultimately, on the performance of that action. There has been some support for this proposition in the sexual domain. Daugherty and Burger (1984) found the age of first coitus of undergraduate students was related to the perceived peer approval of premarital sexual intercourse, but not by parents' or the church's perceived attitudes. It appears that there are gender differences in the influence of peers. For example, Daugherty and Burger showed that for young women, but not men, there was a link between their own attitudes to sex, the number of sexual partners they had, and perceived attitudes to premarital intercourse of their peers. Young women's, but not men's, use of contraception has been shown to be influenced by peer attitudes (Thompson and Spanier 1978), while safer sex practices were more common among young women, but not men, who discussed sexual precautions with their friends (Moore and Rosenthal 1991c).

Udry *et al.* (1985) in summarising studies which assess the relative influences of hormonal and social factors on adolescent sexual behaviour suggest that while both sexes are likely to have friends with similar levels of sexual experience, boys' experience with intercourse is more likely to be related to hormone levels than the influence of friends, while the opposite is true for girls.

The messages that teenage girls receive from others about sex are more likely to be disapproving than the messages given to boys (Daugherty and Burger 1984; Moore and Rosenthal 1991c). This is particularly true about messages from parents, but also applies to attitudes expressed by friends. In this way the female peer network may, once again, act as a brake on early or deviant sexual activity, while among teenage boys this is less likely to be the case. Feldman *et al.* (1992), for example, showed in a longitudinal study of male adolescents that peer acceptance in year 6 (ages 10 to 12 years) was related to having experienced multiple sexual partners by middle high school. They speculated that boys who were more popular had more chances to date, and therefore more chances to become sexually experienced. On the other hand, boys who were rejected by their peers in primary schools also showed higher levels of sexual experience in later adolescence, an association which Feldman and her colleagues linked to the low levels of self-restraint and general misconduct of these boys. These boys exhibited a pattern of 'acting out' of impulses, including sexual impulses.

Although it is clear that parents and peers do influence teenagers' sexual decision-making in various ways, there is another pervasive set of influences to which we now turn.

DISTAL SOCIAL INFLUENCES

The broader social context in which they live their lives plays a significant role in teenagers' sexual beliefs and behaviour. The nature of that context and consequently, its impact, ranges from the overt and overwhelming world of the adolescent subculture, a world in which teenagers are bombarded by media messages about current (and ephemeral) mores, to the less obvious influence of societal institutions such as school, religion, and the law. We address the different contexts in turn.

The youth culture

The day-to-day impact of social control on teenagers is reflected in their commitment to perform in ways appropriate to their role. Western societies, by prolonging the transition to adulthood and by segregating their youth, have given rise to an institutionalised youth culture – more or less standardised ways of thinking, feeling, and acting that are characteristic of a large number of youths.

The power of the youth culture in shaping teenagers' opinions and behaviours can be recognised when we look around at the conformity of youths to current fashions in clothes, music, and leisure activities. The area of sexuality is just as subject to this influence as any other. Adolescents derive much of their information about sexual mores and behaviours from this subculture, which is wider than immediate peers, and which purveys sets of beliefs about what adolescents should be doing, from the point of view of their age-mates. These beliefs are communicated via various media directly targeted at young people. Influences include publications for teenagers, movies and television designed to appeal to this age group, music, songs, rock videos.

Among the print media, magazines (for example, *Dolly*, *Cleo*, or *Rolling Stone*) and romantic fiction (such as the Sweet Valley High series or Mills and Boon romances) are particularly popular among adolescent girls, with boys less directed and more varied in their reading (Sachs *et al.* 1991). Writers such as McRobbie (1982) believe that adolescent fiction contributes to the creation of ideologies about relationships between the sexes, sexual expression and power. For girls, she argues, these ideologies deal with the construction of teenage femininity, such as the nature of attractiveness, the desirability of feminine passive acceptance, and the importance of attracting a man. Teenage boys' interests in a varied diet of adventure, hobbies, non-fiction, and soft-porn such as *Playboy* may encourage a wider range of self-definitions and identities which do not necessarily revolve around sexual attractiveness. The definition of maleness conveyed by boys' reading matter is one characterised by a sense of agency in the sexual as well as in other life areas, that is, a sense of doing, mastery, and control.

Teenagers are also presented with role models in the form of current pop stars. Whereas the teenagers of the 1950s swooned to the sound of Frank Sinatra crooning that 'Love is a many splendoured thing' or 'Our love is here to stay', today's adolescents are more likely to hear explicitly sexual lyrics such as Madonna's 'Erotic, erotic, put your hands all over my body'. Even more explicitly sexual are the lyrics of rap musicians:

> You know it's good for me and it's good for you
> Let Jim Browski [slang for penis] go to work and penetrate.

Videoclips of pop singers or groups have become popular as a means of promoting careers by persuading teenagers to buy records of their favourites. At the same time, these video clips frequently give powerful messages about sexuality, not only in terms of their lyrics but also of their behaviour. Popular music and dancing has been likened to a mating ritual, in which rhythm and simulated sexual movements provide sexual release and indicate attraction (Brook-Taylor 1970).

There are, of course, complex interconnections among these influences, as well as with the word-of-mouth wisdom which is passed on between the 'cliques, crowds and gangs' comprising the set of adolescents in any city, state or country in the Western world. Although there are great individual and group variations in the ways teenagers think about sex, the subculture provides a popular model of what is 'best', 'right', and 'current', of which most young people are aware. This complex set of ideas and values is so pervasive, because of the speed with which ideas are spread by world media, that young people need to make conscious decisions on a regular basis as to whether they accept or reject current trends.

In our highly sexualised society, many of the values and norms of the youth culture concern sexual behaviour. Consequently this subculture probably has more influence on young people's sexual activity than it does on, say, their career choices. Thornburg (1975) suggests that the pressures inherent in the adolescent subculture may thrust young people into heterosexual involvement before they are physically and emotionally ready to deal with it, almost bullying them into premature sexual activity. There is some support for this view of a somewhat malign influence. Cvetkovich and Grote (1980) report that sexual experience among teenagers was strongly predicted by beliefs in the extent of peers' sexual experience and their perceived level of sexual liberalism. Newcomer, Gilbert and Udry (1980) conclude that individual behaviour and attitudes are more closely linked to what adolescents *think* is happening among their peers than what is actually happening. There is a clear belief among some teenagers, at least, that their age-mates are more sexually active than they actually are (McCabe and Collins 1990). Such a belief is likely to affect the behaviours of many young people for whom peer group acceptance and 'fitting in' are important in the maintenance of self-esteem and the movement toward maturity.

Adult models of sexual behaviour

Parents are not the only adult role models available to adolescents. Young people have about them many models of adult lifestyles in which diverse patterns of sexual expression are practised. Examples range through stable monogamous marriages, divorce and recoupling, single parenting, lifestyles characterised by frequent partner changing, and homosexual couples. These days, an adolescent may be almost as likely to watch a parent or other adult agonise about dating and sexual conduct as the reverse. The messages sent by the adult generation about sex are far less clear than they were in the 1950s. Adults seem confused, and their confusion is expressed in worries about relationships, divorce, sexual acting out and sometimes violence. What are the effects of this adult confusion and variety of relationship behaviours on the developing sexuality of young people? One outcome appears to be that adolescents have increased tolerance of sexual diversity and the expressed approval of people 'doing their own thing', even if these behaviours are not engaged in or desired by the adolescent himself or herself (Coleman and Hendry 1990). Beyond this general kind of finding, we know little about the mechanisms by which adult sexual norms affect the youth generation and indeed about the extent of that effect. One way of exploring this further is to examine the influences on young people of various aspects of the wider adult culture, such as the media. Another is to look at the ways in which adults attempt to influence and, to some extent, control adolescent sexual expression directly, through schools, religion, and the law.

Media models of sexual behaviour

On television, movies, and videos adolescents see in their own living-rooms people expressing the whole gamut of sexual behaviours, including violent sexuality. Many popular modern movies have strong sexual themes. In these movies, sex is explicit and not represented, tastefully and discreetly, by waves crashing or reeds blowing in the wind as was the case in the 1940s and 1950s. Today's teenagers are bombarded with scenes of unambiguous sex (usually between unmarried partners), the details of which are portrayed with unprecedented precision. As a result, sex is no longer shrouded in mystery. Teenagers know what sex is and how it is enacted at increasingly earlier ages.

Unfortunately, most films present stereotyped images of the ways men and women relate, and these have many implicit and explicit messages about what is appropriate sexual behaviour. What are the models of sexual behaviour illustrated by popular modern-day films? In some, the message is 'woman as passive victim'. With good luck, the victim-woman will be saved by a knight on a white charger. She is not saved by her own efforts to take charge of her life, but because she ingratiates the man by providing for his needs – being cute, attractive, or good at sex. The popularity of these films attests to the fantasies which they target and activate, a point made persuasively by Walkerdine and other British feminists, and which we discuss in Chapter 5. Another film genre focuses on women who express their own sexual needs rather than a desire to please men, and who attempt to satisfy these needs. These women who are sexual beings on their own terms are often represented as the epitome of evil, bent on destroying true love and sacred family life. Such films might be said to reflect male fears of women who adopt 'masculine' modes of sexuality, but their popularity with men and women alike is disturbing. The third film genre depicts the teenage male fantasy of women as playthings. Women in these films are not serious and, indeed, are hardly real people. Here, sex is a commodity and no self-respecting man would want to relate to these women for any other reason but to attain sexual release. The messages conveyed by these films do not provide strong and positive models of healthy sexual expression for women, nor do they reflect sensitive, intimate, relationship-based sexuality as a particularly attractive option for men.

Sachs *et al.* (1991) point out that young people are socialised into a world characterised by a vast array of media forms. Although it is hard to establish clear lines of influence, we know that adolescents today watch many 'sexy' films, videos, and video clips. These range from the explicitly pornographic to those that might be regarded as 'soft-porn'. In fact, the new technologies such as videos enable today's teenagers (as well as their parents) to circumvent the few safeguards designed to protect minors, such as rating systems of movies ranging from 'general exhibition' to 'R' or 'X' ratings. Most parents do not know what their teenagers are watching at friends' homes, and indeed the prevalence and popularity of 'R' and 'X' rated videos in shops suggests that many are watching these films.

Relationships between the sexes, ideas of attractiveness, and models of sexual expression are presented to adults and adolescents alike through the various media sources. The messages contained in these media representations of life are both direct and subtle. It is likely that these media messages may be especially potent influences on adolescents' sexual behaviour. Because of the strong privacy norms surrounding sex, adolescents have rarely, if ever, seen parents, siblings, or older adults engage in sex. Therefore, it is through the media that they learn the script of what to do, how to do it, and when to do it. It is interesting that the mass media rarely portray planning for sex or consequences of sex, leaving adolescents without a script in these areas. In spite of a recognition of the likely potency of the media in formulating opinions, we know little about how either adults or adolescents are affected by media messages, although there is no shortage of speculation. Nor do we know the extent to which the media shape these opinions or, alternatively, reflect current public attitudes. Many of the media-presented messages about sexuality reflect hedonistic and self-gratificatory values, in opposition to the values usually presented by parents and formal adult institutions such as school, church, and the law. Adolescents are faced therefore with sorting their ways through these various hypocrisies and confusions to develop their own working model for sexual life.

Social institutions

School

Given the apparently limited and difficult role parents have in sex education, the tendency of religions to 'teach only to the converted' (see the next section), and the confusing and often one-sided influence of popular media, there is an important role for schools to play in informing young people and providing a forum for values exploration and clarification about sex. According to a recent article in *The Times*, however, one in four British schools has no policy on sex education (Roberts 1992). Based on a nationwide Sex Education Focus survey, the report considered teacher anxiety (particularly relating to the discussion of homosexuality, AIDS and sexual abuse) as a major factor standing in the way of providing adequate sex education to school students. The need for school-based sex education was emphasised by the response to the report of one parent, on behalf of the National Confederation of Parent-Teacher Associations. This parent commented that the report was 'worrying' because 'many parents rely on teachers in this area'.

In the United States, Nielsen (1991) describes the state of sex education as 'too little too late'. Only 60 per cent of students in the United States receive any sex education before graduating from high school (Forrest and Silverman 1989; Kenney *et al.* 1989). Nielsen notes that in ten states there has been no action with regard to policies or the implementation of sex education in schools, and that only seven states require instruction about pregnancy prevention. On the positive side, while only three states required sex education in 1980, seventeen did so by 1988.

Despite these variations and limitations in the amount and quality of sex education, it appears that young people nevertheless do gain knowledge of sex from school-linked sources. Thornburg (1975) surveyed a large sample of American adolescents from eleven different locations and estimated that about 40 per cent of information about sex was obtained from school literature, about 40 per cent from peers, and about 15 per cent from parents. Allen (1987) concluded from her survey in the United Kingdom that many teenagers received most of their information about sex and contraception from school classes, with friends being a further major source. In Australia, Goldman and Goldman (1982) found that the major sources of children's and teenagers' knowledge about sex were parents, books, and the mass media. Only 19 per cent of these children claimed to have learned most of what they knew about sex from teachers and school sex lessons. As pre-adolescents were included in the Goldmans' sample, however, these figures probably underestimate the number of adolescents who cite school as a major source of sex information.

Schools and teachers, while providing a significant proportion of adolescents with information about sex, are not always perceived as credible sources by young people. In Allen's study (1987), secondary school students were far more likely to rate parents as accurate sources of sex information than teachers and were very unlikely to rate teachers as 'the first person to turn to with a question about sex, contraception or personal relationships'. Goldman and Goldman (1982), comparing sex education across a number of different nations, concluded that lack of trust in teachers' knowledge or discretion served to inhibit many young people in Britain, Australia, and America from approaching their teachers for information or advice about sex. A related issue is that while schools may provide information, we have little evidence that this information is learned, remembered, or acted upon. Nor do we know if it meets the needs of the young people for whom it is designed, or that there is adequate opportunity for the discussion of problems, values, and other concerns. As Currie (1990) points out, adolescents often turn to their friends for information because, although they are aware that the information may not be accurate, they feel more comfortable discussing these issues with friends, and believe that their questions will be treated sympathetically, with understanding and discretion.

It is interesting to consider other reasons why sex education in schools is not more effective than it is. How do we define effectiveness? A closely linked question relates to the goals of programmes. Sex education can range from direct teaching about biological 'plumbing' through to decision-making and value-oriented approaches. The desired outcomes can be an increase in straightforward knowledge about bodily functions, or in sexually responsible behaviour (or even sexual abstinence). Or they can combine these and other attitudes to sexuality in a context which provides the adolescent with a script for dealing with sexual relationships. An example of proposals for the latter comes from the Scottish Health Education Group's (1990) proposal for health and sexuality education in schools, *Promoting Good Health*. In this model, the topic of sexuality is combined with consideration of relationships, while encouraging an exploratory and discussion-based approach to sexual values, and the facilitation of decision-making skills in the sexual domain. The decision process is conceptualised as comprising at least four elements, and teaching in the programme is designed to allow for pupil accessibility to each element. These are: (a) access to, and acceptance of, relevant information; (b) clarification of feelings and related attitudes; (c) investigation of possible alternative actions and probable outcomes for each; and (d) deciding on a course of action that will be right for the individual. The overall aims are outlined below, in order to give an indication of the breadth of focus of the programme.

1. To facilitate communication on sexuality and relationships.
2. To develop knowledge and understanding of physical and emotional development.
3. To develop an awareness of social development and the influences which affect personal choice.
4. To promote responsibility for considerate behaviour and the ability to make informed decisions on sexuality and relationships.
5. To develop skills needed for potential future parents.
6. To increase knowledge of health care services.

(Scottish Health Education Group 1990: 32)

Programmes such as this are usually developed through community, parent, and teacher consultation. Although in the past there appeared to be strong parental resistance to sex education programmes (and in some communities that resistance still exists because of cultural norms), current research shows that, although there is still a vocal minority of 'resisters', the majority of parents are in favour of school programmes (Nielsen 1991). If such programmes are to achieve their aims, parent and community support are important. Equally important is that teaching about sex must be done by trusted and sensitive teachers, secure in their own sexuality and able to cope with discussion of a wide range of views which they do not necessarily share.

Religion

Religiosity has generally been found to be negatively related to premarital sexual behaviour; religious persons regardless of denomination are less likely to be sexually active (Devaney and Hubley 1981; Spanier 1976). This is not surprising, as sexual values encouraging conservatism and restraint are promulgated by most religions. Thus, adolescents who are devout in their religious beliefs are among those least likely to experience early sexual initiation or multiple partnering. Sexual conservatism among religious youths may not simply be the consequence of religious values *per se*. Religious youths are likely to associate with other religious youths. Thus, the norms of the most salient peer group work to enforce the values of religion.

Thornton and Camburn (1987) point out that not only does religious participation reduce the likelihood of premarital sexual experience, but the effect works in the other direction as well. Sexual attitudes and behaviour significantly influence religious involvement. Religious instruction which prohibits premarital sex or encourages its delay puts strains on the individual who has begun sexual activity, with the likely effect of diminishing religious involvement. Today's powerful pressures towards adolescent sexual activity militate against their continued involvement in traditional religion, a situation which can leave young people in a spiritual vacuum in terms of developing values about sex and relationships. There is no shortage of other sources of values, as we have seen. Values adopted by the popular media and the adolescent subculture may well fill this vacuum, but these are often materialistic and concerned with immediate gratification, according to Thornburg (1975). It is not surprising that young people are struggling to find a suitable values framework for thinking about their lives, a framework which incorporates the wish to have fun and experiment with sex, while recognising the powerful emotions which sex elicits, and the responsibilities implicit in establishing relationships. Religion may provide this framework for some, but many others will find religious tenets too sexually restrictive and will look to peers, media influences, and other social institutions to fill this void.

The law

It would be impossible to review, for all Western countries, the laws that deal with adolescent sexual expression. Many countries have such laws, and they provide a broad framework for our decisions about what is deviant adolescent sexuality and what we judge to be normal adolescent experimentation. Age of consent laws, for example, specify an age below which it is illegal to engage in sexual intercourse (usually 14, 15 or 16 years). These laws are a social expression of our beliefs that it is appropriate to protect young people against sexual involvement until they are emotionally and physically ready for it, and that too early sexual activity may be damaging to growth and development. Within such laws, it is often the case that the actions of an older person who has sex with a minor are viewed in a more serious light than, say, the situation in which two minors have sex with each other. In Australia, for example, until recently consensual intercourse with a young girl under 16 years of age was unlawful, irrespective of the age of the girl's partner. The law has now been changed so that intercourse with a girl aged between 12 and 16 years may occur lawfully, provided that her partner is no more than two years older than she is.

Another example of the ways in which the law regulates sexuality concerns an individual's right to be treated as medically adult. These laws deal with the rights of a young person to give consent to medical or surgical treatment without the consent of parents, and the requirement of professional confidentiality on the part of the medical profession. In the United Kingdom, the legal age for consent in this context has been set at 16 years by the Family Law Reform Act (1969, cited in Coleman and Hendry 1990), two years lower than the general age of majority at which, for example, an individual is entitled to vote (Coleman and Hendry 1990). Probably the major implication of this act relates to medical advice and treatment in the sexuality area, such as prescribing contraceptives or termination of a pregnancy. The law, through such acts, recognises the facts of teenage sexuality, the implicit message being that 'if it's going to happen, let's make sure it happens safely'. The hope is that these legal provisions will ensure that contraception is freely available and that if abortions are to occur they can be carried out by qualified medical practitioners under hygienic conditions.

Of course, one difficulty in attempting to regulate sexuality is that these laws are often unenforced and unenforceable. It is one thing to make sexual intercourse between a 15-year-old girl and a 19-year-old boy illegal. It is another to convince the pair in question that what they are doing should cease because it is against the law. Nevertheless, there is a sense in which such laws acknowledge the confusions and misperceptions of parents about their children's sexuality by relieving parents of the need to make decisions. Of course, these laws are not without controversy. For example, the recent Family Law Reform Act in Britain has been the subject of challenges and subsequent legal guidelines regarding interpretation. Laws against homosexuality and laws about engaging in certain sexual acts such as sodomy or oral sex exist in some countries, or states within countries, and are policed with more or less enthusiasm, depending on the social climate of the region and the times.

What is important in considering the effects of any of these laws on adolescent sexuality is that while they govern behaviour through regulation and punishment, the laws also shape attitudes and are, in turn, shaped by the prevailing social mores. It may be said that the law reflects the overt – but not necessarily the implicit – sexual values of a society. The degree to which laws about sexual behaviour actually affect sexual practice has not been systematically studied. It seems likely, however, that laws which are too out of step with current thinking will be far less likely to be obeyed or to influence sexual decision-making. A recent case in Ireland brings home this point. Although abortion is illegal in that country and considered to be morally wrong, it has always been acceptable to seek abortion in the United Kingdom. The case in point was that of a young girl who became pregnant as the result of rape, and who was denied an exit visa because she made clear her reason for travelling to the United Kingdom. Public opinion in Ireland was so strong that it forced a change in the ruling, so that the young teenager could finally travel and have the abortion she and her parents desired. Although the *law* in Ireland has not yet changed, this is a good example of how community values can influence the legal decision-making process and, eventually, the law itself.

FOUR SOCIAL DISCOURSES ABOUT SEXUALITY

Developing sexuality occurs in a culture replete with mixed messages about its acceptability (Brooks-Gunn and Furstenberg 1990). It has been suggested by Fine (1988) that four themes dominate the public and private discourse about sexuality, and these provide conflicting messages about how adolescents should conduct their sex lives. The themes revolve around morality and responsibility, desire, danger, and victimisation.

The discourse of morality, most strongly represented by the parent generation and institutionalised religion, usually focuses on issues such as the moral reprehensibility of sex before marriage. Brooks-Gunn and Furstenberg (1990) argue that framing adolescent sexuality as a moral issue can be counterproductive to encouraging safe and responsible sexual practice because of the underlying message that if intercourse is wrong, then it is wrong to plan for it. The argument against sex education can arise from this moral premise. There is a fear among some parents that discussion of sex with young people may encourage increased sexual activity or indicate tacit parental approval, although we know from research (for example, Kirby *et al.* 1988; Paikoff and Brooks-Gunn 1991) that this is not the case. Arguments about the appropriate moral stance can limit the effectiveness of sex education, as contentious material – such as how to use contraception or the discussion of homosexuality – is omitted because too many parents object to its inclusion. The morality discourse may, however, also include positive messages to teenagers about responsibility for one's own and one's partner's emotional and sexual health. 'Casual sex is alright so long as no-one gets hurt' or 'Sex before marriage is fine if the two people love each other'. Young people who do not accept the traditional moral stance of sexual abstinence in adolescence may feel as if they are in a values vacuum. Statements like those above and the questioning attitude of many adolescents to sexual values can be regarded as attempts to fill this void with a more coherent and meaningful moral framework than is currently being endorsed by the adult generation.

The discourse of desire is Fine's second theme, one which permeates media portrayals of sexuality but is often ignored in parents' or schools' or churches' responses to young people's sexuality. Brooks-Gunn and Furstenberg (1990) suggest that teenagers are discouraged by adults from talking about their longings and feelings of sexual arousal. Most adults are embarrassed and uncomfortable about adolescent sexual feelings and, to quote many a parent, 'would rather not know'. Suppression of desire is also evident in most of society's institutions. The teenager who wishes to articulate and question his or her sexual feelings would be hard-pressed to find a sympathetic teacher, priest, or minister to listen. At the other extreme are those adults who control the mass media and use sexuality as a constant reference through films, magazines, and music. Desire is often the main focus of these presentations of sexuality, with concepts of responsibility in sexual relations rarely emphasised. For example, although modern films show countless depictions of sexual intercourse, contraception or safe sex are almost never mentioned. Media representations of sex are likely to be in extreme opposition to the reality experienced by teenagers in their own homes. This is true both in terms of what parents say to their children about sex, and in the models they present. As we contrast the looks and behaviours of Madonna and Mick Jagger with those of Mum and Dad, the lack of a middle ground for young people in terms of sexual models must indeed be confusing.

The discourse of danger is communicated more frequently to girls, as the possibility of pregnancy, the emotional pain of abandonment, and the social disgrace of loss of reputation. There is a sense, however, in which 'risking all for love' is portrayed as exciting. This has certainly been a theme in modern literature and films. In the era of AIDS, educational and public health sources have attempted to instil in young people of both sexes the dangers of unprotected sex. Emphasis on the dangerous aspect of this activity may be to some extent counterproductive, however, as stressing the danger may also stress the thrill and excitement. The idea that there is risk involved may serve to increase rather than decrease the attraction of an activity for some youths, particularly young boys. For example, we have found that the greatest risk-takers among our 18-year-olds were likely to be young men rather than young women. Some of these sexually active male teenagers, characterised by us as a 'risk-and-be-damned' group, were fully aware of the dangers of their behaviour but took a fatalistic attitude to their risk of being infected with the AIDS virus.

Finally, our society provides many sources of messages arising from the discourse of victimisation. The power balance in sexual encounters is portrayed as residing with men, who are ready to exploit women in the service of their sexual urges. Hence, women are potential victims and must be protected by parents and by society (for example, by means of laws against sexual harassment). The message of this discourse is that women have limited power in sexual negotiation, and the implicit corollary is that they also have limited responsibility. We shall deal with this important issue in later chapters. At this point, we simply note the existence of this fourth discourse.

Conflicts between these four discourses lead to confusion for teenagers about the appropriate way to act. For example, young women who accept media messages (and the messages from their own bodies) that desire and sexual feeling are normal, may find themselves interpreted as 'sluts'. Messages which encourage young women to take responsibility for their own sexuality may conflict with their 'victim' role, or the moralistic expectation that this control can only be exercised through self-denial. Men and boys, too, are drawn into these conflicts and ambiguities. Society conveys the idea that 'exciting' men are powerful, reckless and dangerous, yet there are also strong messages to be responsible and sensitive, and to strive for intimate and mutually fulfilling relationships.

Adolescent sexual development must occur, then, against the backdrop of many and varied social forces, forces which themselves are in a constant state of flux. The way an adolescent balances these forces to produce his or her sexual ideology and behaviour will be unique to each individual. But development does not stop at this point. The resolutions of issues centred around sexuality at adolescence will themselves provide only a framework for adult sexual ideologies and behaviours. In matters of sexuality, there is great potential for change. Thus far, however, we know little about the relationships between adolescent sexual behaviour and lifelong sexual development.

5   Gendered constructions of sexuality

> Man's love is of man's life a thing apart
> 'Tis woman's whole existence.

Byron's words remind us that love and sex have long had different meanings for men and women. In more recent times the difference has been put more crudely with the sexual divide between young men and women characterised as 'Males want more than they get sexually and females get more than they want' (McCabe and Collins 1990: 117). In this chapter we explore differences in the ways adolescents of both sexes behave and would like to behave, how they think about sex, and how they communicate with each other on sexual topics. In doing so, we examine the different expectations that young men and women have about sex roles, as well as the gendered nature of sexual scripts and sexual discourses. We address, also, the impact of social conditioning and of biological sex differences on gender-specific motives for sex and attitudes to permissiveness, as well as gender differences in 'libido' and in intimacy development. The debate about whether a double standard of sexual behaviour still exists is aired and we conclude by discussing the implications for sexual communication of the differences that are observed.

DIFFERENCES IN PSYCHOLOGICAL CONTEXT

Sex roles: masculine or feminine?

Sex, or gender, roles are characteristics, behaviours, and interests defined by a society or culture as appropriate for members of each sex. As such, they have broad implications for sexual behaviour. In Western society, traditionally, appropriate sex roles for men have been as worker, primary breadwinner, head of the household, and holder of leadership roles in the community. These activities are assumed to be paralleled by typically male personality characteristics, such as assertiveness, confidence, bravery, and independence with associated interests in sports, active pursuits, and competition. The female gender role has revolved around the bearing and nurturing of children as well as taking responsibility for household duties. Assumed female traits are warmth, expressiveness, nurturance, dependence, and cooperation, with interests focused around interpersonal concerns rather than those in the intellectual or practical domain.

Traditional roles have been debated hotly and undergone much change in the last two or three decades, so that most activities viewed as appropriate for one gender are now seen as (more or less) acceptable for the other. This is particularly true for women, who are now more likely to be in the paid workforce than not. The man who stays home to look after the children or takes an equal share in child-rearing is less common but certainly not unknown (Lamb 1976; Russell 1982). Feminine characteristics are now viewed more positively (Rust and Lloyd 1982) and girls are expected to be competent and self-confident as well as understanding, kind, and expressive (Curry and Hock 1981). There is no doubt, however, that stereotyping along traditional lines still exists (Williams and Best 1982) and is particularly strong in adolescence (Hansen and Darling 1985; Lewin and Tragoso 1987; Moore and Rosenthal 1980; Simmons and Blyth 1987). Boys appear to hold stronger sex role stereotypes than girls. In their study of junior high school students, Curry and Hock found that boys differentiated male and female gender roles on twenty-nine dimensions, girls on only eight.

The belief that both 'masculine' and 'feminine' traits can happily coexist within the one individual is expressed in the concept of psychological androgyny (Bem 1975; Russell 1978). Many researchers have argued strongly that this coexistence is conducive to adjustment and psychological well-being. Others argue for a masculine model of adjustment (Dusek 1987; Whitely 1983). These latter researchers claim that those individuals, male or female, who have an abundance of 'masculine' qualities are likely to be better adjusted than those who are sex-typed as 'feminine'.

The development of sex-roles, the concept of androgyny, and the relation of these issues to behaviour were briefly discussed in Chapter 2 in the section on sexual socialisation. We consider some further aspects here. An interesting question is whether adolescents' adherence to, or eschewal of, traditional sex roles affects the way they view their developing sexuality and make choices about sexual behaviour.

Sexual behaviour and sex roles

Sexually speaking, the traditional sex role stereotype is for man to be the 'hunter' and initiator of sexual activity, the one with the more powerful and demanding sex drive, the strong one, the powerful figure in a relationship. The traditional woman plays her role through being pleasant, cooperative, placating, flirtatious, and attending to her appearance and the pleasure of the male, while retaining a respectable and ladylike demeanor in public – 'a lady in the kitchen and a whore in the bedroom'. The media and popular culture are replete with male role models for teenage boys which stress strong expression of sexuality coupled with minimal affectional involvement with one's sexual partner. The hard-drinking, fast-living, womanising James Bond is one potent example of this type. For these men (and boys), there is no requirement to keep one's sex drive under control until the right (read good, chaste, pure, committed) woman comes along. Boys who are not so strongly motivated toward sexual gratification or who do not talk – or brag – about their sexual experiences in this way risk derogatory labels that reflect unwelcome attributes such as unattractiveness ('nerd') or having homosexual leanings ('poofter'). Girls are exhorted to be good, but still with the potential to be sexy, waiting for the right man to come along to unleash that potential (Walkerdine 1984). Those who express overt sexuality too soon or too often are 'sluts' or 'molls'; those who are perceived as unattractive or not interested enough in sex are 'dogs' or some similar insulting epithet (Lees 1989). As Lees notes, a young girl's sexual behaviour is a significant contributor to her reputation, in a negative, hostile way. By contrast, that of her male counterpart is determined by a variety of factors – his sporting prowess or his school performance, among others. If a young boy is sexually active, his reputation is likely to be enhanced rather than diminished.

The alternatives for women have been graphically represented as the choice between 'damned whores' or 'God's police' (Summers 1975). The woman who expresses her sexuality is bad; the one who constrains her own sexuality and keeps men in check as well is the pure virgin, the 'good' girl. Although alternative models of sexual expression are available (for example, Madonna's acting out of sexual assertion and control, or the so-called 'Sensitive New-Age Guy'), these models appear not to have had much influence on teenagers' behaviours although they may affect attitudes. We take up this point later in the chapter when issues of permissiveness and the double standard are discussed.

Although much has been written about the ways in which sex role typing is related to sexual behaviour and to relationships between the sexes, there are few research studies. Investigating the relationships between sex role typing and sexual experience in college students, Leary and Snell (1988) and Whitley (1988b) showed that masculinity, but not femininity, was related to young men's likelihood of having engaged in intercourse, to their number of partners, and to other aspects of sexual experience. Young women's sexual activity was also related to levels of masculinity but, in the former study, this only occurred for those with low levels of feminine qualities. Femininity appeared to act as a deterrent to sexual experience. However, femininity relates to relationship quality, as shown in studies by McCabe and Collins (McCabe and Collins 1979; McCabe 1984). They found that androgynous and 'masculine' adolescents were more interested in sexual activity than 'feminine' adolescents, while 'feminine' and androgynous adolescents desired greater affection from a relationship than did teenagers who were sex-typed as 'masculine'. It seems that a combination of masculine and feminine qualities is advantageous in developing dating relationships in which both partners desire sexual activity *and* affection. Couples who are sex-typed, on the other hand, have differing needs which may predispose the relationship to conflict.

SEXUAL SCRIPTS AND DISCOURSES

Sex roles do not tell the whole story about influences on girls' and boys' sexuality. People act differently within the same culture, partly because they follow different 'scripts' (Gagnon and Simon 1973) or behave according to particular 'discourses' (Hollway 1984). Script and discourse analyses examine sexual behaviour from a sociological perspective, capturing the ways in which we are constrained in our actions and attitudes by the social influences around us.

Gagnon and Simon view scripts as learned rules of sexual behaviour that consist of directions for what we will do and plans of action for how we will do it, and with whom. Adolescents do not, initially, develop their sexual scripts from experience, although their experiences become important later. Rather, early scripts arise out of listening to others talk, absorbing the popular culture through watching movies, videos, or television, reading magazines and books. In this way, teenagers get a sense – not always at a conscious or explicit level – of what is appropriate and inappropriate sexually for someone of their age and gender. 'Official' attitudes of a culture may not reflect the true scripts, which can be ascertained by looking more closely at the behaviours within that society. For example, while premarital sex may be officially disapproved of in England and the United States, neither society places many restrictions on its practice. Chaperones are rare and adolescents are left alone in the company of opposite-sex peers. Nor is premarital sex publicly or severely punished, at least in most cultures.

In American society, a common script for sexual development, at least in the past, and currently in more traditional regions, involves elaborate dating procedures, which are approved of by the older generation. These begin at an early age, usually with mixed-sex group activities, and proceed through double and single dates, to 'going steady'. This relationship may culminate in living together or in marriage. During adolescence, however, it is more likely that the relationship will break up with the partners re-forming relationships with others in a process described by Sorensen (1973) as 'serial monogamy'. Similar scripts are often assumed by text-book writers in Britain and Australia (McCabe and Collins 1990; Peterson 1989) but, although there are doubtless similarities, there is also evidence to suggest that the scripts are somewhat different in these three cultures. For example, in a study of Swansea youth, Leonard (1980) concluded that adolescents in his sample had difficulty in describing more committed forms of interaction with the opposite sex and there was 'no formalized, named stage corresponding to American "dating"' (Leonard 1980: 70). Similarly, 'dating' was not a concept favoured by Australian youth in a recent study by the authors (Moore *et al.* 1991). Australian teenagers preferred to describe their interactions in looser, less formal, terminology and apparently began these interactions at an older age than their American counterparts. Some of their comments about dating were as follows.

It sounds like something my mum would do – it sounds American.

I don't really like it, it reminds me of the olden days . . . when they go to a ball or something. I just picture these two people going to a dance or something.

[I]t used to be when the guy took the girl out and paid for everything, and these days it is less formal.

Not only are there likely to be different cultural scripts for prescribing sexual activity, but young people are socialised according to gender-appropriate sexual scripts (Gagnon and Simon 1973; Gordon and Gilgun 1987; Santrock 1990). Teenage girls have learned to link sexual intercourse with love and often rationalise their sexual behaviour by believing that they were carried away by love – that the 'magic of the moment', combined with their desire to satisfy the wishes of their loved one, was the reason for having sex, rather than their own sexual needs or desires. As we shall see later, more girls than boys cite being in love as their main reason for being sexually active. Male sexual scripts stress the satisfaction of their sexual desires. The pleas, 'If you really loved me, you would have sex with me' or 'You wouldn't make me suffer in this way', suggest that some young men are well attuned to the female sexual script, with the male script allowing for the exploitation of young girls' own needs.

Valerie Walkerdine (1984) elaborates on some of these ideas in her intriguingly entitled article, 'Some day my prince will come'. She argues that romantic novels and schoolgirls' adventure stories are powerful vehicles for the socialisation of preadolescent girls into sexual scripts which depict their role as passive, 'good' victims who are saved through the love of a strong, powerful male or a loving and all-encompassing family. Girls are primed with the idea that through selflessness, waiting, and passivity, they will eventually overcome the unwelcome aspects of their role in life. Although they are victims, someone will come along and save them if they are good, and they will live happily ever after. This life script contrasts with the stories familiar to preadolescent boys in which the male hero overcomes victimisation, danger, or cruelty through his own brave efforts. He is active in overcoming problems; she is passive. For young girls, problems are solved by something magical happening. One day the prince comes and takes her away from it all. Such fantasies, says Walkerdine, encourage a passive approach to problem-solving as well as the positive evaluation of the ability to suffer in silence. Both as a general approach to life and in the sexual sphere, this romantic, fairytale (and incorrect) notion of men as saviours rather than partners, as larger-than-life heroes who will change a girl's life from one of boredom or victimisation to something magical and fantastic, is an unsatisfying and unrealistic basis for male–female relationships. Walkerdine's analysis highlights for us an aspect of sexual scripts which is inimical to healthy relationships between the sexes.

Similarly, Wood (1984) discusses the sexual socialisation of boys through the analysis of schoolboys' 'sex talk'. While seemingly good-natured, this can be intimidating to girls, as well as setting up artificial barriers between the sexes as they 'construct' each other in stereotypical and often mythical ways. Wood notes features of this talk, including the loud and joking assessment of women on the basis of their bodily parts, the mixture of fascination and disgust expressed at female bodily functions, the fantasies of invasion and rape, and the projection of 'horniness' onto young women who are sexually attractive to the boys or whose sexuality they find threatening.

In a related, but somewhat different vein, Hollway (1984) looks at stereotyping through the analysis of discourses – that is, systems of understanding that are adopted by individuals in order to interpret their worlds. These discourses are reflected in the ways we talk about sex and relationships. On the basis of her research, Hollway suggests that three discourses represent male–female interactions in Western society. These are the Male Sex Drive discourse, the Have/Hold discourse, and the Permissive discourse. The first of these arises out of the idea that strong biological urges propel men in their relationships with women. Women are considered to be subservient to this male sex drive. Men must have sexual release to be healthy and women need to be persuaded into satisfying this male need through a reciprocal arrangement in which female 'needs' for security and to nurture their young are exchanged for sexual favours. If this strategy fails, force or exploitation may be used. This script implies a relationship in which men have power over women, one which is maintained through men's superior strength and in the service of the male sex drive. Among those who operate according to the Male Sex Drive discourse, the highest value is accorded to men with the largest number of sexual partners (Hugh Hefner of *Playboy* fame may be a real-life example, James Bond a fictional one). This is especially so if they manage to avoid paying for sex with marriage and/or commitment. Women's sex drive is not acknowledged and, in accordance with male views about pure women, there is a belief that women have to be coerced into sex. According to this discourse, women who openly exhibit an interest in sex are considered to be inferior and amenable to exploitation, as loose women who deserve all they get.

The central proposition of the Have/Hold discourse is encapsulated by the Judeo-Christian marriage ideals of monogamy, commitment to partnership, and to family life. The quality of the relationship between partners is compensation for the sacrifice of sexual experimentation and permissiveness on the part of both sexes. Men and women are regarded as equally deserving of satisfaction, although not necessarily in terms of the roles they carry out or the sacrifices they may have to make to achieve these satisfactions. Sex is considered as appropriate only within a committed relationship.

The Permissive discourse, which emerged in the sexually more liberated 1960s, has as its major tenet the proposition that there should be freedom of sexual expression for both sexes, 'so long as no-one gets hurt'. While this discourse accepts female sexual arousal and experimentation as legitimate, the implications with respect to sexual commitment are unclear. For example, a sexually unexciting marriage which may be expected to continue within the Have/Hold and the Male Sex Drive discourses (with the husband taking lovers to satisfy his sex drive in the latter case) may break up within the Permissive discourse. For those couples operating within this discourse, there may be pressure to retain sexual excitement which could interfere with some of the other functions of committed relationships such as rearing children, looking after a partner if they are ill (or just having a bad day), and becoming a financially viable family unit.

While Hollway's discourse analysis of sexual politics is a useful and interesting one, its application to adolescents is as yet unclear. DiMascolo (1991) interviewed young people aged between 18 and 20 about their responses to a range of sexual dilemmas in which, for example, sexual arousal and commitment were juxtaposed. In her relatively select, well-educated sample, all interviewees were interpreted as holding, for the most part, the Have/Hold discourse, although elements of other discourses were present. An attempt to establish the dominant discourse framing the sexual behaviour and attitudes of approximately 160 adolescents aged 15 to 18 from a range of backgrounds and social classes was abandoned in an interview study by the authors (Moore and Rosenthal 1992b). The complexity of the sexual scripts exhibited by these young people was not captured adequately by discourse analysis. Although aspects of each of the discourses could be discerned in many participants' responses, few appeared to be adhering to any one of the Hollway discourses. These teenagers' sexual attitudes and the principles guiding their sexual behaviour involved a complex and often contradictory mix of themes around issues like romance and love, the perceived intensity of sex drives, standards of behaviour for males and females, the nature of exploitation, and the extent to which it was considered appropriate to question and wonder about sexual values. There were some important differences between boys and girls, for example in their attitudes to permissiveness, but there were many similarities as well in male and female views of sexuality.

The idea that we can describe sexual behaviour through recourse to two stereotypes or three discourses, or to a set number of sexual scripts is probably unrealistic. Although such conceptualisations are extremely useful in guiding our understanding of human sexuality, they can lead us to gloss over individual differences and to forget that individuals change over time, behaving differently in different situations. Individuals can also choose – or learn – to be different from prevailing social norms. Nevertheless, the socialising power of roles, scripts and discourses can be strong and it may be difficult to break away from scripts or stereotypical roles which are unsatisfying or which inhibit or retard emotional growth. The history of the women's movement attests to these difficulties, as do the stresses, outlined in Chapter 6, experienced by young people who adopt a homosexual rather than a heterosexual life course.

Sexual scripts, stereotypes and discourses cover many aspects of our sexual lives, and include the reasons why we choose to engage in sex, our attitudes to permissiveness, exploitation, intimacy and commitment, and our actions with respect to these areas of sexuality. They include, also, our beliefs and actions concerning the sexual 'double standard', beliefs about sexual arousal and sexual experimentation, and communication patterns with the opposite sex. In each of these dimensions of sexuality, similarities and differences exist among young men and women. It is to these gender-specific issues that we now turn.

WHY HAVE SEX?

Chilman writes that, as a result of sex role stereotyping, cultural attitudes, and physiological gender differences (such as the fact that male sex organs are more readily stimulated),

[f]emales are more likely to view sexuality in dualistic, ambivalent, self-protective, and dependent terms than males. Males, on the other hand, are more likely to view sexuality in a pleasure-oriented, assertive, achieving, unitary, and less personal fashion.

(Chilman 1980a: 39)

To what extent is this claim supported? There is little research on motives for sexual behaviour among teenagers. Leigh (1989) studied the reasons for having or not having sex among 1000 adults (median age 35, age range 18 to 76) through a systematic random sample of 4000 households. Men attached significantly more importance to pleasure, pleasing a partner, conquest, and relief of tension than did women who were significantly more likely to rate emotional closeness as an important reason for having sex. Among reasons for not having sex, men rated fear of AIDS and fear of rejection more highly than women, while the converse was true for fear of pregnancy, lack of interest, and lack of enjoyment.

Male and female adolescents also have different views about sex.

Boys are more likely to see intercourse as a way of establishing their maturity and of achieving social status, whereas most girls see intercourse as a way of expressing their love and of achieving greater intimacy. As a consequence, boys are more apt to have sex with someone who is a relative stranger, to have more sexual partners, and to disassociate sex from love. Even in their sexual fantasies, boys are more likely to imagine sexual adventures detached from love and emotional intimacy.

(Nielsen 1991: 370)

Where does love fit in? A number of investigators have confirmed that teenage girls, more than boys, report being in love as the main reason for being sexually active (Cassell 1984; Zelnick and Shah 1983). Many other writers have pointed out a gender convergence toward expressed motives for sex and attitudes toward sexual encounters. Certainly, our studies have shown that ideas of love and romance are important aspects of sex for both male and female adolescents in the 1990s. Both boys and girls in our interview research expressed positive evaluations of these aspects of relationships. The desire to experience a loving relationship with 'the right person' is shown by teenagers' responses to the question 'What do the words "romantic love" mean to you?'

I see romantic as roses, candlelit dinner, holding hands, walking down the beach – stuff like that. Someone to talk to, to love, basically.

From movies and things, I see it everywhere. When you think you have the right person, and you have someone forever, and you don't want to break up. You love them and they love you, and you think there is nothing wrong and you are perfect for each other.

When you are really involved with each other and you don't think about anything else except the other person and you are really close.

I think it is more when you have a strong friendship with someone like a girlfriend or your wife or your fiancee . . . it is much different to sex although there might be sex in it, it is different. Romantic love is more sensual and more deep, and it comes from deep inside, where[as] sex – you just want to get it done and it might be over, like a one-night stand.

'Loving, caring and affection' were the primary motivations for having sex among most boys and girls in our middle-class Anglo-Australian sample although physical pleasure or fun was the major motive for some boys and girls. The picture was different for our group of homeless teenagers, with clear differences in the responses of boys and girls. Most of these vulnerable young girls (71 per cent), but few boys (15 per cent), elected loving, caring, and affection as their major reason for engaging in sex. The preferred motive for these boys was sex for physical pleasure or fun (53 per cent). Few homeless girls (8 per cent) used sex to satisfy these goals. Teenagers in our ethnic minority group had yet a different pattern of motives. Sex for pleasure played no part in the girls' sexual behaviour but was the primary motive for some boys (19 per cent). Clearly, among these last two groups of teenagers, there was a mismatch of expectations, with girls looking for something that their likely partners were not wanting or able to give. Many of the homeless boys responded to the harshness of their lives with an unequivocal rejection of romantic values, although this cynical split between romance and sex was not restricted to the most disadvantaged of our male teenagers. What did romantic love mean to these boys?

I try to keep away from all that. Romance is alright I suppose, but fuck the love.

Airy-fairy stuff.

Can't see myself answering that question. Romantic isn't a word to me. You are sexually attracted to them and that's it. There's no romance and all that crap that people say – it's all garbage and it's all bullshit.

While some homeless girls shared their male peers' views about romance and love, most wanted sex with friendship, consideration, love, and romance. These girls appeared to have accepted the full complement of middle-class ideals about partnerships, only more so. Their expression of neediness, and thus vulnerability, coupled with the data we have about the views of sex of their potential partners, does not augur well for these young women's future satisfaction in relationships. This is especially true when seen in the light of their high levels of unsafe sexual behaviours. Our picture of these girls is that their search for love is enacted through sexual encounters, many unsatisfying and not enhancing their sense of self-worth, leading to a cycle of further neediness. The plight of these young girls is poignantly expressed by one 16-year-old's response to the question of why some girls 'sleep around'.

> I think some of them are searching for love and they get their wires crossed, in having a sexual partner – that that is what they are getting from that person. Or they are drunk or on drugs and don't know what they are doing, and it happens. There are different forms of why my friends have different partners. For instance one of my friends does it because she is making money . . . but [it] depends, really. Mainly I think not being in control, being under the influence of drugs, often makes my friends have many sexual partners. I don't think if they were sober or straight they would do it as often.

Research on motives for sex reveals that, among certain groups of teenagers, there are strong differences between boys and girls, while among middle-class and probably more educated teenagers, gender convergence is occurring, with young boys including relationship-oriented motives for sex more often. It is interesting that among these teenagers, girls are acknowledging the contribution of arousal and pleasure as reasons underlying their sexual activity.

LIBIDO: IS THE SEX DRIVE DIFFERENT FOR BOYS AND GIRLS?

Differences between males and females in their beliefs about sexuality, modes of relating sexually, and perceived motives for sex have been at times attributed to differences in strength of sex drive, or libido. In this section we explore the evidence that such differences do exist, and the extent to which they are related to biological sex differences (such as hormone levels) or to socialisation processes.

It is difficult to disentangle the role of hormones from that of social factors in sexual arousal. The fact that levels of testosterone in boys are associated with their sexual activities, including masturbation, provides some evidence that hormones affect drive or arousal; however, the relationship is an association rather than necessarily a causal one. It is quite possible that engaging in sexual activities affects hormone levels rather than vice versa. Another possibility is that hormone levels and sexual activity increase in response to some other factor, such as change in appearance, which may lead to greater attractiveness to the opposite sex. Evidence against appearance being the linking factor comes from the finding that hormone–behaviour links are present independently of secondary sexual characteristic development (Udry *et al.* 1985).

Testosterone levels in females are, of course, much lower than those in males. Furthermore, female sex hormone levels are not directly linked to libido according to Smith (1989) who cites studies in which female libido is decreased after surgical removal of the ovaries and adrenalectomy, but not when ovaries alone are removed. If testosterone alone is the factor associated with sexual arousal, then these data suggest arousal should be greater for males. A complicating factor is that, for girls, hormone levels interact with social factors in the prediction of sexual activities. For example, testosterone levels in girls are associated with sexual interests (masturbation, thinking about sex) but not behaviours (Udry *et al.* 1986). We could infer from this that girls act out their libidinal wishes to a lesser extent than boys. Whether this greater social restraint of sexual expression is also accompanied by changed perceptions of arousal is not clear, as studies which show sex differences in permissive attitudes and motives for sex have not included measures of hormone levels. Goggin (1989) did find differences in self-reported arousal among a group of 18- to 25-year-olds. Young men scored higher than young women on a measure of sexual interest and arousability, which included items such as 'I have a lot of sexual energy', 'I feel quite frustrated if I don't have sex regularly', and 'I have very strong sexual drives'. More research is needed, however, to tease out the physiological predictors of sexual arousal among adolescents, and their interaction with social factors.

We can address the question of gender differences in sex drive from the perspective of behavioural rather than physiological evidence. As we have seen in an earlier chapter, adolescent boys report more masturbatory and other sexual activity than girls (Katchadourian 1990; Luckey and Nass 1969; Sorensen 1973), their attitudes are more liberal, and they are more likely to be aroused by a wider variety of sexual stimuli (Miller and Simon 1980). Dusek (1991) suggests that the sex drive for girls is more diffuse and is likely to be displaced into other areas such as close friendships with other girls, passionate interests in activities such as horse-riding, or 'crushes' on teachers. Thus, sexual urges find a more indirect outlet than heterosexual sex. Furthermore, the quality of the intimate relationship is more important in sexual expression for girls. In support of this belief that the experience of the sex drive is qualitatively different for young men and women, Dusek points to the initial sexual experience, which is likely to occur prior to marriage for both sexes, but in different circumstances.

> The modal male will engage in his initial sexual intercourse with someone with whom he has no particular emotional attachment. He will have sex with her a few times, and then never again. The modal female will be in love with her initial partner and will likely be planning to marry him. The relationship will last some period of time and may result in marriage.
>
> (Dusek 1991: 202)

Although there is certainly evidence of different behaviours and, to some extent, different gender conceptualisations of sexual experience, our knowledge of social conditioning, sex roles, and sexual scripts indicates that these, rather than males' or females' sex drive or libido, may lead at least partially to these differences. Added complexity comes from the knowledge that girls or young women are still likely to be more reluctant than their male counterparts to admit to their sexual behaviours, given that more social disapproval attaches to sexually adventurous females.

What is clear is that society has a strong belief in the fact that males' but not females' sex drive is largely uncontrollable. In our research, young people of both sexes readily expressed this conventional view. Boys' sexual urges were seen as able to be controlled by only 37 per cent of our sample of teenagers, although 87 per cent agreed that this was possible for girls (Moore and Rosenthal 1992b).

> No, the only way they can control it is if they use their hand a lot.

> No, I think if any guy has a chance to root a girl, and if they liked her and she wasn't exactly ugly, they would do it. I think the majority of guys would say 'Yes, go for it', but there might be a small minority that says no. I haven't met that minority yet.

Most of these teenagers thought that girls had greater control over their sex drives because they were more responsible or because their drives were weaker in the first place. There was, however, recognition of exceptions to the general rule. Boys could be restrained and girls could be uncontrolled.

> *Can women control their sexual urges?* I know girls that can, and I know girls that can't. It depends on the girl really. I think that most girls can control it more than guys, definitely. With girls it is different. Guys reach a stage where they don't mature any more, and I think girls keep

maturing, that's the main difference. Girls are more emotional than guys. I think because girls mature more they come to realise that there is more to life than just sexual relationships.

Taking a different slant on the issue of male and female sex drive have been feminists such as Millett (1972) and Koedt (1973). They have argued that female sex drive only seems less strong because the power differential between the sexes leads to sexuality itself being defined as activities and feelings that are more exciting to men. In the *Myth of the Vaginal Orgasm*, Koedt documents how female sexuality has been structured around men's convenience, denying the physical basis of women's sexual pleasure. Hite (1977) also criticises the 'reproductive model' in which sex is defined as penetration, intercourse, and male orgasm. Activities such as foreplay and female orgasm are devalued. Women's lack of power in this phallocentric model of sex leads them to take more passive roles and in fact being less interested in the whole activity.

In summary, our evidence suggests, first, that hormonal and physiological studies point to the possibility of stronger libido in males but more needs to be done to clarify the role of oestrogen in female arousal. Second, gender differences in arousability exist but, as social conditions change, there is evidence that young women are admitting to being aroused by a greater range of stimuli than was previously thought (Miller and Simon 1980). Third, adolescents perceive and accept gender differences in levels of sexual control. Finally, the sex drive manifests itself in different sexual behaviours for teenage boys and girls but some, or even all, of these may be a function of the different social learnings experienced by the sexes and the power differential between them.

INTIMACY AND COMMITMENT

As we have seen, the development of the capacity for emotional as well as physical intimacy, and its culmination in the formation of a life partnership, is regarded as a vital psychological task for young adults. Our focus here is on the ability to share feelings with another, to self-disclose and to listen, to set mutual goals, and to compromise individual desires in order to work toward these 'couple' goals – as well as to share one's body in mutually satisfying sexuality. Intimacy and falling in love are seen as closely associated in our society. Intimacy, or expectations about its development, are often initiated in the charged emotional climate of falling in love.

Do young men and women differ in the ways in which they deal with issues of intimacy and commitment? It seems that they do. Young men frequently interpret their initial sexual experiences as learning and experimentation, and as contributing to their sense of self-definition, rather than as a way to become emotionally close to another. In some cases, sex may be used as a way to ward off emotional closeness, as expressed by the 'love them and leave them' stereotype associated with some young men's behaviour. Young women, on the other hand, usually assume that commitment will accompany physical intimacy, that sex and love automatically go together. These divergent perceptions are likely to give rise to frustration, confusion, and hurt as teenagers explore their sexual feelings. It may be true that a new 'permissiveness with affection' morality is becoming the norm among young people, reducing differences between the sexes in their attitudes to intimacy. Our research suggests otherwise, at least among some groups of adolescents.

In developmental terms, it seems that girls at adolescence are better equipped to handle intimate relationships as a result of their experiences with same-sex friends. Analysis of adolescent friendship patterns shows that, while girls and boys may have a similar number of friends at pre-adolescence and during their teenage years, girls' friendships are characterised by more self-disclosure, discussion of problems, sharing of emotions, and mutual support than boys' friendships (Caldwell and Peplau 1982; Moore and Boldero 1991; Wheeler and Nezlek 1977). We can characterise the difference this way. Boys *do* things with their friends – they play sport, go on outings, ride bicycles, kick a football. When they talk to each other, it is talk characterised by agency – what we are going to do and how we are going to do it. The nearest these boys get to becoming intimate is through shared banter and joking. Girls also have activity-oriented friendships, but their talk is likely to be different. It is about who they are, how they appear to others, how they feel, and how others feel – in other words, intimate, relationship-oriented talk. When romantic relationships begin, girls may have a head start on boys with respect to talking about emotions but are likely to be unprepared for boys' inability and/or unwillingness to express closeness in this way. There is considerable evidence that these mismatches of communication between the sexes are not only characteristic of adolescence but last well into adulthood (Caldwell and Peplau 1982; Fischer 1981), suggesting an on-going problem in sexual understanding.

IS THERE STILL A SEXUAL DOUBLE STANDARD?

'No', says one group of writers (see, for example, McCabe and Collins 1990; Reiss 1971; Steinberg 1985). These researchers document a decline in the popularity of the double standard among adolescents and claim that many teenagers now believe that sexual equality exists, with the same standards for premarital sexual behaviour applying to young people of both sexes. What is sauce for the gander is now sauce for the goose.

The prevailing attitude to sex among teenagers, in this post-1960s period of sexual liberalism, we are told, is one of permissiveness with affection. But permissiveness is not an all-or-none concept. A permissive ideology may apply to some but not all sexual attitudes and to only selected aspects of sexual behaviour as we have found (Moore and Rosenthal 1992b). While most (77 per cent) of our teenagers approved of sex before marriage, relatively few (27 per cent) were comfortable with the idea of one-night-stands.

Many studies have shown that young girls still express less permissive attitudes to sex than do boys (Hornick 1978; Moore and Rosenthal 1992b; Sprecher 1989), although some writers argue that the gender gap is narrowing (Dusek 1991; Kallen and Stephenson 1982; Sorensen 1973). What is clear from our research is that gender differences depend, at least in part, on the particular experience under scrutiny. Girls were as likely as boys to approve of premarital sex but they were more disapproving of one-night-stands than boys and somewhat less approving of infidelity within a steady relationship than their male peers. While premarital sex can be socially interpreted as part of a loving relationship, the other activities do not readily fit a sex-within-commitment ideology that is more consonant with the social conditioning of young girls.

A study by Goggin (1989) confirmed these gender differences among older youths. Young men aged 18 to 25 attending a tertiary institution were more permissive with respect to sexual experimentation, scoring significantly higher than their female peers on a scale which contained items such as 'I could be turned on by watching someone masturbate', 'Group sex might be fun', 'When it comes to sex, I would try anything once', and 'I would like an adventurous sexual partner'. A permissive ideology is also captured by the extent to which one feels guilty about engaging in intercourse. As we have seen in Chapter 1, girls have more negative reactions than boys to their first intercourse, with more girls than boys feeling guilty after the event. Different expectations about sexual behaviour among teenagers were found by Goodchilds and Zellman (1984). Irrespective of their sex, these 14- to 18-year-olds accepted the boy's right to be sexually aggressive and the girl's role to set limits on male sexual overtures. So, while adolescents of both sexes are engaging in intercourse, their feelings about it differ and their levels of psychological comfort have a different flavour.

Sue Lees (1986, 1989) argues that the discourse on adolescent sexuality is still overwhelmingly characterised by a double standard. Reputation is a major issue for girls, she says, so that sexual desire can only be expressed in the context of romantic love and commitment. There is an expectation that both sexes will engage in premarital sex, but girls have to make sure they do so in a circumspect way whereas boys are encouraged to be as active as they like and their reputations are enhanced by more encounters. Girls respond by romanticising their sexual encounters, so they can be interpreted as expressions of caring and love, not as expressions of sexual desire. Such idealisation of sex, while enjoyable and appropriate for certain relationships, is less appropriate for casual and short-term encounters as it renders the romantic young woman highly vulnerable to hurt and disappointment and reduces the likelihood of her being able to take responsibility for her sexual life. 'He will look after me because he loves me' is an all too common refrain among young women.

Recent debate about whether a double standard does or does not exist has ignored the complexity of the issue. Data from our own studies provide evidence that while some aspects of sexual inequality are less common, others remain. We found that more than half of our 16-year-old teenagers had the same reaction to girls or boys who 'sleep around'. This occurred independently of the sex of the judges and reflected views ranging from approval to strong disapproval.

> *What do you think about girls who sleep around?* I think it is okay. Most of my friends think it is okay. Maybe some girls would think it is not acceptable. It depends on who they are sleeping around with. If they had been in a few relationships, and slept with the guys that they had been with, that would be alright. But if they were just sleeping with anyone, it probably wouldn't be accepted as much. [*Boys?*] Similar to females. [It] depends on who they are having sex with.
>
> (Boy)

> [*Girls?*] Personally, I think it disgusting. I know girls who do that, but I feel really different to them. No, I don't like it. It makes her reputation go down from there. Keep away from them. [*Boys?*] The same. Equal rights. If a guy does it, a girl can do it too.
>
> (Girl)

Of those who did judge 'sleeping around' differently for boys and girls, virtually all saw this activity as far more detrimental for girls than boys. The double standards applicable to sexual behaviour are clear in these young people's responses. Sadly, both boys and girls held these views equally.

> [*Girls?*] Sluts, basically. Because they have a mattress on their back, they like having sex. That's the way I look at it, no two ways about it. [*Boys?*] . . . a stud. Good luck to him. It's okay for a guy to be like that.

I don't have to have sex with a guy, so I don't care. That's what the difference is.

(Boy)

[*Girls?*] I think they are sluts basically. [*Boys?*] They are different to girls because they like competing against others, like [a] peer group pressure type of thing. When a guy does something, the other guys do it too. They also like bragging, I think.

(Girl)

Interpretations of sexual experience tell us something of the workings of the double standard. In a survey of about 2000 older adolescents aged 17 to 20 years (Rosenthal *et al.* 1990), we found that young women were more likely to define their sexual encounters as occurring with a regular or steady partner than with a casual partner, while young men were more likely to regard what must be essentially the same encounters as casual. We are aware that the real pattern of adolescent sexual relationships is one of very loosely defined serial monogamy. Teenagers tend to have a succession of partners, with relatively short lead-ups to the start of new relationships (around six months on average in this group, but varying from 'a few hours' to 'a few years'), so in fact the male interpretation of what is going on may be closer to reality. The girls are interpreting, as an indication of love and commitment, encounters which will often turn out to be short-term.

Views about fidelity are also relevant here. Almost all the girls in the above study expected themselves and their partners to be faithful in a long-term relationship, with this pattern consistent across different ethnic groups we tested. Among the boys, most (86 per cent) expected their partners to be faithful, but expectations for their own behaviour were far less stringent and varied quite markedly across groups. On average 75 per cent of young men said they would try to be monogamous in a steady relationship, but for some groups the figure was considerably lower. Teenage boys, while easier on themselves in terms of standards of fidelity, were more likely to take an aggressive approach to partners who strayed. Most respondents of both sexes said they would either 'talk it over' or 'get angry' if they found out that their partner was unfaithful. There were, however, some disturbingly vengeful responses, all from boys, to the question 'What would you do if your partner was unfaithful?'

Beat the shit out of them. Get a bit upset.

Beat her up because she was a fucking slut.

While most boys tended to report some sort of active response to a partner's infidelity – whether it be a reasoned attempt to discuss the matter or an aggressive response – some girls (15 per cent) adopted a stereotyped passive role, replying that they would 'do nothing'. This suggests either a greater tolerance for partners' lapses than was evident for boys or (and possibly more likely) an acceptance of the lesser power that girls hold in these sexual relationships. Whatever the underlying dynamics, it is clear that the meaning of fidelity in steady relationships differs for adolescent girls and boys, with the norms of behaviour being viewed less stringently among boys for themselves but not for their partners.

Summing up, we can say that while the double standard may in fact be disappearing, it has not died altogether, especially among some adolescents such as those from lower social class groups (Lees 1986) or those from cultural groups in which sex roles are emphasised (Rosenthal *et al.* 1990). Even among groups who pay lip service to sexual equality, if one scratches the surface, there are still subtle – and not so subtle – pressures for girls to restrain their sexuality.

NEGOTIATING THE SEXUAL ENCOUNTER

Negotiating the sexual encounter requires that partners are able to communicate with one another about sex. Sexual communication is vital because good communication can enhance people's sex lives by enabling them to understand each other's needs, to avoid misunderstandings – such as the idea that 'no' means 'yes' – and to talk to each other about precautions against pregnancy, sexually transmissible diseases, and AIDS. Boldero *et al.* (1992) found, for example, that among young people, feeling comfortable communicating about condoms with a sexual partner was associated with a greater likelihood of condom use. Such communication is not always straightforward. It can be undermined by embarrassment, defensiveness, fear of rejection, the desire to exploit, or by simply misunderstanding one's partner.

In the area of self-confidence about sex, or sexual self-efficacy, interesting gender differences emerge. Rosenthal *et al.* (1991) found 31 per cent of late adolescent boys, compared with only 9 per cent of girls, were unable or very uncertain about being able to refuse a sexual advance by a partner. Boys also felt less confident of their ability to have a sexual encounter which did not necessarily lead to intercourse. That is, they felt less able than girls to control themselves sexually, to ask a potential partner to wait for sex if precautions were unavailable, to refuse to do something sexually which they did not feel comfortable about, to reject an unwanted sexual advance, and to admit sexual inexperience to experienced peers.

While girls claimed that they felt relatively confident of their ability to 'say no' to unwanted sex (a somewhat surprising finding in the light of concerns about girls' lack of power in the sexual situation), this was not matched by their confidence in expressing sexual drives and wishes, or in taking the initiative in relationships. They were less confident than boys about asking someone (other than a 'steady' partner) for a date, or asking a partner to stimulate them sexually. These young girls also had poorer sexual self-esteem, assessed by perceptions of self-worth on items such as 'I feel comfortable with my sexuality' and 'I am comfortable being affectionate with dating partners'.

There were other problems experienced in sexual communication, as these young girls' responses to the question 'Is it hard to say no to sex' illustrate.

When you are in that situation, I think it is hard to say it. I think you would have to. I wouldn't say it in words, but I would act it out, like move away or whatever. It is very difficult to say no, though.

Yes. Because you are letting the guy down, you are showing him you don't want him as much as he thinks you do. You feel bad.

Research on the way adults talk to each other can enlighten us further on the difficulties which can occur in communication about the emotionally-laden topic of sex. Tannen (1990) concludes that men and women use conversation differently. Women talk to negotiate closeness, to give and seek confirmation of themselves, and to work out ways to gain consensus. Men's talk on the other hand is designed to disguise feeling or vulnerability and to assert power, control and independence. The sexes misunderstand each other's 'talk motives', leading them to non-communicative strategies such as dismissing the talk of the other as trivial ('She's just rambling on as usual'), not registering what has been said because it is couched in tentative language ('Why didn't you come straight out and tell me all this before?'), or interpreting the lack of 'feelings' talk as indicating a genuine lack of feelings rather than an inability to discuss them ('Whenever I bring it up he makes a joke, or walks away'). Others (Jeske and Overman 1984; Lakoff 1973; Parlee 1979) have studied male–female discussions and note that men are more likely to set the topic of conversation, to interrupt, to ignore women's conversational initiatives, and to make assertions. Women are more likely to defer to male conversational opening gambits, to 'work' to keep the conversation going, and to be tentative and questioning in their speech.

Maccoby (1990) concludes, in her review of sex differences in behaviour, that differences in communication style emerge primarily in social situations and are particularly evident in mixed-sex groups. If men and women have different motives for their talk to one another, if they misinterpret each other's conversational styles, and if they use different strategies when they engage in discussion, it is no wonder that misunderstandings so often occur. Such misunderstandings are much more likely in the highly emotionally charged domain of sex, in which myths and fantasies about what the opposite sex is like can be exacerbated by differences in communication styles. Adolescents, because of their inexperience, are probably even more vulnerable than adults to communication breakdowns in the difficult area of sexual negotiation.

In fact, there are few systematic studies of what the sexes really say to one another during courting, sexual preliminaries or during sexual activity but it is an area ripe for research. Unfortunately, our major sources of information – films, television, books, magazines – are likely to perpetuate sex stereotypes and sexual misunderstanding. Understanding more fully the nature of sexual communication may help young people to explain to each other their point of view. In this era of AIDS, such effective communication about safe sex has become a crucial issue. Sex education in schools has a potential role to play here in the facilitation of discussions about sex in which girls and boys can share their values, misunderstandings, and myths as well as learn about their sexual plumbing.

We conclude this chapter by noting that young men and women tend to construct their sexual worlds in different ways, possibly because of biological differences, certainly because of socialisation practices and the power differential between the sexes, and probably because of interactions between these sets of influences. Adolescent sexual worlds are not fixed or static. Rather, they are in a constant state of flux so our conclusions about the 1990s may not be appropriate for the year 2000. Adolescents face the complex task of coming to terms with their own sexuality and learning to relate to the opposite sex (or in some cases the same sex) in a sexual way. All this is set against the background of helpful and unhelpful aspects of sex role stereotyping, issues of power, conflicting social mores, and constantly changing rules for sexual expression. It is to the great credit of teenagers today that most of them are able to steer a path through this minefield to a point where they can establish positive and fulfilling relationships with another.

6 Gay and lesbian adolescence

Mark Goggin

I was 15 years old and I was going through a pretty hard time and stuff. I was feeling pretty low about myself. One day I said I've got to meet someone else like myself. I've got to meet other people because I was in a very isolated position from my family, from the guys at school, as I was going to an all boys school. My parents didn't have any gay friends, I had no gay relatives that I knew of. And I just felt, Oh my God! I'm a freak or something, and I think that was doing a lot of damage to me. So I decided I had nothing to lose and I joined a group and met some other young gay guys. Through accepting myself and my sexuality, I've become proud of myself, happy with myself, more confident about who I am.

(Thomas, 16 years; MacKenzie *et al.* 1992: 13)

Gay and lesbian *adolescence* is a relatively new concept in adolescent sexuality. The recognition of how homosexuality develops in childhood and adolescence is gradually evolving from a past of myths and stigma, toward understanding, support, and acceptance. While the origins of homosexuality are still poorly understood, it is now generally believed by most researchers and health professionals that there is no evidence that homosexuality is pathological in nature but rather is a variation in human sexual behaviour (Bell *et al.* 1981a; Remafedi 1987, 1990; Bidwell and Deisher 1991).

Although society's attitudes toward homosexuality have slowly shifted, stereotypes of young gay boys as effeminate queens or poofs, and young lesbians as tomboys or butch dykes, are still salient. Young gay people are far more than troubled youths whose 'problems' cause them to exhibit deviant behaviour. Rather, growing up with an awareness of same-sex attraction is an enormous and undeniable personal challenge in the face of pervasive social stigma. Despite this, personal acceptance of a gay or lesbian identity as a positive and fulfilling lifestyle is possible.

AN HISTORICAL OVERVIEW

Sexual orientation is widely believed to be determined by early childhood, if not before birth, but its unfolding between childhood and adulthood is not well understood (Bell *et al.* 1981a; Boxer and Cohler 1989; Herdt 1989). Until recently, homosexuality was considered an adult phenomenon and adolescents were thought to be uniformly heterosexual. Youthful homosexual behaviour was regarded as part of the transient experimentation typical of early adolescence. Indeed, studies of fantasies, behaviours and sexual identity show that uncertainty over sexuality is common for adolescents. Only a small minority (about 3 per cent), however, identify as homosexual during adolescence (Michael *et al.* 1988; Remafedi *et al.* 1992; Sonenstein *et al.* 1989).

For a young person, understanding how society will react to a disclosure that 'I'm homosexual' is important. Beliefs that homosexuality is a crime, an illness, or a sin against God have been, and among some sections of the community still are, pervasive. Young people who are attempting to understand their sexual orientation still grapple with the historical stigma attached to homosexuality.

For centuries, homosexual acts were regarded as criminal activities. For example, the English Act of 1533 made buggery (anal intercourse between men) punishable by death (Brown 1989). Historically, what we call 'homosexuality' was not considered a unified set of acts, much less a set of qualities defining particular persons. As Weeks (1977: 12) describes it, 'There was no concept of the homosexual in law, and homosexuality was not regarded as a particular attribute of a certain type of person but as a potential in all sinful creatures.'

Largely, lesbian sex was seen as unimaginable. Most civil laws against same-sex relations were quite explicit about the acts committed by males, but did not specifically mention women.

> Compared with the frequency with which male homosexuality is mentioned, in canon and civil law, especially after the thirteenth century, in penitentials and confessional manuals, in popular sermons and literature . . . the handful of documents which cite the love of women for one another is truly scant.
>
> (Brown 1989: 70)

Within the framework of the criminal law, homosexuality, or at least male homosexuality, was a crime and remains so within some jurisdictions. Within some Christian frameworks, homosexuality was, and is still considered, a sin, a violation of God's law.

From early this century, homosexuality became increasingly regarded as a medical 'illness'. As physicians took over the responsibility for managing this socially unacceptable behaviour from the law and the church, homosexuality was defined as a pathological condition to be investigated, treated and cured. With the early failure of biological explanations and cures for homosexuality, psychoanalytic and behavioural theories proliferated and homosexuality was classified as a psychiatric disorder.

Influenced by political pressure from the gay movement, the American Psychiatric Association removed homosexuality in 1973 as a psychiatric disorder from its official register of psychopathology. The era of homosexuality as an illness was officially over. In the 1970s and 1980s, with more liberal social attitudes towards sexuality, homosexuality was widely decriminalised, openness about homosexuality increased, and gay and lesbian communities developed throughout urban North America, Europe and Australia. These changes and the advent of AIDS changed the social environment in which young people were coming out and the questions that were relevant to ask about lesbian and gay adolescence. For instance, interest in effeminate childhood behaviour in boys as predictive of homosexuality has been replaced by more pressing concerns such as understanding sexual practices and condom use and examining the impact of AIDS in intensifying gay stigma. In these changing social contexts, however, lesbian and gay adolescents must surely be one of the most under-researched groups of adolescents, and the most poorly understood in terms of sexuality.

The dominant themes of adolescent homosexuality are explored in this chapter. Firstly, what is homosexuality and how prevalent is the expression of homosexuality during adolescence? Secondly, what explains the development of homosexuality? Does homosexuality develop from biological or environmental influences? Thirdly, how do young girls and boys come to grips with a sexual orientation other than heterosexual? How do they develop a sexual identity and 'come out' as lesbian or gay? Finally, as we enter the second decade of the rapid spread of HIV among young gay men, the post-AIDS era is examined. What are the increased risks for young gay men, especially those who are HIV positive? What is the likelihood of greater understanding and tolerance of homosexuality in adolescence?

WHAT IS HOMOSEXUALITY?

Homosexuality involves more than only sexual contact with persons of the same sex. Romantic feelings, emotional attraction, fantasies, and definition of self are also involved. A homosexual person is an individual 'whose primary erotic psychological and social interest is in a member of the same sex, even though that interest may not be overtly expressed' (Martin and

Lyon 1972: 1). When describing the development of homosexual sexual identity, there has been a shift in terminology. Homosexual, as a label, is associated with a long history of stigma. Homosexual also emphasises sexual behaviour over strong romantic feelings and intimate behaviour with someone of the same sex. In an effort to create labels that are more positive and connote more than sexual behaviour, 'gay' and 'lesbian' have become the preferred labels. 'Gay', in Western culture, is generally used to describe self-identified homosexual identity. Because of the visibility of male homosexual communities and the relative invisibility of lesbian culture, the word 'gay' has become synonymous with male homosexuality. While some are satisfied that the words 'gay' or 'homosexual' include gay women and men, others are not. With the symptomatic neglect and ignorance of lesbian experience, most gay women prefer 'lesbian' as their label of definition. Using 'lesbian' makes inclusion of gay women explicit and immediately raises important questions. What is lesbian? How is being lesbian different from being gay?

In discussing homosexuality, it is important to define some key concepts, namely, sexual orientation, sexual identity, and sexual behaviour or activity. *Sexual orientation*, often presumed to be innate and unchangeable, is used to describe a person's underlying sexual preferences, heterosexual, bisexual, or homosexual. Sexual orientation has been defined as *a consistent pattern of sexual arousal* toward persons of the same and/or opposite gender (Spitzer 1981), encompassing fantasy, conscious attractions, emotional and romantic feelings, sexual behaviours and possibly other components (Klein *et al.* 1985; Shively and De Cecco 1977).

Sexual identity refers to how a person describes his or her sexual self and how that person expresses that self to others. Typically, sexual identity will be an expression of a person's underlying sexual orientation. For example, a young woman is romantically and sexually attracted to women. For many years she experiences intimate friendships with other girls. Some of the friendships have become sexual at times and these experiences have been pleasurable and satisfying. Her experiences tell her that she is lesbian and she desires a long-term romantic and sexual relationship with another woman. Because she had always assumed she was heterosexual, these feelings for other women are in conflict with her heterosexual identity. Through a process of *coming out* (from her presumed heterosexual identity), described fully later in this chapter, she begins to describe herself as lesbian to herself and others. Through romantic and sexual experiences she has come to develop a sexual identity that matches her sexual orientation.

Sexual orientation and sexual identity, however, do not always match. A young man has grown up in a large family. All his siblings are married and he, too, desires a marriage and a family. This is how he has always planned his life. He believes, as his upbringing has taught him, that these are the experiences that will bring him true happiness. Yet, throughout his adolescence, he has had intense crushes on other boys at school, sometimes leading to sexual experimentation. Despite many close friendships with girls, sexual experiences with girls and attempted relationships lacked intensity, pleasure and romantic attraction. Though he is aware of his sexual attraction to men, he discounts this as a passing phase. As his parents say, 'He just needs to find the right woman.' The idea that he might be gay is abhorrent. Eventually, he marries a long-time school friend. The marriage is without passion and lacks sexual interest. Children add fulfilment to his desire for a family but he remains dissatisfied and troubled. He is aware that his primary sexual orientation is homosexual, although it has never been fully expressed. He chooses to suppress these feelings and adopt a conventional heterosexual identity. Would we describe this young man as heterosexual, homosexual or bisexual? None of these categories is entirely satisfactory.

Sexual orientation is commonly viewed as an either/or choice – one is either heterosexual or homosexual. Yet, when one views human sexual behaviour, the sexual acts people engage in, as distinct from sexual orientation and identity, heterosexuality and homosexuality emerge as matters of degree. This creates unavoidable problems of definition. Exemplifying the difficulties of categorisation, one young boy

> called himself *gay* to a gay AIDS educator and other gay men, described himself as *bisexual* to his brother who knew of his sexual activity with men and women and apparently is *heterosexual* in the eyes of his parents, girlfriend and school mates.
>
> (Davis *et al.* 1991: 13)

As many adolescents questioning their sexual orientation wonder if they are bisexual or homosexual, understanding what bisexuality means becomes important. Bisexuality has been used to describe people who are equally attracted to both sexes. Yet, bisexuality encompasses a number of meanings. There are several types of bisexuality: bisexuality as a real orientation, as a transitory orientation, as a transitional orientation, or as homosexual denial (MacDonald 1981). Bisexuality as a real orientation refers to people with a natural attraction to both sexes that continues into adulthood. An individual with this orientation might or might not be sexually active with more than one partner at a time but would continue to have feelings of attraction to both sexes. Bisexual behaviour can be a transitory experience – a temporary involvement by people who are actually heterosexual or homosexual. Transitory homosexual behaviour may occur in single-sex boarding schools, in prisons, and among male sex workers or prostitutes who work with both men and women. These individuals resume their original orientation after a period of bisexual experiences or experimentation.

Bisexuality can, however, also be a transitional state, or temporary identity (Cass 1979), in which a person is changing from one exclusive orientation to another. The person will remain in the new orientation:

> I had led a traditional life with a husband, two kids and community activities. My best friend and I were very active together. Much to our surprise, we fell in love. We were initially secretive about our sexual relationship and continued our marital lives, but then we both divorced our husbands and moved away to start a life together. The best way I can describe being with her is that life is now like a colour TV, instead of black and white.
>
> (Crooks and Baur 1990: 320)

Finally, bisexuality may sometimes be an attempt to deny exclusive homosexual interests and to avoid the full stigma of homosexual activity (MacDonald 1981). Denial of homosexuality takes many forms as described later in this chapter as part of the identity confusion stage of coming out. Frequently, homosexual feelings are blocked, information and social contact with homosexuals avoided and immersion in heterosexual relationships pursued (Troiden 1989).

Crucial for adolescents is this distinction between transitory homosexual or bisexual behaviour, and homosexual identification. With the meaning of 'homosexual' so often asssociated with sexual acts, confusion and distress can often be caused. For example, a heterosexual girl who has an incidental sexual experience with another girl may feel that this one act makes her homosexual. Because she has been led to believe that sex with another woman makes you a homosexual, she interprets her behaviour as threatening her identity, causing considerable and unnecessary worry. As the following discussion shows, homosexual activity, homosexual fantasies and confusion about sexual orientation are fairly common among adolescents. Only a small minority of adolescents, however, actually develop sexual identities as gay or lesbian. Thus, while homosexual activity may help predict who is gay or lesbian, it does not determine sexual identity. It appears that homosexual activity is integral, but not sufficient in itself, to the development of a homosexual identity.

Kinsey and his associates (Kinsey *et al.* 1948) found frequent homosexual behaviour, with 37 per cent of men reporting at least some overt homosexual experience to the point of orgasm between adolescence and old age. Twenty-five per cent had more than incidental homosexual experience and feelings; 10 per cent were more or less exclusively homosexual for at least three years of their lives; and 4 per cent of men were exclusively homosexual throughout their lives. During late adolescence, one male in three engaged in homosexual behaviour. Later (Kinsey and Gebhard 1953) in a comparable study of American women, the estimated prevalence of female homosexuality was about half the corresponding male figures.

Recently, sexual orientation among adolescents has been studied in a significant way. Remafedi *et al.* (1992) surveyed 34,706 Minnesota high school students aged 12 to 20. Overall, 10.7 per cent were unsure of their sexual orientation; 88.2 per cent described themselves as predominantly heterosexual; 0.7 per cent described themselves as predominantly bisexual and 0.4 per cent as homosexual. The reported prevalence of homosexual attraction (4.5 per cent) exceeded homosexual fantasies (2.6 per cent), sexual behaviour (1 per cent), and homosexual identification (0.4 per cent). The incidence of same-sexual behaviour in this sample was comparable to other studies. Of 18-year-old male students, 2.8 per cent reported homosexual behaviour, equivalent to figures from Sonenstein *et al.* (1989) and Michael *et al.* (1988).

Remafedi and his colleagues found that uncertainty about sexual orientation gradually shifted to heterosexual or homosexual identification with the passage of time and/or increasing sexual experience, with a steady decline in uncertainty with age from 25.9 per cent in 12-year-olds, to 5 per cent in 18-year-old students. Youths who were unsure were more likely to entertain homosexual fantasies and attractions and less likely to have heterosexual sexual experience. Throughout adolescence, the researchers conclude, 'incongruities between attractions, fantasies, behaviours and perceived identities should be anticipated' (Remafedi *et al.* 1992: 7).

Since Kinsey it has been assumed that the incidence of female homosexuality is about half the corresponding male figure. This presumed gender difference in sexual orientation may well be a function of sex role expectations (Remafedi 1992). Unlike men, women may experience close same-sex attachments without homosexual identification (de Monteflores and Schultz 1978). Conversely, because men face more rigid gender codes, they may be more likely to see homosexuality as outside the realm of heterosexuality, and may polarise more markedly in their sexual identifications. However, in Remafedi's study, male–female differences in homosexual identification were less evident and, in fact, a larger proportion of young women than young men reported homosexual attractions and fantasies. Since Kinsey's time, sex role expectations and social attitudes to homosexuality have changed, possibly accounting for this convergence.

While longitudinal research is needed to verify their conclusions,

Remafedi and his colleagues (1992) paint a picture of undifferentiated sexuality in early adolescence with low homosexual identity leading to greater certainty about sexual orientation by late adolescence. Clearly, by late adolescence the vast majority of teenagers identify as heterosexual. Only a minority of youth, with homosexual fantasies, attractions or behaviours, reported a homosexual identity *during* adolescence. Many, however, especially young lesbians, take until their early twenties or longer to openly acknowledge these feelings and self-identify as homosexual (Barbeler 1992; Herdt 1989; Troiden 1989).

HOMOSEXUALITY AND THE DEVELOPMENTAL PERSPECTIVE

The thorny debate about whether homosexuals are born or bred has long fascinated psychologists and scientists. Traditionally, the search for the cause of the disease 'homosexuality' went hand in hand with the search for a cure and the subsequent eradication of homosexuality. Now, the question is more sensibly posed as 'What are the biological mechanisms and the environmental experiences that are involved in the development of homosexuality?'

Homosexuality and biology

From the late nineteenth century with advances in medical science it seemed plausible that homosexuality could be caused by a physiological process. Initially, however, while science failed to pinpoint a congenital deficit, or find physical differences between heterosexual and homosexual men, medical treatments purporting to cure homosexuality abounded. At the turn of the century, cures for homosexuality included castration and vasectomy (Minichiello 1992). In the 1930s and 1940s, hormone therapy (consisting of androgen supplements) was used in the attempt to cure homosexuality, although the data were inconsistent regarding homosexuality and hormone imbalance. Such medical intervention, while it sometimes increased sexual interest, did not result in significant changes in sexual orientation (Money and Ehrhardt 1972). Treatment of homosexuality with electroconvulsive therapy (ECT) persisted into the 1960s.

Gradually, biological theories of homosexuality were replaced by psychoanalytic and behaviourist theories. Following a careful review of the evidence, in a recent study of homosexual people from the Kinsey Institute, Bell *et al.* (1981a) concluded that all environmental explanations of the origin of same-sex behaviour – absent fathers, over-loving mothers, birth order, the labelling theory – are insufficient. A re-evaluation of the biological evidence shows a growing body of knowledge – from hormone, twin, and anatomical studies – supporting biological factors as the primary basis for sexual attraction.

Comparison of hormone levels between adult homosexual men and adult homosexual women has produced contradictory results (Meyer-Bahlburg 1977; Tourney 1980). Even if consistent differences were found, it would remain unknown whether these differences were a cause, or a result, of sexual orientation. Testosterone levels are sensitive to a number of variables including general health, diet, drug use, sexual activity, and stress (Marmor 1980). While many of these variables have been controlled in careful research, hormonal differences could still be a product of the stress and anxiety many homosexual people experience as a result of societal oppression. A recent review of studies concludes that there is no difference in the circulating levels of sex hormones of adult heterosexual and homosexual males (Money 1988).

Hormone levels during prenatal and/or early development may affect sexual orientation. Researchers speculate that hormone imbalances can alter the masculine and feminine development of the fetal brain and that this may contribute to homosexual orientation (Ellis and Ames 1987; Zuger 1989). Laboratory research with animals has demonstrated that hormones given prenatally can masculinize fetal females and demasculinize fetal males. This results in other-sex social and mating behaviour (rams acting like ewes and ewes acting like rams) when the animals mature (Money 1988). Hormones active just before and after birth have been shown to determine the sexual behaviour and brain structure of laboratory rats (Dodson *et al.* 1988). While such fetal research on humans remains unethical, speculation about the physiological effects of hormones on brain development have led to studies looking for anatomical differences between the brains of heterosexual and homosexual males.

Le Vay (1991) showed a difference between homosexual and heterosexual brains, by demonstrating that cells in the interstitial nuclei of the anterior hypothalamus are more densely clustered in gays. The anterior hypothalamus participates in the regulation of typical male sexual behaviour. A similar difference in this part of the hypothalamus was found between heterosexual men and women (Allen *et al.* 1989). Subsequently, Allen and Gorski (1992) found that a cluster of nerves connecting the two sides of the brain, called the anterior commissure, is around 34 per cent bigger in gay males than straight males. Though provocative, logical links between these biological differences and how they affect the development of sexual orientation need to be demonstrated.

Tracing the incidence of homosexuality among monozygotic (identical) twins and dizygotic (fraternal or nonidentical) twins further implicates biology in determining sexual orientation. In a summary of homosexual twin studies, Puterbaugh (1990) concludes that there is between 77 and 88 per cent concordance of homosexuality in monozygotic twins, that is where both twins are homosexual. Dizygotic or fraternal twins, by comparison, show no concordance for homosexuality, or a very slight concordance.

One of the great disappointments of the research in this area is the almost complete absence of research involving lesbians. Recently, however, some controversial twin evidence suggests environmental factors play a greater role in lesbian aetiology than is the case for gay males (Eckert *et al.* 1990). Unlike the concordance of homosexuality among male identical twins, three out of four female identical twins, all reared apart, were discordant for homosexuality. While the findings are descriptive only, the pattern of findings suggest that female homosexuality is a trait most likely acquired after birth, but before menarche, and may be associated with delayed puberty and, just possibly, with larger physique.

Other researchers, whose primary concern has focused on the involvement of various psychosocial factors in the development of homosexuality, also strongly believe that elements of their research point toward biological antecedents. While Bell and colleagues (1981a) see homosexuality as a pattern of feelings and reactions within the child that cannot be traced back to a single social or psychological cause, they believe that a boy or girl is predisposed to be homosexual or heterosexual.

This biological predisposition for homosexuality is evidenced by the strong link between gender nonconformity and adult homosexuality. Gender nonconformity is the extent to which research subjects conformed to stereotypic characteristics of masculinity and femininity during childhood. Both male and female homosexuals were more likely to have experienced far-ranging and deep-seated gender nonconformity than were heterosexuals. Cross-culturally, a comparative study of the United States, Guatemala and Brazil indicated that gender nonconformity, related to childhood toy and activity interests as well as sexual interest in other boys, was a behavioural indicator of adult homosexuality (Whitam 1980). A 15-year longitudinal study that compared gender role behaviour in boys and girls found similar results (Green 1987). Boys who preferred dolls to other toys, disliked rough-and-tumble play and preferred role playing as a female rather than a male, were highly likely to have homosexual orientations later in life. As Bell and his colleagues conclude, 'if there is a biological basis for homosexuality it probably accounts for gender nonconformity as well as for sexual orientation' (Bell *et al.* 1981a: 217).

Homosexuality: psychosocial theories

Different life experiences, gender nonconformity, parental patterning or psychological attributes of the individual are some of the theories often presented as psychosocial explanations for the development of homosexuality. A more popular notion is that homosexuals lack the ability to establish, or are fearful of, heterosexual relations. It is often assumed that lesbianism is due to resentment, fear, or distrust of men rather than attraction to women. Similarly, statements like 'All a lesbian needs is a good lay' or 'He just needs to meet the right woman' reflect the notion that homosexuality is a poor second choice for people who lack satisfactory heterosexual experiences (Crooks and Baur 1990). Actually, gay-identifying adolescents are usually more sexually experienced than their heterosexual peers (Remafedi *et al.* 1992). One study showed about 45 per cent of gay adolescents had at least one sexual experience with a female (Davies *et al.* 1992), while 70 per cent of gay and lesbian adults have had heterosexual sexual experiences (Herdt 1989; Martin and Lyon 1972; Troiden 1989). Gay young men and lesbians did, however, feel differently about dating, tending to engage in fewer types of heterosexual activities with fewer partners than heterosexuals, and finding them less satisfying. Another myth is that homosexuality begins with seduction by an older person. Typically, young gays' and lesbians' first homosexual encounters are with a partner about the same age. Homosexuals are less likely than heterosexuals to have had initial sexual encounters with a stranger or older person (Bell *et al.* 1981a).

Bell and his colleagues do conclude, however, that learning from intense and pleasurable sexual experience is a powerful antecedent to later sexual orientation. Those who learn to masturbate by being stimulated by a person of the same sex, and those whose first orgasm is in homosexual contact are more likely to have a homosexual orientation as adults (Van Wyk 1984). But which comes first? Do the feelings guide the behaviour? What causes the feelings? Does the behaviour shape the feelings? How do the feelings and behaviours interact and how significant is each in developing sexual orientation? These are questions for continued research.

A predominant theory of homosexual development concerns patterns of family relationships and childhood experiences. A number of studies sought to confirm Sigmund Freud's early speculations about homosexuality. Freud (1924, 1935) maintained that the relationship with one's father and mother was a crucial factor. Freud believed humans to be innately bisexual, passing through a homoerotic phase in the process of establishing a heterosexual orientation. Fixating at this homoerotic phase could occur, especially if a male had a poor relationship with his father and an overly close and binding relationship with his mother. Later clinical research sought to confirm these hypotheses with contradictory results. While some research supported the theory of a close-binding intimate mother and a distant father (Bieber *et al.* 1962; Saghir and Robins 1973), others found no such childhood experiences for male homosexuals (Robertson 1972) or differences between homosexual and heterosexual males in their relationships with their mothers (Bene 1965a). Although Bell and his colleagues found some evidence of poor father–son relationships, Boxer and Cohler (1989) report that such poor relationships may be a result rather than a cause of homosexuality, and may arise from defensive distortions of early erotic attachments to their fathers (Isay 1987). Reviews conclude that there is no particular phenomenon of family life that can be singled out as especially consequential for either homosexual or heterosexual development (Bell *et al.* 1981a; Ross and Arrindell 1988).

Implicit in the many psychosocial explanations of homosexuality is the assumption that homosexuality is a less permanent condition than heterosexuality and, thus, may be reversible. Some therapists have provided therapeutic intervention for homosexual or bisexual people who are highly distressed by their orientation and want to develop a heterosexual preference (e.g., Masters and Johnson 1979). Such programmes have been heavily criticised for their claim of converting so-called homosexuals to heterosexual functioning on the grounds that many of their subjects may have been incorrectly labelled as homosexuals when they were in fact bisexual or heterosexual people who had turned to homosexual behaviour because of sexual problems in their heterosexual relationships (Barlow *et al.* 1980; Bell *et al.* 1981a; Zilbergeld and Evans 1980). Currently, most therapists agree that changing the sexual orientation of true homosexuals is probably impossible to achieve (Crooks and Baur 1990). Following the removal from DSM III-R (American Psychiatric Association 1987) of homosexuality as a psychiatric disorder, many therapists and counsellors changed the focus of therapy. Rather than making the assumption that their homosexual clients must be cured, therapists have made it an objective to assist them to love, live and work in a society that harbours considerable hostility towards them (Milligan 1975). This change in therapeutic practice is significant in that it defines the problem as society's negativity toward homosexuality rather than homosexuality itself (Crooks and Baur 1990).

Homophobia

The biological and environmental evidence demonstrating the natural development of homosexuality is increasingly at odds with centuries of fundamental public and religious opinion that homosexuality is unnatural.

Irrational fears of gay people (homophobia) appear to underlie public attitudes that affect the psychological, educative, legal, and political treatment young gays and lesbians currently experience. Concerns that public portrayal of homosexual affection or mere social contact with other homosexuals during adolescence may somehow influence otherwise heterosexual adolescents to 'turn' gay still persist. This is evidenced in public demands to ban safe sex campaigns portraying young gay men (MacKenzie *et al.* 1992). Continuing evidence of the discrimination young gay people face includes higher ages of consent for consenting homosexual sex, laws banning the positive portrayal of homosexuality, and continued harsh penalties for homosexual sex in many parts of the world (Herek and Birrell 1992).

More subtle expression of homophobia is apparent in careful avoidance of any behaviour that might be perceived as homosexual. Same-sex friends or family may refrain from spontaneous embraces, people may shun unfeminine or unmasculine clothing or a woman may decide not to support feminism because she fears being called lesbian. The effect of homophobia on the depth of intimacy in male friendships may be quite significant, although these attitudes can change over time:

> My own reaction to learning that one of my school mates was gay was discomfort. I increasingly avoided him. I am sorry now that I didn't confront myself as to why I felt that way. I was homophobic. And because I didn't deal with that then, it kept me from developing closeness with my other male friends. I lost something in those relationships because I was afraid that being physically and emotionally close to another man meant that I, too, was homosexual. I finally began to explore why I felt so uncomfortable touching or being touched by another man. Today, I am no longer threatened or frightened by physical closeness from another man. I am secure enough to deal with that honestly.
>
> (Crooks and Baur 1990: 326)

THE 'COMING OUT' EXPERIENCE

The process of self-identification as gay or lesbian, and the disclosure of that identity to significant others, notably family and friends, is commonly known as *coming out*. This fascinating, difficult and complex process for the adolescent has been described by many researchers (Cass 1984; Coleman 1982; Ponse 1978; Troiden 1989) and is the focus of the few gay youth self-help books (Alyson 1985; Borhek 1983; Hart 1986; Heron 1983; Kinder and Rampton 1992). Troiden (1989) takes a wide and inclusive view of coming out beginning in childhood and continuing through mature adulthood. He sees the development of a homosexual identity as a series of four stages: sensitisation, identity confusion, identity assumption and identity commitment.

Stage 1: sensitisation

Young lesbians:

> I felt different: unfeminine, ungraceful, not very pretty, kind of a mess.

> I didn't express myself the way other girls would. I never showed feelings. I wasn't emotional.

Young gay males:

> I couldn't stand sports, so naturally that made me different. A ball thrown at me was like a bomb.

> I was indifferent to boys' games, like cops and robbers. I was more interested in watching insects and reflecting on things.
>
> (Bell *et al.* 1981a: 74–86)

The sensitisation stage occurs before puberty. At this time, most lesbians and gay males do not see homosexuality as personally relevant, that is, they assume they are heterosexual, if they think about their sexual status at all. Yet, lesbians and gay males, however, typically acquire social experiences during their childhood that serve later as the bases for seeing homosexuality as personally relevant. . . . In short, childhood experiences sensitise lesbians and gay males to subsequent self definition as homosexual.

(Troiden 1989: 50)

Troiden's picture of sensitisation interweaves a range of research findings. In this 'prehomosexual' period, it is not surprising that the child interprets feeling different in terms of gender metaphors rather than sexual scripts that are used later. Lesbians and gays, for instance, were more likely to report a sense of feeling different to others than heterosexuals, and of feeling more marginalised by involvement in gender-neutral or gender-inappropriate interests (Bell *et al.* 1981a). Lesbians were more likely to feel different because they felt more masculine, more interested in sports, and enjoyed girls' activities less than boys' activities. Similarly, gay young men were more likely to report feeling odd because they did not like sports, or were feminine or were not sexually interested in girls. They were more likely to enjoy solitary gender-neutral activities (drawing, reading, music) rather than boys' activities such as football or baseball (Bell *et al.* 1981a). While feeling different is widely reported, only a minority (20 per cent) of gays and lesbians saw themselves as sexually different before the age of 12, and only 4 per cent labelled this difference as homosexual (Bell *et al.* 1981b).

Stage 2: identity confusion

Lesbians and gay males typically begin to personalise homosexuality during adolescence, when they reflect upon the idea that their feelings and/or behaviours could be regarded as homosexual. Identity confusion arises out of (a) altered perceptions of self, (b) the experience of heterosexual and homosexual arousal and behaviour, (c) the stigma surrounding homosexuality, and (d) inaccurate knowledge about homosexuals and homosexuality (Troiden 1989). The following describe early and late phases of identity uncertainty:

> *Early*: I'm not sure who I am. I'm confused about what sort of person I am and where my life is going. I ask the question, 'Who am I?' 'Am I homosexual?' 'Am I really heterosexual?'
>
> *Late*: I feel that I probably am homosexual, although I'm not definitely sure. I feel distant or cut off from other people. I'm beginning to think that it might help to meet other homosexuals but I'm not sure whether I really want to or not. I prefer to put on a front of being completely heterosexual.

> (Cass 1984: 156)

Generally, the adolescent first defines himself or herself as 'probably' homosexual between the ages of 12 and 17 for gay males (Herdt 1989; Ross 1989), and 16 to 20 for lesbians (Barbeler 1992; Troiden 1989). Cross-cultural evidence suggests that, generally, the more restrictive the culture, the later the age at which homosexual as a self-definition is assumed (Herdt 1989; Ross 1989).

Typical responses to the uncertainties of identity confusion about sexual orientation are to adopt one or more of a range of strategies: denial, repair, avoidance, redefining and acceptance. *Denial* involves attempting to block out homosexual feelings, fantasies or activities. *Repair* involves wholesale efforts to eradicate homosexual feelings and behaviours, often involving professional help. Those who engage in *avoidance* recognise that their feelings are homosexual and that they are unacceptable. Avoidance may take a number of forms. Some inhibit thoughts, behaviours and interests they have learned to associate with homosexuality.

I thought my sexual interest in other girls would go away if I paid more attention to boys and concentrated more on being feminine.

I figured I'd go straight and develop more of an interest in girls if I got even more involved in sports and didn't spend so much time on my art.

(Troiden 1989: 56)

Avoidance may also take the form of withdrawing from the opposite sex so that one's lack of heterosexual responsiveness is not discovered.

I hated dating. I was always afraid I wouldn't get erect when we petted and kissed and that girls would find out I was probably gay.

(Troiden 1989: 56)

Conversely, others may immerse themselves in heterosexual relationships and experiences, including young girls becoming pregnant to 'prove' that they are not lesbian. For others, avoidance involved shunning information about homosexuality, partly out of fear of confirming what is suspected. 'One ingenious defence was to remain as ignorant as possible on the subject of homosexuality' (Troiden 1989: 56). More extreme avoidance strategies may involve expressing anti-homosexual feelings as a way of distancing oneself from individual homoerotic feelings, and escapism, taking drugs or drinking, to find temporary relief. The latter remains a serious health risk with recent studies reporting significant chemical dependency among young gay males (Remafedi 1992) and lesbians (Barbeler 1992).

Redefining homosexual behaviour or feelings forms another strategy in rationalising fears of long-term sexual identity change. Redefinition is reflected through the use of temporary identity (Cass 1979), special case, or situational strategies. As described earlier, for some young lesbians and gay males, seeing themselves as bisexual ('I guess I'm attracted to men and women'), or passing through a transitory phase ('I'm just passing through a phase, I'm really not homosexual'), may or may not reflect their actual sexual interests (Troiden 1989).

Seeing homosexual experiences as a special case, a person may regard his or her homosexual feelings and behaviours as different from other homosexuals, an isolated case, a never-to-be-repeated experience. 'I never thought of my feelings and our lovemaking as lesbian. The whole experience was too beautiful for it to be something so ugly. I didn't think I could ever have those feelings for another woman.' Situational reasons also become another justifiable excuse. 'It only happened because I was drunk.' 'I was at boarding school and everyone did it' (Troiden 1989: 57).

Perceptions of self anchored in the strategies of denial, repair, avoidance or redefinition may be sustained for months, years or permanently. Eventually, however, *acceptance* hopefully arrives as the young person, acknowledging experiences as homosexual, seeks additional sources of information to learn more about his or her sexual feelings.

> From the time I was quite young I felt different from other girls and I felt more masculine than feminine. When I learned that lesbians existed, I had a word that explained why I was different from other girls.
>
> (Reinhart 1982: 26)

Stage 3: identity assumption

Here, homosexual identity becomes both a self-identity and a presented identity, at least to other lesbian or gay friends. At this stage, a young person self-defines as homosexual, initially tolerating and finally accepting that identity. The young person regularly socialises with other lesbians or gay males, experiments sexually and explores the lesbian or gay subculture. Contexts of self-identification as homosexual vary between lesbians and gay males. Most girls who self-identify as lesbian do so in situations of intense affectionate involvements with other women (Cronin 1974; Schafer 1976). For gay males, sociosexual contexts are the usual places of homosexual self-definition – gay bars, clubs and saunas, parties, and public places where men meet for sex (for example, parks, beaches, public toilets). Only a minority, roughly 20 per cent, define themselves in the context of same-sex romantic contexts (Dank 1971; Troiden 1989; Warren 1974) and more recently, in coming out groups (Anderson 1987; Gerstell *et al.* 1989). Initially, being gay or lesbian is tolerated rather than accepted.

> I feel sure I'm gay and I put up with this. I see myself as gay for now but I'm not sure about how I'll be in the future. I'm careful to put across a straight (heterosexual) image. I feel like I want to meet others like myself.
>
> (Adapted from Cass 1984: 156)

Defining oneself as lesbian or gay often occurs shortly after first social contact with other homosexuals, either through deciding to go to a gay bar, club or group, or through learning that a friend or relative is gay (Troiden 1989). If initial social experiences with other gay males or lesbians are positive, feelings of isolation are immediately diminished. The possibilities are opened of learning how to cope with discrimination, feeling good about being gay, neutralising guilt feelings and beginning to understand the range of identities and roles open to lesbians and gays (Gerstell *et al.* 1989; Troiden 1989). Undesirable homosexual experiences, however, may prompt attempts at rejection and abandonment of both identity and behaviour (Troiden 1989).

Struggling with acceptance of their identity, some may continue to rely on avoidance and redefinition strategies. *Passing* as heterosexual, or living a double life, can become a strategy for self-defining as homosexual by concealing sexual preference and behaviour from family, friends and colleagues, by careful – even tortuous – control of information (Humpreys 1972). Alternatively, young gays and lesbians may immerse themselve almost completely in a gay environment, seeking a sense of belonging and inclusion. By minimising heterosexual socialising, and even attaching special significance to their new experiences, their identities become normalised. Acceptance of a gay or lesbian identity occurs at the end of this stage.

> I'm quite sure I'm lesbian. I'm happy about this. I'll tell a few people I'm gay but I'm careful about who. I try to fit in at work and home. I can't see the point in confronting people with being lesbian if it's going to embarrass all concerned.
>
> (Adapted from Cass 1984: 156)

Stage 4: commitment

Commitment involves adopting homosexuality as a way of life. For the committed homosexual, it becomes easier, more attractive, less costly to remain a homosexual than to try to function as a heterosexual (Troiden 1989). Commitment to homosexuality as a way of life occurs from the end of adolescence through adulthood.

> I'm prepared to tell almost anyone that I'm gay. I'm happy about the way I am but I don't feel that being gay is the most important part of me. I mix socially with gay people and straight people, all of whom know I'm gay.
>
> (Cass 1984: 156)

Internal and external changes characterise the commitment stage. Internally, there is a fusion of sexuality and emotionality, feelings that homosexuality is a valid and satisfying self-identity and increased happiness after self-identifying as homosexual. The great majority of gay people report feeling more happy once they reach a certain homosexual self-identity (Troiden 1989). Externally, entering a same-sex love relationship often marks the onset of commitment as does a shift in how stigma is handled. A relationship becomes a concrete manifestation of the synthesis between emotionality and sexuality into a meaningful whole (Coleman 1982). Lesbians appear to enter their first same-sex love relationships between average ages of 22 and 23 (Bell and Weinberg 1978). Gay males' first love affairs occur between the ages of 21 and 24 (Bell and Weinberg 1978; Troiden 1989).

Disclosure to parents, heterosexual audiences, co-workers and employers is another external measure of homosexuality as a way of life (Troiden 1989). Many gays and lesbians continue to use strategies to keep their homosexuality from looming large by continuing to present as heterosexual among workmates, family and other relatives. Others continue to be careful to blend in gender-appropriate ways so that their sexuality is seen as irrelevant in heterosexual interactions. Some gays or lesbians do, however, acquire an ideology that not only destigmatises homosexuality but transforms it from a vice into a virtue and actively pursue educating others and supporting reform to minimise discrimination.

While the accounts of coming out are enormously informative, a common criticism is that they are essentially a developmental psychology of the remembered past (Boxer and Cohler 1989). Early recollection may be coloured by subsequent life experiences. The sense of being different as a child or adolescent may be an adult interpretation of earlier life events. The true chronology of time may be obscured by the passage of time (Remafedi 1987). Little is yet known about how gay and lesbian adolescents experience their lives *as they are living them*, rather than as they are remembered. There is a clear and urgent need for longitudinal studies of coming out that trace the experience of young gays and lesbians as they grow up and develop new sexual identities. Such research could also chart the impact of changing societal attitudes to homosexuality on the coming out process. These changes might be the combined effects of increased recognition, support and education as well as intensified AIDS-related stigma.

HIV/AIDS AND YOUNG GAY ADOLESCENTS

I want to feel joy again but I don't think I can. You can't turn it [the thought of being HIV positive] off, it's always there to take the edge off things. Being carefree, buoyant, feeling how it is to be alive, I'm envious of that in my friends. I want to be normal but fundamentally my base mood is grey, sad, withdrawn.

What do I want? A normal life and all the shit that goes with it. Not just the prospect of getting sick and dying. There is this pressing sense of urgency. You have to work it all out before you die. So I work and work on trying to figure life out. But the payoff is that you die.

(Jim: Author's files)

HIV infections among gay communities, hit earliest and hardest by AIDS throughout Western countries, remain tragically high. Internationally, gay men are disproportionately represented among HIV infections in most Western countries. The current epidemiological picture strongly suggests that young gay and bisexual men are one of the highest risk groups for new HIV infections. While infections among women are increasing in all countries, fortunately for young lesbians, woman-to-woman HIV transmission (i.e. oral-vaginal contact) remains a remote possibility. However, because many lesbian adolescents experience sex with both males and females and some experiment with intravenous drug use (Barbeler 1992), young lesbians are not immune from HIV infection.

It appears likely that a consistently high proportion of young gay and bisexual men in Western countries will be infected with HIV in the next decade. New infections will be constant or increasing in most countries. Because the onset of AIDS takes an average of eight to ten years from infection, many of those who were infected in their teens and early twenties will develop AIDS in their late twenties. Internationally, the picture of HIV infections is uncertain, except that it is dramatically worse than notified AIDS cases and more prevalant among young people. For instance, HIV infections among young gay men (younger than 24 years) in Australia and the United Kingdom represent about 19 to 20 per cent of all HIV infections in those countries, in contrast to the 4 to 5 per cent of notified AIDS cases.

As epidemiologists have noted, HIV surveillance figures provide only a picture of newly discovered HIV infections which underestimate actual HIV infections (Crofts 1992). Indeed, younger gay men who may be at risk of HIV infection or who are already infected appear less likely than older men to have taken an HIV antibody test. While 79 per cent of gay adult men had taken an HIV test (Dunne *et al.* 1992), studies of gay adolescents (aged 20 and younger) show that 20 per cent of Australian gay youths (Gold *et al.* 1992), 36 per cent of English gay youths (Davies *et al.* 1992), and 40 per cent of American gay youths had taken an HIV test (Remafedi *et al.* 1992). Under-reporting of new HIV infections among gay male adolescents aged 20 or younger, therefore, seems probable. Fears of a 'second wave' of HIV infection among young gay men have become a reality in San Francisco with a recent study showing very high rates of infection among this group. For example, 49 per cent of young African-American gays attending STD clinics in the San Francisco Bay Area were HIV infected (Kellogg *et al.* 1991).

The primary mode of new HIV infections among these young gay men is unprotected anal intercourse although needle sharing is not uncommon (Remafedi *et al.* 1992) and concerns about transmission through oral sex persist. A recent study showed that 43 per cent of young gay men (younger than 25 years) had engaged in unprotected anal intercourse in the last six months, supporting the finding that young gay adults had more unprotected anal sex with more partners than older gay men (Ekstrand and Coates 1990; Valdiserri *et al.* 1988).

Gay adolescent sexual risk-taking may be more moderate. Among gay adolescents, recent studies show those engaging in unprotected anal intercourse was between 21 per cent (for English gays in the last month; Davies *et al.* 1992) and 31 per cent (for any of the last three sexual partners for Americans; Remafedi, 1992). In contrast to American studies, Davies *et al.* (1992) found English gay adolescents used condoms more consistently than older gay and bisexual men. While more younger gays engaged in anal intercourse than older gay men, this appears to be due to higher numbers of regular, monogamous relationships. Being in a relationship has been shown to be a major predictor of unsafe sexual behaviour for gay adolescents and young gay adults (Hay *et al.* 1990; Remafedi 1992). Choosing relationships as a protection against HIV remains a questionable strategy. From this research, the imperatives for educating gay adolescents are emphasising the pleasures of nonpenetrative sex, exploring the pitfalls of unprotected anal sex in relationships, and promoting awareness of the dangers of unsafe sex occurring when drugs or alcohol are used.

Young gay males continue to be over-represented among new HIV infections. Development of effective educational strategies has largely failed. A decade into the AIDS epidemic and the plight of young gay males remains grim:

> Things are going very badly indeed at almost all levels of HIV/AIDS education and prevention work for young gay males throughout Europe . . . it reflects a crisis of European culture which remains deeply and profoundly homophobic across all known social and national boundaries.

> (Watney 1992: 27)

There are urgent needs to understand the reasons behind continuing HIV infection among young gay adolescents in Western countries. The need for education and counselling of young gay people in the face of intensified discrimination due to AIDS has never been greater. Although the dominant social climate of stigma and oppression towards gays prevails, there are some grounds for believing that more tolerant community attitudes are forming. Recent research has considerably enhanced our understanding of the sexual lives of gay adolescents. Model programmes for sexual minority youths have arisen from the spirit of youth advocacy and the imperative for AIDS prevention. These hold the promise of social recognition and validation of the sexual identities and experiences of lesbian and gay adolescents.

I always put on a brave front. I prepared myself for the (HIV positive) result even though deep down it hurt. I closed off from the feelings and emotions. I've got some people to talk to, it's just . . . I get a bit down and it's too hard to talk about. Sometimes it feels like the end of the world. I love my family and they all love me but my sexuality always hinders that relationship subconsciously. I didn't let them get too close because they didn't know who I was. I certainly learnt that if you don't deal with things, they come back. I'm not looking forward to telling my mother and my father. They're not aware of homosexuality, let alone HIV. I don't want to feel disappointment and guilt. I've learnt that my sexuality is more important than HIV. The relationship I'm in now, it's shown me I can handle it. I'm proud that I was strong all the way through. It showed me I didn't have to worry about not being loved. Even David could accept it [HIV] if love was there. It's given me hope and confidence.

(Joshua: Author's files)

The risk of HIV/AIDS for sexually active young gay males is high, and is recognised as such in many quarters. Risk among heterosexuals in Western nations is, however, potentially likely to increase to gay levels or beyond in the next decade, but this danger is often not taken so seriously by public health authorities or by the young people themselves. In the next two chapters, we discuss sexual risk-taking among adolescents in general, beginning with the threats posed to health by AIDS and other sexually transmissible diseases, and in Chapter 8, continuing this theme through the discussion of unplanned pregnancy and abortion among young people.

7 Sexual risk I

AIDS and sexually transmissible diseases

In this chapter we return to a consideration of the sexual health of all adolescents, from the point of view of the health risks involved in unprotected intercourse. The so-called sexual revolution of the 1960s brought with it a new freedom for young people, but it also brought a realisation of the consequences of that freedom – in particular, the need for effective contraception as a means of preventing unwanted pregnancies. More recently, there has been an increasing awareness of the risk of sexually transmissible diseases (STDs) for those sexually active people who have multiple partners. Although the actual incidence of STDs in the community is difficult to ascertain accurately, some trends are apparent from the surveillance data that exist. In Western society, STDs are predominantly diseases of adolescents and young adults. Moreover, the pattern of disease prevalence has changed in recent years with syphilis and gonorrhoea, the best known STDs, no longer being the most commonly reported. Of the STDs which are prevalent today, chlamydia may have particularly unfortunate consequences for young women – who are much more likely than young men to be infected. The most common complication of chlamydia for young women is spread of the infection to the upper genital tract, leading to pelvic inflammatory disease, the major cause of tubal damage resulting in ectopic pregnancy and infertility.

Other common STDs include genital herpes simplex and genital warts (human papilloma virus – HPV). Genital herpes is being diagnosed with increasing frequency and has been reported since the 1970s as affecting as much as 15 per cent of the population (Gallois and Callan 1990). In young women, genital herpes is a significant problem because it may be asymptomatic and there is a strong likelihood that the infection will be transmitted from mother to infant if the infection is in an active phase during birth. A similar possibility exists for genital warts (HPV), another STD whose incidence is reported to be increasing. Of particular concern is the association now known to exist between HPV infection and the development of carcinoma of the cervix. With all STDs, the risk of infection is greatly reduced if appropriate precautions are taken during sexual activity – in particular, the use of condoms during penetrative sex. While the threat of disease as a result of sexual activity has long been with us, it is the advent of AIDS as a global health threat that has led to a more active focus on sexual safety. Strictures against unsafe (unprotected) sex have accelerated in recent years with the realisation that AIDS is one sexually transmitted disease for which a cure has not yet been found and which appears to carry with it, ultimately, a sentence of death. In the remainder of this chapter, we look at the impact of this contemporary disease on adolescent sexuality.

AIDS AND ADOLESCENT SEXUAL BEHAVIOUR

While AIDS was initially regarded in the Western world as a disease restricted to male homosexuals, it is now clear that the heterosexual community, and especially young people, are vulnerable to HIV infection and AIDS. Although the number of adolescents among diagnosed AIDS cases is low (about 1 per cent in Western countries), more than 20 per cent of AIDS sufferers are in their 20s. Given the long lead time from infection to diagnosis, the inescapable conclusion is that many were infected in their teens. Reports from New York indicate that heterosexual transmission of the HIV virus is more widespread among adolescents than adults, leading one researcher to question whether adolescents are the 'next wave' of the AIDS epidemic (Hein 1989a). Recent figures (Hein 1992) reveal that AIDS, unheard of before 1981, is now ranked sixth among causes of death among young people aged 15 to 24 in the United States. Among this group, AIDS deaths have increased a hundredfold between 1981 and 1987. Among 13- to 21-year-olds, the number of reported cases of AIDS is doubling every 14 months, but the incidence of HIV-infected young people is unknown. Of the reported cases of HIV infection at the end of 1991 in the United States, 31 per cent were within the 13 to 29 age group. Addressing the mode of transmission of HIV among adolescents, Hein (1992) reports that the adolescent ratio of male to female cases is 3:1 in New York and 7:1 in other parts of the United States. Across America, adolescents with AIDS are less likely to have been infected as a result of homosexual activity or IV drug use, and more likely to have acquired AIDS from blood transfusions or from heterosexual transmission. It is noteworthy that almost half of the AIDS cases of female adolescents are due to heterosexual spread.

It is clear that the virus has entered some adolescent subgroups already, with similar figures to the American ones reported in Australia (National Centre in HIV Epidemiology and Clinical Research 1992). It is not surprising that the theme of adolescent vulnerability has been taken up forcefully by the popular press with anxiety-arousing headlines such as 'AIDS message fails to make impression on youth' and 'Warning: Teens the new AIDS risk group'. Dramatic claims such as these may overstate the likelihood of HIV infection among young people since they fail to do justice to the variability among adolescents in terms of their sexual behaviours and sexual ideologies. This is a view put compellingly by Warwick and Aggleton (1990) in their analysis of researchers' representations of adolescence and their review of themes in research studies of adolescents and AIDS. It is a view supported by even the most cursory reading of studies which document the importance of context in the development and nature of young people's sexual beliefs and behaviours. Nevertheless, there are grounds for concern about the potential for risk of HIV infection among some adolescent subgroups. At the very least, we need to ask questions about the sexual behaviour and responses to the threat of AIDS of different adolescent subgroups. To what extent are adolescents engaging in sexual behaviour that puts themselves at risk of HIV infection? Are they heeding messages about safe sex – particularly the need to use condoms as protection against HIV infection? Do adolescents perceive themselves to be at risk? If not, why not? Can adolescents be persuaded to change unsafe practices which may leave them at risk of AIDS?

As we have seen in an earlier chapter, recent studies in a number of Western countries show a trend to sexual liberalism among adolescents – the incidence of sexual intercourse is rapidly increasing and the age of initiation of sex is declining (Abrams *et al.* 1990; Hein 1989b; King *et al.* 1989; Rollins 1989). It seems that in the 1980s and 1990s premarital sex is normative by the end of high school although there is wide variation among young people in the age at which they begin to be sexually active.

The fact of relatively high levels of sexual activity does not, in itself, give cause for alarm. Coupled with this, however, is the finding that many sexually active adolescents have multiple partners and that unprotected intercourse or inconsistent use of condoms is common, especially with partners who are regarded as 'steady' or long-term (e.g. Abrams *et al.* 1990; Hein 1989b; Kegeles *et al.* 1988; Rosenthal *et al.* 1990; Rollins 1989; Turtle *et al.* 1989). For example, our homeless 16-year-old boys reported an average of twelve, and the girls an average of seven, sexual partners in the preceding six months, with the maximum for both being a hundred partners – compared with a maximum of five for non-homeless youths. It is this apparent failure of some adolescents to take on board the messages of safe sex, now being targeted at them via mass media and school education programmes, that is addressed in this chapter.

SOME SEXUAL MYTHS

Why do so many sexually active young people engage in behaviour which appears to place them at risk of HIV infection? This apparently foolhardy behaviour can, in part, be explained by the prevalence of some inappropriate beliefs or myths about sexuality and AIDS. The first of these we might call the 'trusting to love' myth. Many young people appear to justify their non-use of condoms with the belief that condoms are unnecessary because their current relationship is monogamous and promises to be long-term. For example, Abbott's study of adolescent girls showed that 55 per cent believed that having sex only with a steady boyfriend was a safe option, and this was the main change they had made to protect themselves (Abbott 1988). In another study, Gallois *et al.* (1989) found that a majority of their sexually active heterosexuals kept themselves safe from infection by having sex only within what they believed to be an exclusive, monogamous relationship. Several other studies (Crawford *et al.* 1990; Holland *et al.* 1990; Nix *et al.* 1988; Rosenthal *et al.* 1990) reveal that young people are less likely to use condoms with regular than casual partners, with young women using this strategy more than young men. These consistently higher levels of risk-taking with regular partners suggest that adolescents may have acknowledged the AIDS threat in casual encounters, but have yet to realise that in the fickle world of adolescent relationships, sex with regular partners also may entail a high level of risk. It is clear that the meaning of a 'regular' relationship varies, both in terms of duration and fidelity. Among our samples of adolescents, the period defining a relationship as regular ranged from one month to marriage, with a modal time of six months. For some adolescents, serial monogamy – or a succession of 'permanent' relationships – is the norm, confirming earlier findings with American adolescents reported by Sorensen (1973). There were also alarming cultural and gender differences in beliefs about monogamy in so-called steady relationships. While girls held firm views about their own and their partner's fidelity, at least 25 per cent of boys, and more in some groups, expected their partner to be faithful but did not require the same commitment of themselves.

Adolescents who believe in the safety of a steady partner do not seem to have understood the dangers of serial relationships, failing to take into consideration the sexual history of their partner as well as his or her present behaviour. It appears that girls, in particular, operate with rose-coloured glasses, taking the view that sex is about romance and love, and therefore trust. Trust becomes a significant element in making decisions about using condoms.

Are there any situations when you wouldn't use a condom? Yeah . . . if

I've been with a partner for a very long time. I know him. I know what he's all about.

[Yes] Once it is a relationship and it has been going on for a while and you really care about them. . . . It is more serious.

As Holland *et al.* (1990) graphically put it: 'If love is assumed to be the greatest prophylactic, then trust comes a close second'. A further complicating factor associated with particular types of relationships is the reluctance of young girls to describe themselves as having casual sex, for fear of the harm to their reputation which may result from this breaching of culturally approved feminine behaviour (Lees 1986). The other side to this dilemma is the expectation and hope held by many young girls that relationships of short duration will last. If young girls' relationships are conceived of as steady until proven otherwise, condom use is unlikely or, at best, will be inconsistent.

The issue of knowing one's partner has been addressed in a recent study by Ingham *et al.* (1991). Contrary to the findings reported above, they found that, whereas length of relationship was not related to condom use in young men, young women were considerably more likely to report condom use when intercourse occurred with someone they had known for a longer period. Both, however, were *less* likely to use condoms with partners whose sexual history – whether virgin or non-virgin – was not known. These are troubling findings. The researchers suggest that these young people, and young women especially, consider that casual acquaintance prior to a relationship developing is sufficient to convince them of the lack of risk involved in intercourse. Compounding the problem is the fact that most of these young people reported being aware of campaigns stressing the risk of HIV infection but few considered that the issue was relevant to their own lives.

Do you consider the risk of AIDS? No, I'm not involved in that sort of scene.

All of the people that I have gone out with before, I have known beforehand and have known that they haven't been into that sort of thing. That they are pretty clean.

(Two sexually active homeless 16-year-olds)

This is a common theme among heterosexual adolescents in their responses to the threat of AIDS – the 'not-me' myth. It is clear that most adolescents have not personalised the risk of HIV/AIDS, perceiving the illness as a threat to others, not themselves. This is consistent with the belief that adolescents' thinking is characterised, in part, by the 'personal fable'. The personal fable reflects a kind of cognitive egocentrism, or belief that one is special, unique, and invulnerable to the risks and hazards that befall other people. Much has been made of adolescents' perceived invulnerability to unpleasant events and their belief that, although others may suffer the consequences of dangerous and risky actions, they are somehow immune (see, for example, Elkind 1985; Lapsley and Murphy 1985). Adolescents' belief that 'it can't happen to me' has been shown to influence risk-taking in a variety of health-related situations including smoking and contraceptive use. In a recent study of British adolescents, Abrams *et al.* (1990) found high levels of concern about the presence of the HIV virus in the community, but little evidence of concern about their own levels of risk. In our own work with Australian adolescents, it is apparent that not only do many feel themselves to be invulnerable to the threat of AIDS, but also that concerns about HIV infection rarely figure in their decision-making about whether or not to have intercourse (Moore and Rosenthal 1991a; Rosenthal *et al.* 1992b).

Closer exploration of the reasons underlying the failure of these adolescents to take on board the messages of safe sex suggests a number of processes are at work. In part, what seems likely to be happening here is that these young people have linked HIV/AIDS to risk groups, rather than risk behaviours. Moore and Rosenthal (1991a) showed that those youths who perceived themselves to be least at risk have a strong stereotype of an AIDS victim. This stereotype is likely to be maintained because few adolescents have ever known or even met an AIDS sufferer. Given that social representations of HIV/AIDS include theories about the type of person who will become infected (homosexuals, drug users, prostitutes), and in the absence of personal knowledge of a sufferer, it seems reasonable to assume that the stereotype held by these heterosexual youths is of someone unlike themselves. This stereotyping serves a distancing function by allowing individuals either to ignore the possibility that some or even many of those who are infected may not fit the stereotype, or to concentrate only on superficial differences between themselves and the stereotype, thus failing to see fundamental similarities (such as in sexual behaviours). In fact, it is a strategy that may well be counterproductive as a protective technique as it mitigates against the likelihood of changing one's own behaviour to safer options.

The illusion of invulnerability may also be fostered by engaging in risky acts which have no (immediate) negative consequences (Kasperson *et al.* 1988). Thus, adolescents who repeatedly engage in unsafe sex without becoming infected are likely to deny the riskiness of that behaviour. Perceptions of risk are also influenced by beliefs about control. Most of the adolescents in our study believed that they could completely control their risk of HIV/AIDS, a finding similar to that reported by Abrams *et al.* (1990). However, those who perceived themselves to be most at risk of HIV/AIDS were those who believed themselves to be least able to control the risk of infection. The importance of a perceived sense of control over events was confirmed when perceptions of STD risk were assessed in a later study by the authors (Moore and Rosenthal 1992a). Plainly, issues of personal mastery and the ability to take responsibility for one's sexuality are touched on here, a point we shall return to later.

While the notion of personal invulnerability provides a compelling and frequently invoked explanation of adolescents' risk-taking behaviour, we must be careful not to assume a simple and direct relationship between low perceptions of risk and actual risky behaviour. In fact, there appears to be only a weak link between the two. For some adolescents, perceptions of low HIV/AIDS risk are associated with risky sexual behaviour; for others, there seems to be a realistic appraisal of low risk, based on their safe sexual activity. A third group, which we have labelled 'risk-and-be-damned', gives cause for concern because of their risky behaviours *and* their realistic perceptions of relatively high levels of risk. What is of interest is that this group – mostly males – doubted their control over avoiding AIDS. We are uncertain as to the meaning of this lack of control. It may arise from youths' general sense of fatalism – a sense that there is nothing they can do to alter the course of fate – or from doubts about their ability to use condoms or control their sexual urges. Whatever the reason, it is clear that characterising adolescent risk-taking merely as resulting from beliefs in invulnerability is to oversimplify the processes at work in determining their responses to HIV/AIDS. Some adolescents knowingly take risks with an understanding of their possible consequences. This suggests that there may be a link between a general psychological risk-taking trait and sexual risk-taking, a possibility confirmed by Breakwell *et al.* (1991). They found that individuals who describe themselves as willing to take risks were less likely than low-riskers to intend to use condoms in sexual encounters.

Adolescents' confidence that they are not at risk may well stem from another myth or misconception, namely that 'you can tell by looking' whether or not people are infected. In one study, a significant number of young men claimed, mistakenly, that a woman's appearance was an accurate guide to her likelihood of being infected (Chapman and Hodgson 1988). Use of physical characteristics as a justification for unsafe sexual behaviour has been found in studies of young homosexuals as well as heterosexuals by Gold and his colleagues (Gold *et al.* 1992; Gold and Skinner 1992). It seems that inferences about the likelihood of infection of one's partner, based on that partner's healthy, clean and/or beautiful physical appearance, are not uncommon among these young people. What might be the origins of such inferences? Gold suggests several possibilities. First, they may not know that, because HIV has a long incubation period, one cannot tell from appearances who is infected. Alternatively, they may be drawing incorrect inferences by generalising from frequently encountered diseases. Most diseases do, in fact, have short incubation periods, so that for these diseases, it is true that one can tell by looking. Both these possibilities are implausible since these young people have high levels of knowledge about HIV transmission and are unlikely to be ignorant of its long incubation period. It may be that adolescents are merely drawing on the socially constructed equation of beauty with good health – a link reinforced endlessly by the media. Whatever the basis for their misconception, it is vital that adolescents learn to look beneath the external packaging to the realities of transmission of HIV.

ARE THERE REAL OBSTACLES TO SAFE SEX?

We have seen that, for some adolescents, responses to HIV/AIDS are influenced by misconceptions about themselves and their partners. Are there other, reality-based obstacles to their adoption of safe sex practices? In addressing this question, researchers have assumed that sexual behaviour, like other behaviours, can be predicted from an individual's attitudes, beliefs, and values. Thus, adolescents' sexual behaviour has been conceptualised as arising out of a process of rational decision-making. For example, adolescents who have good levels of knowledge about HIV transmission will avoid unsafe behaviours; the adolescent who perceives that there are high costs in using condoms is less likely to use condoms than one whose attitudes are positive. When we check these assumptions, we find that they do not provide an adequate or indeed accurate explanation of adolescent sexual behaviour.

Early surveys of adolescents' knowledge of HIV transmission (e.g. DiClemente *et al.* 1986; Strunin and Hingson 1987) suggested that substantial numbers of teenagers had misconceptions about the ways in which HIV is transmitted, and that these misconceptions were more apparent among minority group youths and those who were poorly educated. Knowledge levels were independent of whether or not teenagers were sexually active or used drugs. By 1988, it seemed that almost all the American youths surveyed had learned the major modes of HIV transmission and misconceptions had diminished, although some remained (Hingson and Strunin 1992). Somewhat worryingly, these studies revealed that the few teenagers whose knowledge was inadequate were found disproportionately among groups where the risk of exposure to the virus is high.

Like their American peers, Australian youths appear to be well informed about HIV/AIDS. In most recent studies (e.g. Rosenthal *et al.* 1990: Turtle *et al.* 1989), adolescents have shown reasonably high levels of knowledge about HIV transmission and AIDS although there is evidence of uneven knowledge in some groups. As in the United States, ethnicity plays a role in levels of knowledge. Not only were there lower levels of knowledge among youths of non-English-speaking backgrounds but also, in these groups, young women were less well-informed about HIV and safe sex practices than their male counterparts. Other studies have confirmed the existence of misunderstandings and inaccurate information. For example, although the role of blood in the transmission of HIV appears to be widely understood, a large minority of adolescents fail to recognise that HIV could be transmitted through vaginal fluids, and many confuse disease prevention with contraception, believing that condoms need not be used if other means of contraception are being employed (Greig and Raphael 1989; McCamish *et al.* 1988; Wyn and Stewart 1991).

Unfortunately, even these misperceptions may underestimate the gaps in teenagers' real understanding of HIV transmission and prevention of AIDS. Many educators have drawn attention to the differences between 'factual knowledge' and 'understanding', and the dangers of inferring the latter from the former. In the context of HIV/AIDS it is imperative that we distinguish between a superficial level of knowledge, perhaps derived from media campaigns, and a thorough understanding of the issue, grounded in appropriate education programmes. In a welcome shift in focus, questions are now being asked about the nature of children's and adolescents' knowledge. A comprehensive study of 14- to 15-year-olds, designed to tap their actual understanding of HIV/AIDS as distinct from an ability to produce facts without necessarily understanding their basis has revealed considerable gaps in understanding (Slattery 1991). While most (90 per cent) knew that sexual behaviour is linked to HIV transmission, and many (68 per cent) were aware of the dangers of contact with blood, the majority of these adolescents showed little or no understanding of the precise nature of the danger. Many of these young teenagers believed that someone was more likely to contract HIV if they came into contact with menstrual blood than blood from a leg wound.

In another task, Slattery asked her teenagers to rank in order certain activities in terms of HIV risk. Although they were able to rank correctly the most risky activities, Slattery concluded that it would be unwise to conclude with confidence that these young people had high levels of understanding. In ranking anal sex as a high risk activity, some students mentioned the physiological reasons for this, but many referred to how distasteful they found the behaviours, rather than the physiology involved.

Furthermore, Slattery found that students had to struggle with the notion of a virgin female having AIDS or being HIV positive, even though IV drug use was listed by them as the riskiest behaviour. Slattery concludes from her study that, while these young adolescents do know some specific facts about HIV/AIDS, only half of them express acceptable levels of understanding and accurate knowledge.

A similar conclusion arises from an interesting study by Waters (1992) which compared the levels of factual knowledge expressed using a standard questionnaire format with responses to an in-depth interview. Waters found that children as young as 10 years of age had high levels of 'knowledge' as assessed by the questionnaire, but the interviews showed that true understanding of AIDS was very limited for many of these, and even older, children. Here are two 15-year-olds who had most items correct on the true-false questionnaire, but their interview responses showed that their 'understanding' of HIV/AIDS differed dramatically.

> *How does someone get AIDS?* The two most common ways of getting AIDS arc through unprotected sex and sharing needles. But the person may not get AIDS; they might just become a carrier of the HIV virus. *How does unprotected sex cause AIDS?* If the man does not wear a condom, he can pass the virus through his semen or get it from the woman's fluids. *How would you know if you had AIDS?* I wouldn't know for a long time. *Why is that?* Well, the symptoms of AIDS do not show up for years because there is a long incubation period. *What do you mean by symptoms?* The person actually catches other viruses and diseases more easily because AIDS has affected their immunity. *What happens during the incubation period?* The AIDS virus kills off the immune system.

> *How does someone get AIDS?* By having sex [*said in a tentative manner*]. *How does having sex cause AIDS?* It's from the blood or something. *Can you tell me anything more?* It just goes through the organs. *Would you know if someone had AIDS?* Yes, I think I would. *Can you explain to me why you think you would know?* They would look really sick. Don't they lose their hair or something? *(Pause)* I think they can get rashes as well.

> (Waters 1992)

One other recent study (Walsh and Bibace 1991) has fitted young children's and teenagers' reasoning about AIDS into a cognitive-developmental sequence. These researchers report that children's causal thinking about AIDS parallels the ways in which young children think about illness in general, from a prelogical to a formal logical way of reasoning. One important implication of these studies is the need to tailor AIDS educational programmes to children's levels of cognitive development, so that the information they receive matches their ability to comprehend.

While it is clear that accurate information about AIDS and transmission of HIV is important, it appears that knowledge is a necessary but not sufficient cause for action. Of considerable concern is the increasing evidence that knowledge is not reflected in these adolescents' behaviour. Several studies have shown that higher levels of knowledge are substantially unrelated to safe sex practices (Keller *et al.* 1988; Richard and van der Pligt 1991; Turtle *et al.* 1989). A study of teenagers over one year in the United States (Kegeles *et al.* 1988) revealed the disturbing finding that knowing that condoms prevented transmission of HIV did not result in greater intention to use condoms. Nor did this knowledge lead to actual increased condom use.

This gap between knowledge and behaviour is consistent with Abbott's finding that 99 per cent of the young women she surveyed thought that, because of AIDS, they would need to make behavioural changes (Abbott 1988). Of those who were sexually active, half had not made any changes at all. Another study bears on this important issue. Turtle and her colleagues (Turtle *et al.* 1989) gave parallel questionnaires to two sets of students selected at random, one asking about behaviours, the other about AIDS beliefs. They found a marked discrepancy between knowledge and performance of safe sexual behaviours, measured by questions about condom use in casual sexual encounters, and about drug use and blood transfusions. For example, 92 per cent of their 'beliefs' group answered 'always' to the question 'Should you use a condom as a safeguard against AIDS in vaginal sex with a casual partner?' In their 'behaviours' group, only 26 per cent had actually done so. Of the beliefs group, 86 per cent thought that a potential partner should be asked questions about IV drug use; only 6 per cent of the behaviours group had done this. Of course, we do not know if Turtle's beliefs group would actually follow up their intentions with the appropriate behaviour, but this sort of discrepancy is in line with other findings which imply that knowledge and beliefs are not necessarily clearly linked with behaviour.

One of the key AIDS prevention messages is the importance of consistent condom use. Unfortunately, condoms have not been regarded positively in the past. Earlier studies of contraceptive preferences showed that the pill was the most-favoured method, with condoms relatively low in popularity (see Morrison 1985 for a review). As we have seen in an earlier chapter, reasons for non-use of condoms vary. For some teenagers, the critical problem is one of knowing how and where to obtain condoms, and having the courage to purchase them. Others have negative attitudes centred around issues of premeditation (and concerns about one's reputation if one appears to be 'prepared' for sex) and the spontaneous, unplanned nature of sex. For other young people, using condoms has unpleasant consequences for sexual pleasure by reducing sensation – a view often expressed in vivid comments such as 'having showers in raincoats' or 'washing your feet with your socks on'. An additional source of difficulty with insisting on condom use has been noted recently. In this era of AIDS and other STDs, some young people feel that to ask a partner to use condoms, or to insist on using this precaution oneself, is tantamount to implying that the partner may be infected or, at least, sexually promiscuous. Such an implicit lack of trust does not fit with the idealised attitudes to sexuality which many teenagers, especially girls, still hold (Buzwell *et al.* 1992).

Recent attempts to socialise the condom (encapsulated in Australia by the catchy slogan 'Tell him if it's not on, it's not on') have been designed to reduce resistance to using condoms. While dislike of condoms is still reported by many teenagers (see, for example, Chapman and Hodgson 1988; Holland *et al.* 1991; Worth 1989), there is some evidence that negative attitudes are breaking down, and that the benefits of condom use are being recognised (Chapman *et al.* 1990; Klitsch 1990; Moore and Rosenthal 1991b). Despite this, and although both positive and negative attitudes to condoms are associated with intentions to use condoms in the future, it seems that whether or not condoms are actually used depends on young peoples' *negative* attitudes to their use (Boldero *et al.* 1992; Moore and Rosenthal 1991b), a finding that is particularly clear for young girls. Adding further complexity to this picture is the finding reported by Richard and van der Pligt (1991) that attitudes to condom use were predictive of actual use in a sample of monogamous adolescents but not in a group with multiple sexual partners. They suggest that teenagers who believe themselves to be in a monogamous relationship and who have negative attitudes to condoms assume that they can, with safety, dispense with this AIDS precaution, a choice that is not open to teenagers with multiple partners.

Another belief about condoms that relates particularly to sexual risk taking with casual partners is an unwillingness to take personal responsibility for AIDS precautions. In our study we found that teenagers who held the view that this responsibility lay with one's partner and who were more likely to make excuses for not initiating a discussion about condoms or other precautions were engaging in more risky behaviours. It seems that casual sexual situations may be characterised by less comfort about communication. This is particularly problematic, as participants in casual encounters usually know less about each other than do those in regular relationships.

WHY GOOD INTENTIONS FAIL

The message that condoms are an acceptable (and indeed obligatory) accessory to sexual intercourse appears to have been only partially acted on by today's adolescents. What, apart from their own negative attitudes, are the factors that intervene between adolescents' good intentions to use condoms (Boldero *et al.* 1992; Kashima *et al.* 1992) and their frequent failure to do so?

In attempting to answer this question, some researchers have drawn on the concept of self-efficacy (e.g. Bandura 1982). Just as a perceived sense of mastery in other health-related domains is predictive of healthier patterns of behaviour in that domain, it is expected that a sense of sexual self-efficacy or mastery will be associated with safer sexual practices. In fact, as we noted earlier, many adolescents lack the confidence necessary to deal with condoms. For example, only half of our 18-year-olds felt confident that they could purchase a condom; half that they could discuss the use of a condom with a potential partner; and less than half felt that they could carry a condom with them 'just in case'. Lack of mastery of their sexual world is evident in other ways. We found two particularly important areas where levels of confidence varied. These were adolescents' ability to be assertive about their sexual needs (including communicating the desire to use a condom), and the ability to say no to unwanted sexual activity (including refusing to have unsafe sex). In both areas a sense of sexual self-efficacy or perceived competence was related positively to safe sex practices. In a similar vein Breakwell and her colleagues (Breakwell *et al.* 1991) explored young virgins' perceptions of three aspects of sexual control or mastery – choice of a trustworthy sexual partner, condom use, and confidence in dealing with sexual relationships. They found that perceived control in the first two areas predicted *intentions* to use a condom, especially for female virgins. While these findings are encouraging, we must remember that, in the area of condom use, there appears to be a wide gap between intentions and behaviour. We do not know, therefore, whether Breakwell's young virgins would retain their sense of control if put to the test in an actual sexual situation. Our strong hunch is that many of them would not. One interesting aspect of Breakwell's study is that these young girls felt themselves to be more in control of partner choice and condom decisions than did the young boys. To some extent this unexpected sex difference in favour of perceptions of greater control by girls was confirmed by sexually experienced young people in another study (Rosenthal *et al.* 1991). In this study, it became clear that there were differences in the skills needed to deal with sexual matters. Young girls' sense of sexual mastery appears to be based on being responsible about the consequences of sex and being able to say no to unwanted sexual activity – perhaps because they have more experience of saying no to sex than do young boys. On the other hand, the boys were more able than their female counterparts to assert their sexual needs and to initiate sexual activities, a finding consistent with gender differences in norms and experience.

These findings might suggest some flaws in one of the most commonly held views about the process of sexual negotiation, namely that girls have less power or control over this process than do boys and this makes it difficult for them to insist on safe sex. Before rejecting this view of a gendered power imbalance in favour of one of gender equality, we should remember that the girls in one study were virgins whose sense of control reflected a guess about a hypothetical situation, with no assurance that their control would survive the reality of a sexual encounter. In the second study, most girls were well-educated and middle-class. It is unlikely that their competence in the sexual domain would be matched by their less privileged sisters.

In fact, there are substantial grounds for believing that the sexual world of adolescents is well and truly sex-differentiated in terms of power and that this has a profound effect on how adolescents respond to sexual situations. We have seen in an earlier chapter that the politics of heterosexuality are extremely complex and involve contradictory discourses and practices. Holland and her colleagues make this point strongly in arguing that young women are coping with conflicting social pressures in dealing with sex. In raising the issue of using condoms, these young girls fly in the face of social convention which denies sexual activity to respectable young women. Thus they find themselves putting their reputation on the line, risking being labelled as 'easy' or a slut (Moore and Rosenthal 1992b). In a society where sex for young women is constructed as 'the relinquishment of control in the face of love' (Holland *et al.* 1991), the contradictions between this and the rational discourse of safer sex and 'premeditated' condom use are apparent. As Holland and others have concluded, if we are to understand the variable patterns of condom use by young women (and young men) we must take account of these gendered power relations and the contradictory pressures exerted on adolescents by the social context.

Perhaps the most important aspects of the everyday social context for adolescents are the beliefs about and attitudes to condom use of family and peers (see Chapter 4). Indeed, most models of decision-making (e.g. Fishbein and Ajzen 1975; Ajzen and Fishbein 1980) take account of the potential influence of individuals' subjective norms for 'good' or 'correct' behaviour, derived from their perceptions of the attitudes and practices of salient others. Studies of sexual behaviour using Fishbein and Ajzen's model report that positive normative beliefs about the importance of contraception are related to young women's intentions to use the pill as a contraceptive. However, in two recent studies of condom use, the importance attached to using condoms by parents and friends did not predict adolescents' actual use of condoms (Boldero *et al.* 1992; Richard and van der Pligt 1991). Why were these adolescents, contrary to expectation, not influenced in their behaviour by perceived social norms about condom use? We speculate that condom use usually requires both partners to communicate and to agree before the behaviour occurs. Using a condom is not a private act, carried out well in advance of a sexual encounter – unlike taking a contraceptive pill. The negotiated, shared aspect of using condoms is likely to add considerably to the difficulties in dealing with condoms that we have already described for some adolescents. Because of this, the immediate context of the sexual encounter may have a more powerful influence on adolescents' sexual decisions to use a condom than any distal normative influences.

It is not surprising, then, that there are difficulties in applying general models of decision-making, albeit ones that have been successfully used to explain a variety of illness or health-related behaviours, to sexual behaviour. One other popular model of health behaviour that has been extended to the study of sexual risk-taking is the Health Beliefs Model (Janz and Becker 1984). The hope here is that the factors which appear to govern positive, health-sustaining or health-promoting responses to illness will produce safer sexual practices. According to the model, people make a rational cost-benefit analysis in deciding whether to adopt preventive behaviour. Unfortunately, it is becoming clear that concerns such as the seriousness of the illness and the individual's susceptibility to that illness which have considerable explanatory value in many areas of health-related behaviour – and which are key components of the Health Beliefs Model together with perceptions of the barriers and benefits of preventive action (in the case of safe sex, using condoms) – do not fare so well in the less predictable and irrationally governed world of sex (Rosenthal *et al.* 1992b).

TAKING CONTEXT INTO ACCOUNT

Plainly, sex is more than a matter of making rational decisions in advance of the act and independent of its context. As further evidence for this we can consider the regrettable gap between good intentions and actual behaviour. Many adolescents, when questioned, assert that they intend to use condoms in subsequent sexual activity. Most are able to act on their intentions but for some (and these are a not-insubstantial minority), good intentions fail (Boldero *et al.* 1992; Kashima *et al.* 1992; Rosenthal and Shepherd 1993). Why is it so hard for some young people to maintain their professed intentions at the critical moment? We have identified several critical determinants of condom use which arise out of the immediate sexual context. As might be expected, high levels of sexual arousal at the time of the encounter seem to reduce the likelihood of using condoms (Boldero *et al.* 1992; Emmons *et al.* 1986; Goggin 1989). It may be that sexual arousal operates in a similar fashion to the effects of arousal on other tasks. For highly aroused young people, the encounter alone becomes the focus and the issue of whether or not to use a condom receives little or no attention. Overtraining, a common technique used in other stress-related performance situations, may be the answer to arousal-induced failure to use condoms. For some young people the difficulties in dealing with condoms may be overcome if they are taught to negotiate about and use condoms in sexual situations almost as if they were on automatic pilot.

A second significant contextual factor is the ability to communicate with a partner about his or her past sexual history and about using condoms – not an easy task, as we have seen, especially for adolescents brought up in cultures where discussion of sexual matters is, or has been, taboo. Asked about their willingness to discuss a partner's sexual history, these 16-year-olds responded as follows.

If you have just met her that night, you don't want to say have you gone to the doctor or whatever before we have sex. It is a bit hard to say that sort of thing.

(Boy)

Probably not. Because it is embarassing. What do you say? Usually I sleep with people I know and I know they haven't got any diseases.

(Girl)

Condom use is reported more often by those adolescents who communicate with each other, highlighting our earlier point that the decision to use a condom involves both partners. We know that many adolescents report disturbingly low levels of confidence in their ability to discuss the use of condoms with their partners and many believe that they are unable to take the initiative in expressing their sexual needs. It is important, then, that adolescents be taught the skills which will enable them to communicate confidently and accurately in a climate of mutual acceptance.

HAVE ADOLESCENTS CHANGED THEIR SEXUAL BEHAVIOUR?

Considerable energy has been devoted to educating adolescents to adopt safer sexual practices in spite of the likely difficulties in persuading adolescents to change their behaviour. How successful has the 'safe sex' message been? What evidence is there that adolescents have taken heed of the messages that they have received? One of the difficulties in assessing the extent, if any, of uptake of safe sex is the problem of measuring behaviour change accurately. We are, of course, unable to adopt the most reliable strategy – actual observations of behaviour. Instead the strategy has been to ask people directly whether they have changed their behaviour in response to HIV/AIDS, without taking into account the reasons underlying their subjective reports. For example, there may be no change because respondents are already practising safe sex independently of the HIV/AIDS threat, or change, if reported, may not have eliminated the risk of HIV infection. Alternatively, reports of change may be motivated by the need to provide a socially desirable response rather than be an objective account of behaviour. Another strategy, which obtains information from individuals at more than one point in time, yields more compelling data about the magnitude and direction of change. By comparing individuals' responses about their actual behaviour over two or more different periods, and even at specific sexual encounters, we are able to detect changes in behaviour without having to resort to direct questioning.

Such follow-up studies of change have been remarkably few in number. Almost without exception, inferences about change have been made by comparing different cohorts, with increasing knowledge and safe sex behaviour, and more positive attitudes to condoms among more recent (or younger) cohorts cited as evidence for positive change. An Australian cross-sectional study of first-year college students over several years (Kippax and Crawford 1991) suggests an increase in college students' awareness of the danger of unprotected sex since younger students were more likely than older students to use condoms with both regular and casual partners, although the numbers always using condoms were disturbingly low for both groups.

Evidence that educational strategies may be successful in shaping the sexual attitudes and practices of young people comes from a study evaluating a recent Australian television campaign targeted at young people. Conducted over a six-month period, this campaign focused adolescents' attention on the benefits of using condoms as well as the dangers of making assumptions about the sexual history of one's partner(s). Surveys revealed an increased rate of endorsement by adolescents of condoms as a preventive measure and more positive attitudes to condoms generally. Post-campaign surveys revealed increases in the percentage of young people reporting that they had used condoms, bought condoms, carried condoms, and insisted on condom use over the past six months.

While such cross-sectional studies give some cause for optimism about change, there is little evidence available with regard to individual change over time in response to HIV/AIDS. One longitudinal study examined change over one year in attitudes towards and use of condoms among adolescents in San Francisco, a city where HIV/AIDS is highly prevalent, and thus salient (Kegeles *et al.* 1988). While these adolescents viewed the condom as an effective prevention measure and believed that it was important to avoid sexually transmitted diseases, very few reported always using condoms. Neither their condom use nor their intentions to use condoms increased over the year, and they continued to have multiple partners. Further evidence that the process of changing behaviour among adolescents may be difficult comes from a six-month follow-up study of Australian youths which revealed little evidence of behaviour change over this period (Rosenthal and Shepherd 1992). In fact, of those few adolescents who changed their behaviour, half changed in the direction of greater, rather than less, risk.

PREVENTING AIDS: SCHOOLS AND THE MASS MEDIA AS AGENTS OF CHANGE

The sparse research on behaviour change implies that persuading teenagers to change their sexual habits is not an easy task, and is one which requires sensitivity to the needs and nature of the target population. The major avenues for educating teenagers about the risks of HIV/AIDS, apart from parents, continue to be schools and the mass media. Reviews of school health education programmes, including education about HIV/AIDS in Britain, Australia, and the United States (Clift and Stears 1991; Goldman and Goldman 1992; Kirby 1992) suggest that, while a start has been made in getting HIV/AIDS onto the school health agenda, much remains to be done. Clift and Stear's survey of secondary schools in the south-east of England revealed alarming gaps in the provision of education about HIV/AIDS, especially in the training of teachers. Only one-third of teachers had received some form of specialist training on issues related to HIV/AIDS and most teachers were reluctant to be explicit about risks and prevention associated with sexual activity.

Similar problems were found in Australian schools, with adequate delivery of health education programmes impeded by lack of appropriate courses available for teachers (Goldman and Goldman 1992). Although, in Australia, there is a policy of providing HIV-relevant education in schools and there exists a variety of creative and imaginative programmes, the reality is that there are many impediments to this occurring at all, let alone in an effective way. Many of the difficulties encountered in establishing effective programmes in schools arise from the controversial nature of the topic which gives rise to unique social, economic, political, and legal problems. Teachers may well feel insecure in dealing with these complexities, especially if they have been poorly trained and have inadequate resources at their disposal.

In the United States, Kirby (1992) reports that there is widespread support for AIDS education in schools, both from parents and from educators, but the programmes that are in place are also subject to the same problems as those in other countries. One particular problem is that it is extremely difficult to implement comprehensive sex education programmes, including HIV/AIDS education, that extend across the school years. Both in the United States and Australia, many schools introduce these programmes late in secondary school, at a time when a substantial number of adolescents have already left school and many are already sexually active.

What about the media, and particularly TV, as educational tools? Although most information about HIV/AIDS is gained from the mass media (and considerable government funds for AIDS education are used for this purpose), the media are not regarded by adolescents as highly credible sources (Abrams *et al.* 1990). In spite of this, TV, judiciously used, is a cost-effective method of getting messages about HIV/AIDS across to adolescents. Certainly, the mass media have been effective in the fight against smoking, drinking and driving, illicit drug use, and, in Australia, excessive sun-tanning which leads to skin cancer (see Romer and Hornik 1992 for a review of the American research). TV campaigns in Australia and the United States appear to have been successful in increasing awareness of HIV/AIDS and, in the United States, increasing teenagers' use of testing and counselling services. As Romer and Hornik note, perhaps the most effective outcome of blanket media campaigns has been to raise awareness of HIV/AIDS as a health issue.

We need now to continue with more carefully targeted campaigns. One such campaign is reported in the Netherlands where TV campaigns have succeeded in changing the cultural meaning of 'safe sex' for young people. Over the period of the campaign, there was a dramatic increase in the association of safe sex with condom use and reduction in number of sexual partners. Campaigns designed to create norms favourable for the existence of safe sex practices have also had some success in both Australia and the United States. In the former, the focus has been on 'socialising the condom', by giving messages that condoms are fun, easy to use, and do not reduce sexual pleasure. In the United States, the message has one of peer support for safe sex – friends would insist on a condom being used, and on asking about a partner's sexual history.

There is an important message for AIDS educators from the research discussed in this chapter. If we are to prevent adolescents from becoming the 'next wave' of an AIDS epidemic it is abundantly clear that we must explore the framework in which young people view their sexuality and their sexual relationships. No longer is it acceptable to treat adolescents as a homogeneous group, assuming that all young people share a common response to the AIDS threat and producing general, all-purpose AIDS educational programmes based on that assumption. Rather, programmes designed to reduce sexual risk must be targeted at specific groups and focus on the needs and resources of these groups. Some of the ways in which this can be achieved have already been alluded to. In particular, efforts to persuade adolescents to use condoms may not be successful unless they are gender-specific. Other programmes need to take account of accurate and inaccurate risk-perceptions. For example, the information required to reduce the AIDS-related risk of highly sexually active homeless adolescents is very different from that needed for the 'worried well' adolescent whose sexual behaviour places him or her at little or no risk. It appears also that educators may have to look at the informational sources that they use. Abrams and his colleagues (Abrams *et al.* 1990) suggest that AIDS education may be more effective if it is provided by health professionals working in conjunction with well-trained peer educators in a school setting. Ensuring that credible educators are presenting programmes tailored for the specific needs of different audiences is bound to improve the impact of large-scale media campaigns.

WHAT OF THE FUTURE?

What have we found out about youths' sexual behaviour in the era of AIDS? We know that young people's sexual behaviour does not follow a rule-governed script but is strongly influenced by the moment-to-moment context and by beliefs about unequal gendered relationships. Their behaviour is governed by many factors, some rational, some less so. We know that the reasons given by young men and women for engaging in sex differ. In spite of apparent changes in society, young men are still more likely than young women to have multiple partners, to regard themselves as needing sex, to approve of casual sex, and to seek sex for physical pleasure. Young women, on the other hand, stress the need for emotional commitment to a sexual partner and feel uncomfortable about sex with a one-night-stand. It appears that love and romance are still potent forces in the sexual world of the female adolescent. Small wonder, then, that young people engage in sexual behaviour that does not seem to be rationally governed, in the light of current knowledge about AIDS. If adolescents are to take sexually responsible decisions, they must be aware of the meaning and obligations attached to love and relationships. They must understand that communication with a partner about his or her sexual history and about using condoms is crucial and does not imply a questionable past. Given that trusting one's partner is likely to lead to less cautious sexual behaviour, it is important that such trust is not misplaced, and that the information received is accurate.

What of the future? It is possible that, as the impact of AIDS in the heterosexual community increases, adolescent sexual behaviour will become more conservative. Fewer partners and more frequent use of condoms are one possible option. Alternatively, adolescents may return to the pre-1960 days of premarital chastity, when non-penetrative sex was a preferred and often-used substitute for sexual intercourse. Whatever their chosen path, today's adolescents will have to live with the danger of AIDS and their sexual decisions must be guided accordingly.

8　Sexual risk II
Pregnancy and abortion

As we have seen, many young people are sexually active at an early age, and many fail to use adequate – or indeed any – measures to avoid conception or sexually transmissible diseases. Since unprotected sexual activity is now a common feature of teenage life, teenage pregnancy can no longer be dismissed as a remote possibility and an infrequent occurrence, limited to a small number of 'immoral' or 'promiscuous' adolescents. Premarital teenage pregnancy, like premarital sex, has had a bad press in our society, with frequent and worrying reports of a teenage baby boom, as well as stories about the dire consequences of young (and often single) motherhood for both infant and mother. For pregnant young women who choose alternative paths to that of motherhood, such as abortion or adoption, negative outcomes are equally assumed.

In the context of societal concerns about the care and cost of teenage pregnancies, it is essential that we understand the dynamics underlying this 'maladaptive' behaviour on the part of many adolescents, as well as the outcomes of that behaviour. As Sue Sharpe puts it in her book reporting interviews with teenage mothers, '[t]eenage mothers are not a significantly large group, nor are they a particularly increasing "problem" in this country, but their lives are quite different to those of other girls of the same age without children' (Sharpe 1987). In making this point, Sharpe also raises the question of whether the perceived 'epidemic of teenage pregnancies' (Alan Guttmacher Institute 1976) is a reality, or whether today's teenage mothers are no more numerous than their sisters of yesteryear.

FACTS AND FIGURES

One out of every 10 women aged 15–19 becomes pregnant each year in the United States. Of the pregnancies, five out of every six are unintended – 92 percent of those conceived premaritally, and half of those conceived in marriage.

(Trussell 1988: 262).

These are dramatic and disturbing figures accounting, according to Trussell, for about 837,000 pregnancies, plus another 23,000 among those aged 14 and younger. Another report (Richmond 1979) puts the percentage of births to adolescents as one-fifth of all births in the United States. In other countries, the figure is much lower. For example, in Australia, 5.7 per cent of all births are to teenagers (Littlejohn 1992), a figure similar to British statistics reported by Hudson and Ineichen (1991) for 1971, the peak year for teenage births.

A glance at the research literature reveals some inconsistencies in the reported figures for pregnancies and births, suggesting that accurate data are difficult to obtain. Phoenix (1991) makes this point in her analysis of demographic trends in teenage motherhood, a caution echoed by Hofferth and Hayes (1987a). In calculating and interpreting teenage conception and birth rates, Phoenix, in England, and Siedlecky (1984), in Australia, remind us that inaccuracies are likely to arise. For example, in the case of pregnancy rates, the incidence of abortion in the population is included in calculations, but not that of spontaneous miscarriage. Nevertheless, the magnitude of the numbers of pregnancies and births to teenagers that are reported gives cause for concern. Whether they imply a 'baby boom' among this group is not clear.

Trussell reports that the proportion of pregnancies in the United States has changed little in the past fifteen years. Other researchers have suggested that, in fact, there has been a fall in teenage fertility rates, since the 1970s when the so-called epidemic of teenage parenthood first came to the attention of a concerned public (Chilman 1980b; Furstenberg *et al.* 1989; Phoenix 1991). In other industrialised countries, teenage pregnancies and births occur far less frequently than in the United States (Jones *et al.* 1986; Trussell 1988; Werner 1988). In England and Wales, Phoenix reports, birth rates for teenagers are not much higher now than they were in the 1950s, with a rapid fall from a peak in the mid-1970s. She concludes that early motherhood is now less common in these countries and in the United States than it has been for most of the past two decades. In Australia, a similar picture to that in Britain emerges. There was a steady increase in teenage birth rates between the 1940s and early 1970s, with a subsequent decline until 1982. By that time there had been a 50 per cent reduction in births to teenage mothers – from 55.2 per thousand to 27.4 (Siedlecky 1984).

What has increased, it has been argued, is a rise in the proportion of babies born to adolescents outside of marriage. Bury (1984) reported that in the decade of the 1970s in Britain, the number of pregnant teenagers who married was halved. By the late 1980s, teenagers had become the first age group in Britain, as in the United States and Canada, in which the majority (over 70 per cent) were single when they gave birth. In the United States, too, young women are less likely than in the past to marry in order to legitimate their baby's birth, although the marriage rates for older pregnant teenagers is somewhat higher than for those who are younger (Hofferth and Hayes 1987a). Trussell, writing in the late 1980s, suggests that about 75 per cent of 15- to 19-year-olds will deal with their pregnancies outside the context of marriage, a figure that rises to almost all younger pregnant teenagers. This is in stark contrast to the early 1950s when less than a third of babies born to teenage mothers were conceived out of wedlock (Furstenberg *et al.* 1989). These figures are confirmed by Australian data where there has been a marked decline in maritally conceived births and ex-nuptial conceptions legitimised by marriage and a corresponding increase in conceptions and births outside of marriage (Siedlecky 1984).

However, to talk about a plateau or decline in the teenage birth rate may mask important social features of the phenomenon. We shall deal with these in later sections of this chapter. It is sufficient to refer briefly here to two likely contributing factors. First, the decline in birth rate may have occurred largely because of teenagers' increased access to, or choice of, abortion as a means of dealing with an unwanted pregnancy. A number of writers such as Sharpe (1987) and Zelnik *et al.* (1981) have endorsed this proposition. Second, there is a need to take demographic factors into account. For example, it is quite possible, argues Siedlecky in accounting for the fact that the 1970s decline in teenage birth rates appears to be levelling off, that there are two opposing trends among teenagers. In some groups – the well-educated, the affluent – there may still be a declining birth rate; in others – the unemployed or socially disadvantaged – rates of teenage pregnancy and birth may actually be increasing.

Inspection of the data available for the United States and Great Britain confirms Siedlecky's conclusion that the incidence of teenage pregnancy is unevenly spread over different groups of teenagers. As Hudson and Incichen (1991) observe: 'Teenage motherhood remains overwhelmingly a working class affair'. Particularly at risk, it seems, are adolescents who are poor and adolescents of colour. The association between low socioeconomic status and teenage pregnancy has long been noted (e.g. Presser 1974; Ross and Sawhill 1975; Zelnik *et al.* 1981). In a more recent study, Trussell (1988) estimates that about 77 per cent of births among teenagers will occur to those whose family incomes are well under the poverty level. The high levels of teenage pregnancy and motherhood among African-Americans in the United States (Furstenberg *et al.* 1989;

Hofferth and Hayes 1987a; Zelnik *et al.* 1981) may also have their genesis, at least in part, in the poverty that prevails for many of these people.

In addition to social class and race, we need to take into account the differences in pregnancy and birth rates between younger and older teenagers. Although the pattern of declining birth rates in recent years applies to all cohorts, there are more births to older than to younger adolescents. In England and Wales, 1980 figures show that 18- and 19-year-olds accounted for more than two-thirds, and those under 17 years accounted for less than one-fifth, of teenage births (Phoenix 1991). In part, this difference can be accounted for by the greater proportion of terminations of pregnancy in the latter group, an issue we take up later in this chapter.

What can we conclude about teenage pregnancy and motherhood from these figures? It appears that teenage births are less common now than they were several decades ago and that fewer of these young women than before are giving birth within the institution of marriage. There are, however, considerable national and subcultural differences within this context of an overall decline in teenage pregnancy. In most Western, industrialised countries the number of teenagers who conceive and become mothers is relatively low. In the United States the numbers are much higher, and enough to be regarded as a significant social problem, especially among the poor, the blacks, and the otherwise socially disadvantaged. Why do these differences exist? We turn now to the reasons why some young girls become pregnant.

WHY DO TEENAGERS BECOME PREGNANT?

Why do so many teenagers fail to use contraception or use methods of birth control inefficiently? Two stereotypes are usually called upon as explanations of teenage pregnancy. The first is that the pregnancy is planned, but as a deliberate manoeuvre to get some sort of financial benefit or material gain such as welfare payments or subsidised housing. The second is that teenagers become pregnant accidentally because they are incapable of planning contraception adequately. Neither stereotype, the research shows, captures accurately or completely the reality of teenage pregnancies. In several British studies reported by Phoenix (1991), it was rare for young women questioned about why they wanted to have a baby to supply a reason relating to material gain. In a study of Australian pregnant teenagers, not one gave such a reason for her pregnancy (Littlejohn 1992). The incentive of welfare is likewise insufficient as an explanation in the United States, where there is little or no support for the belief that young women have babies in order to be eligible for welfare (Furstenberg 1976; Moore and Caldwell 1977; Presser 1974; Ross and Sawhill 1975).

The second stereotype – teenage pregnancy as the unwanted outcome of incompetent or non-use of contraception – appears, on the face of it, a more likely explanation. And yet the evidence we have suggests that this is an oversimplification of what occurs. Indeed, for some young women, their pregnancy is *not* accidental and unwanted. Rather, having a baby is a planned and deliberate choice. While we might ask why young teenagers would want to take on the responsibilities of motherhood, the fact remains that a significant number of pregnancies are regarded as positive, planned events (Morrison 1985; Phoenix 1991; Simms and Smith 1986). For these young women, the decision to become a mother is often influenced by social factors such as having a mother who had her own first child earlier than average, having friends who are themselves young mothers, and having a stable relationship – which may or may not be marriage – with a partner.

Some young girls admit that getting pregnant is a planned strategy which enables them to avoid sex! If sex is seen as an unpleasant but unavoidable activity, if your boyfriend treats you as his sexual possession, free to use you sexually as, and when, he pleases, then being pregnant is a way of buying some status, as well as temporary 'freedom'. As one 15-year-old mother quoted by Hudson and Ineichen put it:

> It was great when I's pregnant – wouldn't let him near me and he respected that – I dunno if he went anywhere else for it. I didn't care anyway. I was glad to have meself to meself . . . . I wouldn't mind getting pregnant again – just to have the peace and quiet.
>
> (Hudson and Ineichen 1991: 42)

Nevertheless, it seems that most teenage pregnancies are not planned (Furstenberg 1976; Zelnick and Kantner 1980). For example, Phoenix reports that 82 per cent of pregnant adolescent girls in one study had not 'planned' to get pregnant. When she explored attitudes to conception of these young mothers-to-be, Phoenix found that the majority held one of two positions. The first group had not thought about the possibility that they might conceive; the second did not want to conceive when they did. Among the former we would expect to find those teenagers with a limited understanding of the reproductive process who failed to use contraception at all. In some ways, these young women are reminiscent of the 'invulnerable' adolescents described in the previous chapter. These are the young people who believe that they are unlikely to suffer the negative consequences of their actions, and hence take risks that others would not. In her Australian study, Littlejohn (1992) found that 20 per cent of pregnant teenagers did not think they needed to use contraception because they couldn't get pregnant. In a comprehensive review of adolescent contraceptive behaviour, Morrison (1985) concludes that at least one-third, and often more than half, of sexually active adolescents have erroneous beliefs about their own fertility.

Members of the second group, the 'inconvenient' conceivers, are likely to include those young people for whom contraception had failed, one way or another. For some, inadequate knowledge about effective contraception is a problem (Ineichen 1986; Morrison 1985); for others, negative attitudes to contraception or problems associated with obtaining contraceptives are a deterrent (Morrison 1985). But there is another group for whom an unplanned pregnancy occurs. These are the contraceptively 'unprepared' young people for whom sexual activity is regarded as – and often is – a spontaneous, unplanned event. A substantial number of adolescents report that they did not use contraception because they were not planning to have intercourse (Morrison 1985).

The reasons why some youths use effective contraception and others do not are many and varied. We have seen in an earlier chapter how parents' behaviour and attitudes influence young people's decisions to contracept. What other factors are associated with effective contraception? Hofferth and Hayes (1987a) report that age of sexual initiation is important – the older the adolescent girl at the time of initiation, the more likely she is to use contraception and to use it effectively. When there is a stable and committed male–female relationship, contraceptives are more likely to be used than when there are no romantic ties between sexual partners. Although this finding is inconsistent with that reported for condom use in the previous chapter, a partial explanation may be that adolescents in committed relationships are more likely to use oral contraceptives (Kantner and Zelnik 1972; Luker 1975). There is substantial support for the view that girls who have clear educational goals and those who are achieving well in school are more likely than their less achieving and ambitious peers to use effective contraception. Finally, girls who feel good about themselves, who feel that they have some degree of control over their lives, who have a sense of equality with their male partners – in short those who have high levels of 'ego strength' – are likely to be good contraceptors.

Whatever the reason for contraceptive avoidance or failure, those young women who have to deal with an unplanned pregnancy must choose between a number of possible options. It is to this decision-making process that we now turn.

RESOLUTION OF TEENAGE PREGNANCIES: 'MAKING THE CHOICE'

While it may be easier for teenagers to get pregnant today than ever before, there is greater acceptance of a variety of possible outcomes. The ready availability of legal abortions has enabled more young people to choose termination of pregnancy as an option. At the same time, there has been a shift in attitudes so that the birth of a baby out of wedlock is no longer stigmatised in the way that it once was. Today, pregnant teenage girls are able to choose to keep their child, and rear it either alone or with the support of their partner. Alternatively, they may avoid motherhood by choosing either abortion or adoption. Each of these choices depends on a variety of factors and each brings with it different consequences.

Abortion

The legalisation of abortion that has occurred in many parts of the world has brought with it a substantial increase in the number of terminations of teenage pregnancies (Bury 1984; Chilman 1980b; Phoenix 1991; Siedlecky 1984). Zelnik and his colleagues (1981) report that over the five-year period of their study there was a substantial drop in the number of pregnancies that ended as live births (from 79 per cent in 1971 to 65 per cent in 1976). Hofferth (1987a) estimates that the percentage of teenage pregnancies terminated by abortion almost doubled between 1974 and 1980, with a levelling off in abortion rate since then. A similar trend is reported among Australian adolescents by Siedlecky (1985). Today, it is estimated that roughly 40 per cent of pregnancies to teenagers in the United States end in abortion (Hayes 1987), one of the highest abortion rates for teenagers in any developed country (Jones *et al.* 1985). In Britain, the numbers of teenage pregnancies which we know are terminated have risen over the past 20 years, with teenagers having a higher abortion rate than other women in the mid-1980s (Hudson and Ineichen 1991). The large number of adolescents who opt for abortion leads us to ask: what are the factors that are associated with this decision and what are the consequences of the decision to terminate a pregnancy for these young women?

It appears that now, more than in the past, younger teenagers are more likely to choose abortion as an option than those who are older (Hofferth 1987b; Hudson and Ineichen 1991; Olson 1980; Siedlecky 1985). Based on her 1980 review, Chilman suggests that teenage abortees are more likely than those who carry their pregnancies to full-term to be contraceptive users, single, have high educational or occupational aspirations, and to be of higher socioeconomic status (Chilman 1980b). A more recent review by Hayes (1987) confirms these conclusions, noting also the significant impact of religion as well as parents', especially mothers', attitudes to abortion. Positive peer (and boyfriend) attitudes to abortion are related to pregnant teenagers' decision to abort, while adolescents who report knowing other unmarried teenage mothers report that they are less likely to make this choice (Eisen *et al.* 1983). Although there are claims of substantial racial differences in abortion rates with black adolescents less likely to abort than their white peers (Fischman 1977; Hayes 1987), Hofferth argues that this black–white difference varies according to age, with similar ratios for 19-year-olds, and higher rates of abortion for older black women than whites.

Even within a social context in which abortion is seen as a legal option for teenagers, there are grounds for concern about the health consequences of this decision. Teenagers are less likely than older women to obtain abortions in the safer, earlier months of pregnancy (Hayes 1987; Strobino 1987). Data from the United States show that only 34 per cent of abortions to girls younger than 16 are performed in the first eight weeks of pregnancy, while 14 per cent are performed at 16 weeks and later (Alan Guttmacher Institute 1981). This delay is likely to result in increased health risks. While young women who have chosen to terminate their pregnancy do not, in general, appear to have a higher incidence of negative health outcomes than do older women, Strobino (1987) argues that there has been insufficient long-term and careful follow-up of these teenagers for such conclusions to be drawn with confidence. Moreover, there is evidence that these young women are at greater risk of cervical trauma which in turn may have long-term negative implications for future conception and pregnancy outcomes (Siedlecky 1985; Strobino 1987).

Few studies examine the psychological consequences of abortion for young girls. There is something of a paradox in the situation where abortion is now readily available to most young women in most Western countries but it still stirs strong negative feelings among teenagers. In one British study, only 38 per cent of boys and girls approved of abortion, 49 per cent disapproved, and the remainder had mixed feelings. The teenagers for whom abortion is most likely to be a reality, girls, and especially working-class girls, are the ones who have the least positive attitudes. This would suggest that the decision to abort an unwanted pregnancy is likely to engender conflict for many of these young girls. One view is that, while abortion may be seen as a quick and easy solution, the consequences of abortion may be distressing and long-term (Hudson and Ineichen 1991). Sharpe (1987) is one who argues that teenagers cope well with abortion and that long-term psychological stress is uncommon, although there may be short-term, transient episodes of guilt or depression.

For some teenagers, the decision is easily made and has no negative consequences; for others, abortion is an event replete with ambivalence. This letter to one dispenser of advice to young girls captures something of the dilemma faced by teenagers.

Six weeks ago I found out I was pregnant. [My boyfriend and I] spent the next day crying together. I decided the only thing I could do was have an abortion. . . . Ray was totally against the abortion. He said I was being selfish. Then he gave me a choice; me, him and the baby or just me. After a million tears, I chose just me. . . . [H]e paid for half the abortion. . . . He also said he didn't love me anymore, would never forgive me and that we had no future together. I was so hurt I wanted to die. I trusted him and couldn't believe he turned on me. . . . We're back together now, but I feel so guilty for having the abortion. . . . Every time I see a baby, I cry.

(Weston 1988: 190)

One measure of the ambivalence surrounding abortion, suggested by an experienced abortion counsellor (Allanson, personal communication), is the attachment that the pregnant young girl has already developed to her baby. Some of these teenagers describe having fantasies about the sex of the baby, what it might look like, how it might grow up. Some even report giving the baby a name. Allanson has found that these young girls have particular difficulty in making the decision whether or not to proceed with an abortion, and argues that they are likely to be among those who subsequently regret a decision to abort. In an area where decision-making is so complex and determined by so many factors, the inner voice of the young girl is often forgotten. Exploration of her fantasies and dreams is one promising way of allowing that voice to be heard.

For young women who do choose abortion as the means of dealing with an unwanted pregnancy, access to good counselling support is essential so that the decision whether or not to abort can be made after a careful, informed, and thoughtful appraisal of the situation. When abortion is chosen under pressure or in haste, the likelihood of negative outcomes is increased. For some, the process is akin to one of mourning, in which the natural stages of grief and loss must be worked through. The teenager who chooses to terminate her pregnancy needs to feel that that decision is the right one for her.

Giving up the baby: choosing adoption

Adoption of her baby was long the option of choice for teenagers facing unwanted pregnancies. However, since the advent of legalised abortion and a reduction in the social stigma attached to unwed motherhood, this option appears to have fallen out of favour. Hayes (1987) reports that it is impossible to derive precise estimates of the number of teenagers in the United States who currently choose this means of resolving an unwanted pregnancy. There is some evidence that the numbers of young women who gave up their babies for adoption declined in the 1970s (Bachrach 1986). By 1982, only 7.4 per cent of white teenagers and fewer than 1 per cent of blacks reported having given up a child for adoption. As Furstenberg and his colleagues note (Furstenberg *et al.* 1989), there has never been a widespread tradition of formal adoption among some groups such as African-Americans, so that current low rates are not surprising.

The sparse literature on adoption makes it impossible to draw strong conclusions about why teenagers choose this option rather than any other. One study (Resnick 1984) suggests that teenagers who plan to adopt out their babies are more like those who choose abortion than teens who decide to keep their babies. The consequences of adoption are likewise little researched, although one small study indicates that relinquishing one's baby may be less problematic for teenagers than choosing to continue in the parenting role (McLaughlin *et al.* 1988).

Keeping the baby

Why do some teenagers choose to continue with a pregnancy and to take on the responsibilities of parenthood, often without a partner to provide emotional and material support? Here we shall focus on the factors which are strongly associated with this decision for unwed teenagers, leaving the consequences of that decision for later. The major 'causes' of teenage illegitimacy are summarised by Chilman (1980a) and include a variety of social as well as psychological factors. Taking a broad sociological perspective, Chilman asserts that unwed parenthood is associated with changes in society which have led to the two-parent family becoming less important for the economic well-being of parents and children. Equally, she notes that changes in cultural norms have resulted in out-of-wedlock children – and their mothers – no longer being stigmatised as they once were. Another key factor, she argues, is the inability of society to keep pace with changing sexual mores, so that the recent and dramatic increase in young people's sexual activity has not been matched by the provision of adequate community family planning services.

There is also considerable research to suggest that race plays a significant role in a teenager's decision to keep her child. Although the rate of child-bearing among unmarried white teenagers in the United States is increasing, the figure has always been high for black teenagers. In fact, in the early 1980s almost all births to black teenagers under 15 and nearly 90 per cent to those aged between 15 and 19 occurred outside of marriage. This high rate of ex-nuptial births may be attributed to the high rates of sexual activity of these young women, and their greater reluctance to use abortion as a means of dealing with an unwanted pregnancy (Chilman 1980b; Hayes 1987). The diversity within black families means that single parenting is less unusual and more socially acceptable in these communities than in white communities. Because of this, support for the single mother is more likely to be forthcoming among black families than among non-blacks. There is a suggestion, too, that these girls – and those of other ethnic groups in similar positions – may perceive motherhood as a rare gratification in a life devoid of opportunity. When life offers little but continuing unemployment, poverty and difficult family circumstances, it would not be surprising if teenage girls sought comfort in the prospect of bearing and rearing a child. For these disadvantaged young women, willingness to bear a child outside of marriage may well be related to the perceived benefits of doing so. Before we accept this appealing hypothesis too readily, we should note, however, that the implied link between bleak social and economic prospects and contraceptive behaviour has not been supported in at least one study reported by Hayes (1987).

One factor that does seem to have a complex impact is the availability and source of financial assistance to unwed mothers-to-be. Several studies have shown that the decision to carry a premarital pregnancy to term is influenced by the availability of financial aid from the young woman's family of origin, as well as the availability of public aid. However, as we noted earlier, the weight of evidence suggests that unmarried teenage girls do not get pregnant in order to receive public assistance. Rather, it is likely that unmarried mothers are drawn from the ranks of low-income, female-headed families, many of whom are receiving welfare assistance themselves. It has been suggested that if welfare assistance is available, many young women will choose to continue with a pregnancy, rather than contemplate a termination. Again, the evidence for this conclusion is thin, with at least one study (Moore and Caldwell 1977) revealing little evidence for any connection between the availability of welfare and choosing single parenthood over other options.

Apart from issues of class, race, and economics, young girls give many reasons for keeping their babies. Becoming a mother may not be a real matter of choice. Some young girls fail to realise, perhaps because they have erratic periods, that they are pregnant until too late to do anything but have the baby. Some may deny the pregnancy hoping that 'it will go away' if they don't think about it. Others may be frightened of telling people until after the time when an abortion would be possible. But motherhood is seen by some young girls as having positive (although possibly short-term) consequences for their lives. Apart from having an object to call their own and to love, for some young girls a baby may be seen as a means of keeping a boyfriend's interest, of complying with his wishes to keep the baby, or of achieving status because of their new 'adult' role as mother. Not all reasons for choosing to keep the baby have such a positive basis. Sometimes pregnancy can be used as an excuse for avoiding difficulties associated with school, a strategy that may continue even after the birth of the baby. Sometimes the young girl will respond to hostile family pressure to give up the baby by becoming determined to keep the child even if it means leaving the family home.

One particularly disturbing reason for the young teenager to involuntarily choose motherhood is because of poor or inadequate medical advice. While most doctors do their best to help the young girl decide among the options open to her, others are less helpful. In one study reported by Hudson and Ineichen (1991), patients claimed that 21 per cent of all doctors consulted made no effort to help teenage girls obtain abortions. A second study revealed that 20 per cent of the pregnant girls who continued with their pregnancy had wanted an abortion but were either too late or had their wish thwarted. Given these difficulties, it is not surprising that some teenage girls have little confidence in the medical profession as a source of guidance and assistance.

CHOOSING PARENTHOOD: CONSEQUENCES FOR TEENAGERS

While we have relatively little research to draw on in determining the consequences for teenagers of choosing abortion or adoption as the outcome of an unwanted pregnancy, the decision to keep the baby and the consequences of that decision have been the focus of considerable research. Here, the spotlight has extended to include not only the young mother, but also the father as well as the new-born and developing infant.

Teenage motherhood

The disadvantages of teenage motherhood are many and well documented. They range from concerns about health outcomes, interpersonal and relationship difficulties, and interruptions to the normative life trajectory, to economic consequences. Surveying the literature, we can only agree with Campbell's conclusion of more than twenty years ago: 'The girl who has an illegitimate child at the age of 16 suddenly has 90 percent of her life's script written for her' (Campbell 1968: 238).

Research on health risks and outcomes shows that pregnant teenagers have higher rates of complications, maternal morbidity and mortality, premature and/or low birthweight babies, and perinatal deaths – stillbirth and death within the first 28 days – than older women (Siedlecky 1985;

Strobino 1987). Risks are especially serious for the youngest of these teenage mothers. These poor outcomes are often due to neglect of their own physical health by these young mothers-to-be. For example, it is argued that poor access to antenatal care, poor attendance at these centres, and, sometimes, denial of pregnancy until a relatively late stage contributes to the increased risk of premature births for young teenagers. Littlejohn (1992) suggests that the provision of clinics catering specifically for adolescents would significantly improve attendance and pregnancy outcomes. Although adequate antenatal care would no doubt reduce the incidence of pregnancy complications, there remains the problem that many teenage mothers, as we have already seen, live under conditions which make good health care difficult to sustain.

When we turn to psychological consequences of teenage motherhood, the picture is more positive. Early studies of pregnant and parenting teenagers concluded that they suffer major psychological distress (see Barth *et al.* 1983 for a review). For example, one such study reported a high suicide rate among pregnant adolescents (Gabrielson *et al.* 1970). It should be recognised, however, that this research was conducted in the days when adolescents' sexual activity was considered unacceptable and shameful. Although recent studies of psychological correlates of out-of-wedlock teenage pregnancies have been few, Barth and his colleagues found that levels of psychological distress among their pregnant and parenting teenagers were lower than might have been expected. They decided that teenage pregnancy and motherhood are not in and of themselves as incapacitating as once thought. Rather, contextual factors such as socioeconomic status and social supports predicted well-being better among their pregnant and non-pregnant, parenting and non-parenting adolescents than did parenting status. But the picture was not all rosy, with some ill-effects of pregnancy showing up in the form of somewhat lower levels of self-esteem and a tendency towards higher depression scores. Quite clearly, although the severe psychological reaction to their pregnancy and parenthood has given way in the face of changes in society, today's teenage mothers need adequate material and social support if psychological dysfunction is to be avoided.

One particular concern of researchers has been the impact of early motherhood on teenagers' normal life trajectory. One of the key tasks for adolescents in Western cultures is the achievement of a sense of autonomy and self-identity. How does becoming a mother affect a young girl's capacity to work through these complex issues? For many teenage mothers, dependence on family for financial and emotional support is prolonged, and much of the energy which would normally be devoted to acquiring self-knowledge and psychological independence is necessarily diverted to child care. Another crucial aspect of adolescent development likely to be affected by early motherhood is the establishment of close relationships with peers of both sexes. The demands of a small baby are likely to mitigate against this developmental goal. Caught up in the burden of caring for a demanding infant or toddler, teenage girls may well find that they have little time or energy for establishing and maintaining friendships with their peers, especially those who are not so burdened. Many a young mother is likely to find, also, that the traditional patterns of heterosexual contact, beginning with dating, may be denied her. The logistics of organising such a simple and taken-for-granted activity as going on a date may be beyond many teenage mothers, and many young boys may be uninterested in dating these young girls.

The implications of early motherhood for later outcomes are likely to be considerable. What effect, for example, is there on the educational attainment of these young women? Since education substantially influences later life chances, through income and occupational opportunities, this is a particularly important issue. The research shows unequivocally that teenage mothers drop out of school earlier and are less likely to go on to college or university study than older mothers (see Hofferth 1987b for a review). This is true even when factors such as socioeconomic status and academic aptitude are held constant. But impending or actual motherhood may not be the sole or critical factor operating here. Chilman and others have noted that some of the characteristics of teenage school dropouts (such as being impulsive, lacking in long-term goals, and coming from unhappy families) are similar to those which lead to becoming an unmarried adolescent mother.

It could be argued that regular high schools are, even today, hostile and difficult environments for pregnant young women so that there is little incentive to remain at school or to return after the baby's birth. However Furstenberg (1976) found that the provision of special schools for pregnant teenagers did not substantially increase the likelihood of their continued schooling over and above that of girls in ordinary high schools. There is now good evidence that pregnant teenagers have lower grades and lower school motivation before becoming pregnant than their non-pregnant peers so that it may be unrealistic to expect that these special schools will have a substantial impact. It would seem that for girls who have the ability and motivation to continue with their education, pregnancy and motherhood does not necessarily mean the end of their dreams. There is encouraging evidence, too, that differences in educational attainment between teenagers who give birth and those who do not may diminish over time, and that many teenage mothers who interrupt their schooling do resume their educational careers later in life.

There is no question that the interruption to schooling or termination of education that often follows pregnancy and early motherhood has implications for the economic well-being of these young women. What are the economic consequences of early motherhood? Most studies show that teenage mothers are less likely than older mothers to find stable and well-paid employment. Once again, we should be wary of assuming a direct link between early motherhood and poor job prospects. Several writers have pointed out that the employment of young women is just as dependent on the conditions of the labour market and personal characteristics as it is on high educational attainment. Nevertheless, it is true that teenagers who begin child-rearing at an early age are economically disadvantaged. Because they left school at an earlier age and are likely to have more children (Hofferth 1987b), their ability to find employment in higher status jobs and earn high wages is diminished, and they must use their earnings to support a larger family. Although the differences in income between early and later child-rearing decrease over time, these teenage mothers are at greater risk of poverty throughout their lifetime. Because of this, they are likely to rely on public welfare and it has been shown that long-term welfare dependency is a consequence of early child-bearing. However, Furstenberg and his colleagues (1989) point out that many of these young mothers enter the workforce when they are older and their children reach school age, thereby substantially reducing the proportion of those who are on welfare. Nevertheless, they conclude that 'early childbearers will not achieve complete economic parity with women who postpone parenthood until they are adults.'

To what extent is the interruption by premature parenthood of the normal maturational cycle of workforce experience before 'marriage' and child-rearing likely to affect these young women's intimate relationships and marital outcomes? Once again, the picture painted by the research is dismal. We know that many teenage mothers raise their children as single parents (Oz and Fine 1988). It seems that, for some, early child-bearing accelerates the pace of marriage or cohabiting; it also accelerates the pace of separation and divorce (Hayes 1987). But premarital pregnancy or childbirth does not necessarily prevent a stable, happy relationship, be it marriage or cohabiting. Furstenberg's work shows that marriages are most likely to last if the couple had a longstanding, committed relationship prior to the child's birth (Furstenberg 1976). By contrast, those couples in his sample whose marriages failed were likely to have married after the birth of the baby rather than before, and were experiencing difficult economic circumstances – often because they had two or more children. If these marriages are to work and to survive, they must have a sound economic, social, and emotional basis.

The children of teenage mothers

There appear to be considerable health risks for children of teenage mothers. Infants of these young women have a higher likelihood of low birthweight and of dying within the first year of life than those of older mothers. Indeed, the prevailing wisdom is that these children face a bleak future with increased risk of parental neglect, child abuse, abandonment, and other forms of parental mistreatment (Furstenberg *et al.* 1987). The reasons for this, it is argued, are to be found in the young mother's immaturity, lack of parenting skills, and inadequate financial resources.

Concerns about parenting competence led to a number of studies of teenagers and their children. Many of these suggest that teenage mothers are less responsive to their infants than are older mothers, and engage in more physical and less verbal interaction. There is considerable evidence in the child-rearing literature to indicate that this parenting style is one that impedes optimal cognitive and social development in children. So we might expect poor outcomes for the children of these mothers. And, indeed, this appears to be the case for some children and adolescents. Hayes (1987) concludes that 'the available research suggests that having a teenage mother negatively affects a child's development, and the effects do not decrease over time'. This conclusion is supported by other research from the United States (Furstenberg *et al.* 1989). The developmental disadvantage of children born to teenage mothers compared with those of older mothers is reflected in deficits in cognitive functioning, in problems in social functioning (for example, higher levels of aggression and lower self-control) and later school motivation and achievement. These difficulties appear to persist into adolescence and may be more pronounced for sons than daughters.

A less pessimistic view of the outcomes for children of teenage mothers comes from work in Great Britain. Phoenix (1991) suggests that the deleterious effects of mother's youthfulness disappear or diminish when other important social and economic characteristics are controlled for, although she concedes that children of very young mothers are likely to be at risk, both from the point of view of their health and their subsequent social and psychological development. Reporting the findings of a rare longitudinal study of young mothers, Phoenix concluded that the responses of many of these teenagers to pregnancy and motherhood were not very different from those of older women. On the whole, the children were well cared for by their young mothers, most of whom took full-time responsibility for child care. These mothers were not ignorant of the need to provide a stimulating environment and good nutrition so that their children could develop to their maximum potential. When the children's developmental status was assessed, test scores revealed normal variability, and were related to the usual sorts of factors, such as co-operativeness of the child and satisfaction with motherhood.

These somewhat conflicting views may be the outcome of different methodologies and different samples. Certainly there is evidence from the United States that there some children of teenage mothers escape the risks. Researchers are now turning to the task of identifying risk-protective factors, especially those features of the mother's environment which serve as a buffer against negative outcomes. One promising area involves an examination of the relationship between children's outcomes and the timing and sequence of events in the lives of their mothers. For example, resumption of education by the mother and entry into a stable marriage appear to influence positively the child's later academic performance. Quite clearly, the outcomes for children of young mothers are determined by a complex set of issues. To argue that these outcomes are inevitably negative is to overlook the possibility that teenage mothers can reclaim their lives.

What about the fathers?

It seems that fathers, young or old, have long been invisible participants in the act of procreation and parenthood. In the case of partners of teenage mothers, there are particular difficulties involved in researching and writing them into the family formation process. Most pregnant young women become known to service agencies because they seek medical help. The fathers of these babies are sometimes unknown or, if known, may be fearful of disapproval or reluctant to accept responsibility for on-going support of mother and child. For these reasons, they are likely to be wary of contacts with service providers or even researchers. In a rare review of research on teenage fathers, Parke and Neville (1987) argue that we need to recognise that male partners of adolescent mothers represent a wide range of ages and are not necessarily adolescents themselves. So any attempts to understand the impact of fatherhood need to take account of their current life stage and developmental status. Nevertheless we shall limit our brief analysis to teenage fathers, while acknowledging that this oversimplifies the issue.

A substantial minority of teenage fathers never acknowledge their paternity, partly through ignorance, partly through disbelief, and partly because they refuse to accept the responsibilities of fatherhood. Furstenberg reports that in one study, many young fathers doubted their ability to support their new family, either financially or emotionally. In another of the few studies of partners of teenage mothers, Simms and Smith (1986) were able to locate 59 per cent of the young men six months after the birth. Not surprisingly, fathers who had negative attitudes to the pregnancy, who were 'missing' from their baby's life, or who were teenagers themselves were difficult to recruit and were underrepresented. The fathers interviewed presented a somewhat rosy view of parenting, no doubt because the least satisfied young men did not participate, but they also added to the depressing picture of ignorance about, and apathy towards, pregnancy and contraception that is characteristic of many young mothers. Often the decision about parenting is taken out of these young men's hands, when their partner seeks an abortion without discussing the matter with the father-to-be. For some, this is a situation which can lead to conflict and considerable distress for the father who feels that his wishes and needs are being ignored.

When the pregnancy is carried to term and the baby arrives, it is too often the case that boys continue to behave in the ways that have been socially conditioned. They retain their macho, dominant, tough image, and may find it difficult to deal with the demands of a dependent infant and an inexperienced young mother. Some resolve this problem by leaving, escaping from their new responsibilities. Hudson and Ineichen (1991) argue forcefully that government and other agencies must address the needs of these young boys, teaching them to accept their parental responsibility. Only by recognising that young fathers need support in the same way that young mothers do are we likely to reduce the number of absent fathers in these young families.

It is clear that early fatherhood, like early motherhood, may interfere with the usual processes of adolescent development, in particular those of identity achievement and emancipation from the family, as well as limiting educational and occupational opportunities. The last outcomes are likely to be dependent on whether the young father accepts the social and economic responsibilities associated with this role. While it appears that early timing of fatherhood may accelerate the rate of dropout from the educational system, an alternative interpretation is that young men who leave school early may be more likely to become teenage fathers. When it comes to employment prospects, it seems that those fathers who are living with their children are more likely to be employed than are absent fathers. But, reflecting their lower educational attainment, these young fathers, like young mothers, are underrepresented in higher status occupations.

Turning to the contribution of the young father to his new family, it seems that teenage fathers, even if married, have difficulty in providing support for their partners. Parke and Neville counter the 'common misconception' that adolescent fathers have little contact with their offspring, suggesting that there is considerable variability in desire for involvement as well as actual care of the child. Nevertheless, it does seem that the contribution of many unmarried fathers is limited to an occasional visit, rather than a serious effort to take responsibility for their children. In analysing paternal involvement, Parke and Neville make the interesting observation that mothers (and their parents) can function as gatekeepers. For some fathers, access to their infants and children may be restricted, thus limiting the degree of paternal involvement in infant and child care even when they keenly desire the opportunity to participate in child-rearing.

It seems that the available research is too sparse to draw any firm conclusions about teenage fathers' interest in their children and their competence in infant care. On the other hand there is tentative evidence that contact with their teenage fathers has a positive effect on children, enhancing their social and cognitive development. Of course, fathers may have an indirect effect, too, through their relationships with the mother or other family members. Here again, the picture is mixed. While some young fathers support their partners socially, emotionally, and financially, others do not. Having a supportive partner has a positive impact on maternal–infant involvement but, overall, the level of support that these young men offer is not high (Parke and Neville 1987). Turning once again to Phoenix's longitudinal study, we find little cause for optimism about the role of these young men in the lives of their young families. Phoenix reports that a sizeable minority of relationships come to an end during the pregnancy and that most male partners did not provide the emotional and material support that the young women desired. Especially disturbing to these young mothers was the incidence of infidelity among their male partners. Equally disturbing is the suggestion that poor fathering may indirectly increase the likelihood of child abuse by the mother (Bolton and Belsky 1986). One important buffer against child maltreatment for these young parents is the presence of support from the young fathers' families.

It seems that there are many unanswered questions about the consequences of teenage fatherhood – for the young fathers themselves, for their partners, and for their children. Why do some young fathers accept their family responsibilities and obligations? How effective are these young men as parents (and as partners)? What is the effect of these young fathers on their children's development? These and other questions need to be addressed before we can fully understand what it means to father a child while still a teenager.

TEENAGE PREGNANCY: WHERE TO?

Our discussion of teenage pregnancy and parenthood has highlighted the variability of outcomes for those concerned. It is clear that, for some, pregnancy is unplanned and the baby unwanted. For others, the decision to

have a baby at an early age brings in its wake a series of negative consequences. Teenage parenthood may prove to be a difficult and disruptive
choice, resulting in serious and permanent limitations to life's
opportunities. But there is yet another group. Not all teenage parents,
especially mothers, experience difficulties. A substantial number complete
their schooling, marry (and do not divorce), find rewarding employment,
and their children develop along patterns which are not different from those
of children of older parents. In spite of the very serious hurdles that these
young people encounter, they are able to realise their ambitions and life
plans.

What are the factors that protect these successful young parents from
difficulties and distress? We have mentioned some of these in passing. The
importance of adequate social support in mediating the stress for young
mothers, whether this comes from the child's father, parents, or other
family members, has been well documented (see, for example, Barth *et al.*
1983). Not surprisingly, socioeconomic level contributes substantially. To
be poor and undereducated is likely to decrease significantly the likelihood
of well-being for these young parents and their offspring. One factor to
which we have not yet paid attention is the interpretation given to teenage
pregnancy within the society. Is teenage pregnancy seen to be a normative
phenomenon or is it assumed to be disruptive of young people's normal life
trajectory? In some cultures, it is clear that parenting at a youthful age is
accepted and incorporated into everyday life. The African-American
culture in the United States provides an excellent example, in the West, of
this process. In many studies, we find that parenthood at an early age is less
disruptive of their everyday lives for young black women than for their
white counterparts.

By contrast, in other cultures teenage pregnancy and parenting is seen to
require special programmes to assist these young parents and their children.
Considerable funds are spent to prevent teen pregnancy as well as providing
services to ameliorate problems after conception occurs. These include
provision of antenatal care, health and parenting programmes, and a variety
of comprehensive care programmes. There are some programmes which
have been directed to promoting educational or occupational opportunities,
including the provision of alternative schools for pregnant girls. It is not
appropriate for us to outline in detail the variety of programmes designed to
overcome the negative health, social, and economic consequences of early
child-rearing (see, for example, Hayes 1987 and Hudson and Ineichen 1991
for reviews). Rather, we wish to make the point that the responses to
teenage pregnancy are, to some extent, culturally bound as well as
dependent on individual characteristics.

What is striking about the research findings is that teenage parents are not a homogeneous group. Clearly many of the problems that beset these young people are not a function of their premature parenthood but are shared by their non-parenting peers. What is also apparent are the gaps that exist in our knowledge of the impact of early pregnancy and parenthood. We have mentioned the dearth of research on teenage fathers. What is also missing from the research are the voices of these young mothers and fathers. In spite of the plethora of books dealing with teenage pregnancy, and with the notable exceptions of British writers such as Sharpe (1987), Hudson and Ineichen (1991), and Phoenix (1991), researchers have neglected the phenomenology of early motherhood and fatherhood. We have little idea of what it actually feels like to become a mother or father when one is little more than a child. We know, from a reading of these British researchers' interviews with pregnant teenagers and young mothers, that individuals experience these events in many different ways. Teenage pregnancy and/or parenthood may be a monumental handicap to well-being and achievement. Even when this is the case, many young women, while regretting lost opportunities, cannot imagine themselves without their children and are happy as parents. As the words of this young mother testify:

[S]ometimes I say to myself I wish I never had her. Maybe I would probably have had a boyfriend. . . . Sometimes when I've got money problems I say to myself if I didn't have her I'd probably be well off now . . . but then when I think of her I say no. She's mine, and I'm happy she's here. You know I can sit down and play with her and give her the love I never really had from my father when I was small . . . and I'm two parents in one really.

(Phoenix 1991: 242)

9 Adventurers, exploiters and victims

Some aspects of adolescent sexuality can be described as maladaptive, troubled, or troubling. We include here sexual behaviours which may result in a sexual identity that is insecure or uncertain. Or they may reflect a desire to achieve experimental conquest, to escape from unpleasant experiences, or to satisfy peer pressures. They may satisfy a drive for dominance or submissiveness, express a pathological need, or reflect the presence of self-destructive urges or alienation from society's institutions. These worrying aspects of sexuality may be self-regulated, as in early onset of sexual activity, or be the result of external forces over which the adolescent has little or no control, as in rape. Whether the impetus is internal or external, voluntary or involuntary, the common feature of these behaviours is that the outcome for the teenager is inimical to current and future life adjustment generally, and sexual adjustment in particular.

ADOLESCENT SEXUALITY AS DEVIANCE?

Adolescents' propensity for risk-taking, their experimentation with adult behaviours, their drive towards autonomy, and their openness to peer influences has been thought to make them vulnerable to maladaptive sexual behaviours. These include precocious sexual intercourse (often referred to quaintly in the literature as 'early sexual debut'), and sex with a succession of changing partners. These behaviours have commonly been regarded in the research literature as deviant and problematic, 'socially defined as a problem, a source of concern, or as undesirable by the norms of conventional society and the institutions of adult authority' (Jessor and Jessor 1977: 33). Although engaging in sexual activity becomes normative with increasing age, for young adolescents it is behaviour that parents do not condone. Why is this the case? The particular focus on initiation of sexual activity is due to its special place as a transition behaviour. Like many behaviours which reflect the transition from child to adult, sexual activity, if ill-timed, may be detrimental to the psychological, emotional, and social well-being and development of the adolescent.

It is not only teenage sexual behaviour that raises parents' and society's anxiety levels. Other adolescent behaviours which cause concern include substance use, drinking, smoking, truancy, and delinquency, as well as further forms of antisocial behaviour. Given their assumed common aetiology – which arises from the fact that adolescence is a time of testing boundaries – it is no wonder that researchers have explored the possibility of links between all these problem behaviours. Indeed, it has been argued that they all form part of a syndrome of mildly deviant behaviours (Jessor and Jessor 1977). There is abundant evidence for an association between early sexual activity and other non-sexual misconduct or behaviours considered inappropriate for adolescents (e.g. Donovan and Jessor 1985; Elliott and Morse 1989; Ensminger 1987; Rodgers and Rowe 1990). The link between delinquency and precocious sexual activity is clear in a study of more than 1000 adolescents admitted to a juvenile detention facility in the United States (Weber *et al.* 1989). In support of their conclusion that delinquent teenagers are at particularly high risk of initiating sexual intercourse at an early age, Weber and his colleagues reported that 40 per cent of African-American boys and 20 per cent of non-blacks had engaged in 'volitional' (that is, non-coerced) sexual intercourse by age 10. These compare with the figure of 17 per cent reported by Sorenson (1973) for a representative sample of American adolescents. For the young girls in Weber's sample, the average age of sexual initiation was 13 years, compared with Sorenson's girls of whom only 7 per cent reported being sexually active prior to age 13.

The belief that teenage problem behaviours, including precocious sexual behaviour, form part of a syndrome of deviant behaviours came from the classic study by Jessor and Jessor (1977). In a longitudinal study of high-schoolers and college students, Jessor and Jessor found a positive association between all of the problem behaviours studied (problem drinking, marijuana use, delinquent behaviour, and sexual intercourse) for both age groups. Moreover, these behaviours were found to correlate negatively with measures of conformity and conventional behaviour such as church attendance and school performance, and positively with personality measures reflecting unconventionality. From these findings, Jessor and Jessor concluded that early transition to nonvirginity is linked with the transition to other problem behaviours.

This conclusion leads us to ask two questions. First, to what extent are non-normative or risky sexual behaviours other than early sexual initiation associated with non-sexual problem behaviours and thus part of Jessor and Jessor's problem behaviour syndrome? Second, do these problem behaviours emerge at the same time or is there a particular sequence in which they occur? Metzler and her colleagues have addressed the first issue (Metzler *et al.* 1992). In three independent samples of teenagers (from 14 to 18 years of age) they found high correlations between a number of sexual behaviours which included nonvirgin status, multiple sexual partners, and sex with casual and/or promiscuous partners. Furthermore, there were high correlations between a composite measure of sexual risk and other problem behaviours such as smoking, alcohol and marijuana use, and antisocial behaviour. We might conclude from this work and other research that links early sexual activity with risky sexual practices such as unprotected intercourse and intercourse with multiple partners (Chilman 1980a; Hayes 1987; Thornton 1990) that Jessor and Jessor's problem behaviour syndrome may be extended to include risky sexual behaviours other than precocious sexual activity. This link holds up in our studies of risk-taking among older adolescents in which sexual risk (multiple partnering, unprotected intercourse) was found to be correlated with risky (fast) driving and smoking (Moore and Rosenthal 1992a).

Although there may be strong grounds for considering these behaviours to be parts of a whole, there is little evidence as to whether there are causal relationships between them. Does being sexually precocious lead to other problem behaviours, such as drinking or smoking? Is the direction of causality the other way round? Or, as Jessor and Jessor seem to imply, is there an underlying cause, common to uptake of all these problem behaviours? Elliott and Morse (1989) have examined the temporal ordering of these behaviours, seeking the existence of a clear developmental progression into multiproblem patterns of behaviour. They also sought to establish whether the different problem behaviours could be regarded as causally related to each other. With regard to temporal ordering, they found that the most common, but not the only, sequence was for both drug use and delinquency to precede onset of sexual activity. They concluded that '[w]hile it cannot be said that this developmental sequence is invariant or that any one behaviour is necessary for the *emergence* of another, the evidence does suggest a typical sequence or developmental progression' (Elliott and Morse 1989: 50). It seems from this study that initiation of sexual activity *follows* entry into other non-normative forms of adolescent behaviour. The researchers argue from their findings that engaging in early sexual activity is highly dependent on the young teenager's delinquent and drug-use status and reflects a general tendency on the part of these teenagers to engage in risky behaviour.

The attempt to link problem behaviours with underlying psychological causes has largely hinged on identifying these behaviours as deviant, and interpreting them as having only negative outcomes. Teenagers at risk of engaging in these behaviours are seen as rebellious and alienated from traditional institutions of society, especially the family and school. Personality characteristics associated with this construct of social deviance include impulsivity and sensation-seeking. In an interesting paper, Chassin *et al.* (1989) propose that negative behaviours may be associated with a positive, constructive form of teenage unconventionality, reflecting independence and creativity, as well as with the anticonventionality associated with 'destructive' deviance. This view of so-called problem behaviours as having an adaptive function and playing a constructive role in adolescent development has been persuasively argued by Silbereisen and his colleagues (Silbereisen *et al.* 1987; Silbereisen and Noack 1988). Chassin's study of health-related behaviours such as smoking and participation in sport and/or exercise suggests that 'constructive' and 'destructive' deviance can be regarded as independent, and representing different pathways to adolescent health-related behaviours. They conclude that

> one type of adolescent at risk for substance use is unconventional, creative, independent, and assertive. However, these adolescents are not in rebellion against traditional socializing agents such as the family and the school and they also engage in relatively higher levels of health-protective behaviors.
>
> (Chassin *et al.* 1989: 261)

We do not know if these alternative pathways, via a positive, constructive independence or a destructive, rebellious anticonformity, operate for problem sexual behaviour but there is some evidence that there are both positive (through peer acceptance) and negative (through peer rejection) paths to early multiple partnering (Feldman *et al.* 1992). This evidence is suggestive of the distinction that Chassin and her colleagues wish to draw and which downplays somewhat the maladaptive aspects of sexual precocity and other 'deviant' expressions of teenage sexuality. But, although we may wish to focus on the more positive features of some teenage sexual behaviours that have been defined as undesirable, there is little question about the harmful nature of the behaviour to which we now turn.

ADOLESCENT PROSTITUTION

It is tempting to describe adolescent prostitution as a relatively new phenomenon, attributable to the 'breakdown of modern society'. In fact, teenage prostitution has been a fact of life for most of recorded history and was even enshrined in law in some countries. England, in the nineteenth century, saw fit to regulate the age of prostitution, setting the minimum age at 12 until 1874, and at 16 in 1885. Brown (1979) in her review of teenage prostitution makes the point that although male prostitution may be equally as common as female, the legal and moral codes are designed to deal with female prostitution exclusively. This view of prostitution as a female activity is reflected in research where there are few studies of teenage homosexual prostitution, in spite of the dangers of this activity in the era of HIV/AIDS.

There does seem to have been an increase in the incidence of female teenage prostitution recently in many countries (see, for example, Firme *et al.* 1991), with some teenagers as young as 12 reported as turning eight to ten 'tricks' per night in some cities (Hersch 1988). Figures reported by Garbarino (1985) indicate that over the decade of the 1970s there was a 160 per cent increase in prostitution among teenagers below 18 years of age in the United States. This figure is based on crime reports and undoubtedly significantly underestimates the actual number of teenagers who are engaged in prostitution. Most researchers acknowledge that arrests and court statistics are inaccurate indicators of the incidence of teenage prostitution and recognise the impossibility of obtaining an accurate count. Several note the alarming increase in arrests of young prostitutes, with the average age declining and one study showing that 60 per cent of the 200 street prostitutes surveyed in San Francisco were younger than 17 and some were 10 and 11 years old.

So adolescent prostitution is a serious problem, with young prostitutes being the rule rather than the exception. What, then, are the factors which have led to this disturbing social problem? Why would a young girl enter this hazardous profession when the evidence shows that the outcomes are likely to be both 'dangerous and developmentally debilitating' (Garbarino 1985: 490)? The paths to prostitution vary, but a common characteristic is that the young girl is living in an environment which is unhappy, unrewarding or hostile. These young girls may have to cope with problems of family stress, poverty, crime, substance abuse, lack of education and/or unemployment – any or all of these are likely to lead to prostitution as a means of survival. Firme and her colleagues argue that prostitution is the product of socialisation stresses, with young girls either being pushed into or pulled towards prostitution by social forces.

In the former case, young women voluntarily enter the profession as a consequence of 'passive' neglect. The causes for this include educational deprivation or failure in the classroom, poverty or dead-end employment, and the absence of family support structures. For these young women, prostitution may provide a sense of adventure, as well as money to satisfy their needs. As one teenage prostitute put it:

I only did one job to try it out at first. I'd never done it before although a friend of mine had been working the streets for two months and had made a lot of cash. . . . [Then] I did three jobs and made about $300. So did my friend. The next morning we couldn't believe it. We woke up and we had all this money. We went out and bought all this make-up and these clothes and everything. I really got into the work. Like I didn't enjoy it then and I couldn't really handle it, but I really got off on all the money.

(Wilson and Arnold 1986: 63)

Some girls talk of their need for excitement and a hectic, action-packed life that is different from the dull, ordinary routine they experience at home. With few, if any, positive role models, marriage and motherhood do not figure high on these girls' life agendas. For them, working on the streets is seen as 'a relatively rational, compelling opportunity among otherwise boring alternatives' (Firme *et al.* 1991: 494). Firme found the opportunity to forsake menial, routine, and poorly paid work to be the most compelling reason for her Brazilian teenage girls' entry into prostitution. She concludes that one of the main reasons for teenage prostitution in Third World countries is economic deprivation, so that prostitution is simply one of the most appealing work opportunities available to these girls.

In contrast, in wealthier Western countries, it seems that most teenage prostitution is not voluntary and is caused by home and family stresses. These young girls are often pushed into prostitution by difficult family circumstances which cause them to leave home, usually with poor survival skills. Brown's review of the scanty research on teenage prostitution (Brown 1979) indicated that alienation from their family, often caused by family dissolution, marital violence, or other disruptions to family life, and parental neglect or abuse – either physical or sexual – are the most potent sources of young girls' entry into prostitution. There is some evidence that the vast majority of adolescent prostitutes have been victims of incest or sexual abuse (Newton-Ruddy and Handelsman 1986). These girls feel themselves to be unloved at home and abused. For some, prostitution – at least in the beginning – is a means of seeking the love, care, and intimacy which has been lacking in their lives.

There are other routes to prostitution, as Brown notes. Some girls find themselves in occupations such as bar waitresses or dancers where flirtatiousness is the required mode of interacting with men and which provide easy opportunity for the step into prostitution. Others may have engaged in sexual 'promiscuity' and found themselves stigmatised and labelled as sluts or whores. As Brown notes, 'that labeling may then create a vicious cycle of increased deviant behaviour; the girl who sees herself as rejected by mainstream culture for her sexual activity may come to identify with, and thus see prostitution as a viable lifestyle' (Brown 1979: 673). Other teenagers may be caught up in the cycle of providing funds for their drug habit.

> So the money I make which might be in the one hundred mark tonight, well I'll spend it all by the morning getting a score of stuff. I tried getting off the stuff, like I tried to get a regular job and get out of the game, but it is never easy. Well all my friends are down here and I don't know nobody else.
>
> (Wilson and Arnold 1986: 63)

The prospects for these (often) very young girls, undereducated and unskilled, are grim indeed. They are ready targets for the 'charms' of pimps – often not much older than themselves – who trade on their prey's naivety and need for love and shelter. Baizerman and his colleagues (Baizerman *et al.* 1979) describe in graphic detail one process of recruitment by a pimp. Often the process is slow and the young victim may be initiated by another girl who is 'in the game', with the 'target' not aware that she is being recruited for prostitution. Contact is made by the pimp who begins to work on the girl, building her trust in, and need for, his presence. Finally, when the young girl's dependence on the relationship is established, the shift to sex for money with other men is proposed by the pimp and accepted by the young girl, now in his thrall. Of course, not all prostitutes begin in this way. As we have said, some enter the occupation voluntarily, fully aware of the choice they have made. Others have a less benign introduction to prostitution. Although the idea of 'white slavery' has less currency now than in the past, it has not disappeared. There is still evidence that young runaway girls are forcibly recruited by unscrupulous individuals, held captive, raped, often initiated into injecting drugs, and then pushed into prostitution (Brown 1979).

Whether they have become prostitutes voluntarily or otherwise, there is no doubt that these young girls have taken a path which has many hazards. Forced perversion, customer rape, robbery, and physical violence are but some of the dangers encountered (Garbarino 1985). Here is one Australian teenage prostitute's description of the harshness and very real dangers of her work.

> [Y]ou know you can get some really nice guys, I don't know they are just really nice. They seem to care but they really don't I suppose . . . and then you get the mugs, you really do most of the time . . . they get half an hour and they think they own you and they want to maul you and they say would you like this and if you say you don't, then they go ahead and

do it anyway . . . [with one guy] we did the usual, then he started coming down real heavy because he had too much grog and he was smacking me around the face. . . . He wanted to do all sorts of weird things and then he belted me . . . and I went unconscious. He rang the boss and he came and took me to the hospital, but you know that the guy never gets charged with anything. . . . I can't do nothing about these other creeps who come on real heavy. . . . Yeah, we had two girls killed in the other place. They all said suicide and drugs but even the police knew what was going on.

(Wilson and Arnold 1986: 64)

We have seen that prostitution may be associated with initiation into hard drugs which leaves the young girl with a lifelong dependency. Another major risk for teenage prostitutes is that their occupation places them at considerable risk of contracting a sexually transmissible disease. These range from the deadly HIV, through to other non-fatal but potentially serious conditions. Many girls have disturbingly low levels of knowledge about STDs. Some learn from experience that the consequences of these diseases can be infertility or cancer. At a more psychological level, by entering prostitution at an early age, these young women open themselves to subsequent physical and emotional risks. They have little schooling and few interests or skills which could enhance their personal growth. What happens when these girls are 'used up' so that they can no longer ply their trade because of illness, use of drugs, lack of physical stamina, or even pregnancy? Unfortunately they may never have the opportunity to acquire the skills which will enable them to leave what can only be regarded as a dead-end job.

Given that the outlook for teenage prostitutes is bleak, what can be done to reduce prostitution among these young girls? Brown argues forcefully for a shift away from the present juvenile justice system which deals with girls' 'sexual deviance' in a harsh and insensitive way. She claims that the sexual stigmatisation that is the inevitable consequence of contact with this system merely serves to push these girls towards deviant groups and away from the desired goal of behaving in accordance with acceptable cultural norms. Brown recommends that the process of self-denigration which is set in train must be short-circuited by providing appropriate educational opportunities for these young girls, including sex education and education about human relationships, a view supported by Baizerman and his colleagues. Second, she argues that positive role models – drawn from the ranks of teachers, youth workers, correctional officers, among others – are needed to fill the gap left by inadequate parenting. Baizerman also adopts a pragmatic approach which suggests the need to use youth workers on the streets to counsel young prostitutes, as well as the provision of shelters or 'safe houses' where girls can escape from the demands of their pimps and leave the world of prostitution.

Realistically speaking, it is unlikely, particularly in times of economic hardship and high levels of unemployment, that teenage prostitution will cease. If a young girl can earn large sums of money each day, even though she has to share her earnings with her pimp, she is unlikely to settle for a minimum-waged job. Nor are we likely to be able to ensure a happy and fulfilling, trouble-free home life for all our teenage girls. What we can do is to ensure that young girls who are in difficult circumstances have alternatives to prostitution, and that those who wish to escape from prostitution can do so.

Before leaving the topic of teenage prostitution, we should refer to the meagre information about male juvenile prostitution, by which is almost always meant homosexual prostitution. As Wilson and Arnold (1986) point out, there is no legitimising ideology for homosexual prostitution as there is with heterosexual prostitution, which condones the practice while condemning the female prostitute. Furthermore, in Australia, and possibly other Western countries, male prostitution takes place in the context of an anti-homosexual culture which stigmatises homosexuality rather than the practice of prostitution.

The dangers of homosexual spread of HIV/AIDS make the behaviours of these young boys of particular concern to the community. Male prostitutes are likely to be young, unemployed, from a disadvantaged social background, and usually not strictly homosexual. As might be expected, young male prostitutes do not form one homogeneous group. In one study, Allen (1980) classified the young boys into four groups. Full-time professionals constituted the first group, practising their trade in bars or as street hustlers. Very young and usually school dropouts and runaways, these boys adopted a macho posture and were likely to have girlfriends or wives. These young boys, whose experience of the world of prostitution is likely to be transitory, had the lowest status of all the male prostitutes. The second group, also full-time, were the call boys, working through phone contact. Allen likens this group to the female mistress. More attractive and somewhat older and better educated than the street hustlers, they may have a 'permanent' liaison with an older man. The hope of most of these young boys is that they will find a benefactor who will provide long-term financial and emotional support, or even an alternative means of steady employment.

[H]e really looked after me and we did everything. I felt really good

because I didn't have to worry about where I'd sleep or how to get food
. . . he was like a big brother or a father or a mother maybe. I never loved
him or anything like that. . . . But he was really sort of a gentle person
even though he hassled me. . . . Yeah, I think he loved me because it was
more than the fucking. He knew more about me than my mum and dad
ever did.

(Wilson and Arnold 1986: 72)

Another group consisted of part-time prostitutes for whom prostitution is
used as a means of supplementing their income. Usually hustlers, they may
be call boys, or work for a pimp. These boys are often students who need
extra money for a particular purpose. For them, prostitution appears to be a
convenient means to a specific end, and poses few problems of adjustment.
The final group, also part-timers, were part of a 'peer-delinquent culture'
whose purpose was to harass homosexuals. Allen suggests that these boys
may be homosexuals themselves, but their hostile and aggressive behaviour
towards the homosexuals that they pick up is a mechanism for denying their
own sexual orientation.

The similarities between boys and girls engaged in prostitution are
marked. Most full-time male prostitutes were runaways and had low levels
of education. Their family backgrounds are similar to those of their female
peers, with evidence for considerable family discord, violence, lack of love,
and rejection by parents. Like female prostitutes of the same age, these boys
lack a stable, intact family upbringing and most have a high need for love
and affection (Garbarino 1985). Father absence appears to be an important
factor among teenage male prostitutes, but the psychological consequences
of the lack of a male model may be compensated for by the camaraderie that
develops among these boys. Wilson and Arnold add another dimension to
male prostitution, suggesting that for some boys life on the streets provides
the thrills afforded by games of chance. In the case of prostitution, '[t]he
only commodity that these young people really own is themselves and so
they gamble their lives, their bodies, their freedom, and their future often
against all odds for kicks and thrills' (Wilson and Arnold 1986: 75).
Tragically, in this post-AIDS era, the odds are often stacked against these
young boys. And, as with girls, there is the danger that few life skills are
learned. These boys, like their female counterparts, are likely to lead lives
which are severely limited and unrewarding.

While there is no question that some young male prostitutes are
exploited, it is also evident that there are some young boys who use
prostitution to exploit others. This theme of exploitation is one that we
pursue in the next section, although the focus is on heterosexual sexual
relationships.

ADOLESCENT SEX OFFENDERS

Davis and Leitenberg (1987) report that in the United States about 20 per cent of all rapes and 30 to 50 per cent of all cases of child sexual abuse can be attributed to adolescents. Further, approximately 50 per cent of adult sex offenders report that their first sexual offence occurred during their teenage years. Offences range from rape through indecent assault (sexual fondling or touching, usually short of penetration), sexual assault, exhibitionism, voyeurism, to obscene telephone calls. Most adolescent sex offenders are male and are more likely than non-offending males to have had a history of physical (and probably sexual) abuse and to have witnessed family violence (Lewis *et al.* 1981: McCord *et al.* 1962; Van Ness 1984). Burgess *et al.* (1988) report a study of incarcerated serial rapists which revealed that their repetition of sexually aggressive behaviour began at adolescence, with the onset of rape fantasies and behaviours.

In nearly two-thirds of cases of adolescent sex offences, young children are the victims. Almost all are girls, and acquaintances or relatives of the offender (Davis and Leitenberg 1987). Clinical material has suggested several psychological characteristics of adolescent sex offenders, such as feelings of masculine inadequacy, low self-esteem, anger towards women, poor social skills, and atypical erotic fantasies. However, there are often serious methodological flaws in these studies, in particular the failure to use a matched control group of non-sex-offending male teenagers. A study by Blaske and his colleagues (1989) overcomes this criticism by comparing four groups of 13- to 17-year-old boys on measures of individual functioning and family and peer relationships. Included were sex offenders, assault offenders, nonviolent offenders, and non-delinquent boys. Sex offenders reported higher rates of anxiety than the other groups, were less emotionally bonded to peers, felt more estranged in their relationships with others, had poorer communication with their mothers, and were more likely to come from dysfunctional families.

One problem in establishing the characteristics of sex offenders is that the available information refers to those offenders who have been convicted. It is well known that assailants often avoid conviction because of the difficulties associated with proving, beyond reasonable doubt, that they have been guilty of an offence. Compounding the difficulty is the fact that many sexual crimes are unreported because of victims' fear and shame, and the further trauma that physical examination, questioning, and court appearance involves for those who have been raped. The unfortunate and still present tendency for society to 'blame the victim' in cases of rape can make court appearances even more traumatic for the assaulted woman and render conviction of her assailant unlikely unless there is overwhelming evidence against him. Society's readiness to endorse a position of blaming the victim arises from a complex rape mythology. One element is the belief that women with a sexually active history are always willing to consent to sex or that they forfeit their right of choice. Other pervasive beliefs are that women who dress in a so-called provocative way are considered to be 'asking for it', that women enjoy men forcing them to have sex, and that the rules of courtship decree that when a woman says 'no' to sex she means 'yes'.

Myths about rape, together with sexist attitudes and beliefs, provide a framework for justifications of sexual coercion and force. Even if the myths are not completely accepted, elements of victim blame remain, even among the well educated. A recent study (Wallis 1992), surveying community attitudes to child abuse found that about one-quarter of the randomly selected adults believed that, in some cases, blame rested with the child. Men were twice as likely to hold this attitude than women and, although it was more prevalent in blue collar workers, this view of diminished perpetrator responsibility pervaded all social classes and education levels. Hollway's Male Sex Drive discourse (discussed in Chapter 5) describes a social context which legitimises sexual coercion. The belief that masculine biological urges are so strong that they must be satisfied at any cost, together with the corresponding belief that those who do not exhibit such strong sex drives are not 'real men', puts pressures on men to display their sexual prowess and their ability to 'score'. Further, this discourse en-courages the interpretation of male–female encounters as basically sexual, with other options such as friendship or non-sexual intimacy not taken seriously. Young men socialised according to this discourse who find their sexual drives thwarted may feel justified in expressing anger and forcing their partners to engage in unwanted sexual behaviour.

Rape mythology may account for the guilty and shameful feelings characteristic of many rape victims, a topic we will explore in the next section. Not surprisingly, young women feel that the odds are stacked against them in the case of rape. Because of this there is likely to be a high rate of non-reporting, especially of the phenomenon known as date rape. According to various reports (Carlson 1987; Levine and Kanin 1987; Nielsen 1991; O'Keeffe *et al.* 1986; Warshaw 1990), a growing number of young males are forcing their dates to have intercourse or perform other sexual acts against their will, often with the use of physical force. Young women may be loath to report these rapes for fear that their consent to the date is interpreted as consent to the rape. In fact, the very use of the term date rape serves to trivialise the event, inappropriately, making it seem less serious than 'real' rape.

Not surprisingly, those who hold these myths about rape are more likely to engage in victim blame (Blumberg and Lester 1991). Distressingly, these myths are held by both sexes but are more common among young and adult men than among girls and women (Blumberg and Lester 1991). Of course, judges and juries are just as likely to have stereotyped and unsubstantiated beliefs about rape as are other members of the public, providing a further barrier to justice and compassion for rape victims. There has been considerable debate over appropriate law reforms so that the victims are treated with greater fairness and justice in cases of rape. In some countries, a woman's past sexual history is not admissible evidence in rape trials, a reform designed to work against the myth that women 'ask for' rape by their demeanour and sexuality. In this way, the law ensures that it is the perpetrator, not the victim, who is on trial.

As we have argued, the incidence of rape and sexual molestation is much higher than reported, a claim that is supported by studies in various countries. For example, in New Zealand, Gavey (1991) found that 52 per cent of female university students reported that they had experienced some form of sexual victimisation. Twenty-five per cent reported rape or attempted rape, a figure almost identical to that obtained by surveys of college students in the United States. Among high school girls, Klingman and Vicary (1992) reported that 23 per cent had experienced some form of unwanted sexual activity by dates or boyfriends, and that 15 per cent had experienced date rape. Unwanted sexual experiences had occurred for 15 per cent of a large sample of high-schoolers surveyed by Erickson and Rapkin (1991). These included willingly engaging in sexual activity that was later regretted (for example, while under the influence of alcohol), as well as experiences in which the participant was unwilling at the time. Girls were far more likely to have had such experiences than boys, especially those of childhood sexual abuse or rape. Turning the question around from asking respondents about their experiences of being sexually abused, Fromuth *et al.* (1991) obtained information from male college students, via an extensive questionnaire in which items about various sexual activities were embedded, about perpetration of abusive behaviour. Of these young men, 3 per cent reported activity that met the criterion for sexual molestation of a younger child. Most of the victimisation experiences were initiated by the young men, and most involved female victims. Molesters were more likely than non-molesters to endorse rape myths and to have been sexually victimised themselves as children.

Why is rape and sexual coercion so common? Katchadourian (1990) argues that the use of sexual coercion and the various justifications for this unwanted and unsought behaviour appear to be already established among many young men by the time of adolescence. One disturbing clue to young boys' behaviour comes from a study in which 15- and 16-year-olds were asked about their views on the relationships between the sexes, including the phenomenon of rape (Szirom 1988). The girls ranked rape as a highly important topic for them to know more about. For these young women and others like them, rape is a salient issue in their lives, something to fear as they sit alone in a house at night or venture onto the streets after dark – and, increasingly, during the daylight hours. The young boys interviewed by Szirom saw rape as unimportant in their lives because they believed it was unlikely to happen to them. Szirom concluded that, while these young men purported to condemn rape, they did not interpret the pressure for intercourse which they exerted on young women as in any way related to rape. It seems that for young men there is a clear distinction between urging a date to engage in sexual activity which is unwanted and resisted, and the attacks on women described so vividly in the media.

Confirming this confused view of rape, a recent study of Australian youth (Roberts 1992) found that one in three 14-year-old boys surveyed by Brisbane's Domestic Violence Resource Centre believed it was reasonable to rape a girl if she 'led him on'. About 10 per cent thought rape was acceptable if 'they had dated a long time' or if 'the girl was stoned or drunk', while 14 per cent believed that a girl who had had intercourse with other boys was a permissible rape target. Twenty-three per cent were similarly inclined if the girl 'says she is going to have sex with him then changes her mind'. Many of these young boys believed that a girl meant yes when she said no to sex, using spurious justifications for their beliefs such as 'she was smiling when she said it'.

Among the sample of 16-year-old boys from all social classes interviewed by the authors (Moore and Rosenthal 1992b), there was clear evidence of exploitative views about sexual relationships as well as aggression towards girls who were not prepared to be sexually accommodating. Three examples follow.

If you wanted to have sex and your partner did not, would you try to persuade them to have sex? How? Yes mate. Root the fucking bitch in the fucking arse.

Sure, give her a stern talking to.

Sure mate, shove it in.

Disturbingly, young girls who were perceived to be sexually liberated, in that they engaged in the same activities as their male peers, were the frequent targets of aggressive attitudes on the part of these same young men. They were regarded as fair game for exploitation or even rape. Many boys who might not consider rape or physical force were not averse to strong persuasion in order to get their own way sexually. A variety of techniques such as shaming, teasing, trickery, and perseverance were considered appropriate.

> *If you wanted to have sex and your partner didn't, would you try to persuade them to have sex?* Yes, I would try. I would touch them and stare at them.

> What I would do is carry on for a little bit by saying 'come on, come on, are you sure?', and I would tease them and shit like that . . . and after about half an hour or so, and they still say no, I would let up. I would say 'don't worry, give me a blow job or a hand job instead'.

> Yes, I would try to convince her. In a short term relationship, you would tell her she is not normal, and everyone else is doing it.

> I would try to persuade her, maybe with a bit of force. I wouldn't rape the girl, but kiss her and so on, touch her vagina, her bosoms, try to stimulate her, and if she didn't want to, I would give up and just talk to her and see what is wrong.

> Yes, probably try to get her drunk and talk her into it.

Many young men saw sexual persuasion as part of the game of male–female interaction and failed to recognise that their persistent attempts at sexual conquest could be regarded as more than gentle seduction. The following two example answers to the question about sexual persuasion illustrate this point.

> Most definitely, it is all part of the game. I would say 'come on, come on, it's not that big.' You have to say those things to virgins because they are scared.

> Morally, I would say no, but really I would say yes. It's like yes and no. I would just keep on with what we were doing, and give her a bit of time.

In all, over two-thirds of the teenage boys interviewed said they would try to convince a reluctant female partner to have sex. They appeared to regard their partner's reticence as a weak barrier to intercourse, one which it was part of the male role to overcome. While seduction is very different to rape, there is some sense of a continuum in the boys' methods of achieving their sexual goals – methods which ranged from seemingly harmless persistence and titillation through to the clearly unacceptable techniques of derogation and force. Our data unfortunately do not address the issue of whether these young women accepted this male behaviour although the boys themselves, not surprisingly, seemed to believe that girls both expect and encourage it.

Previously discussed studies of perceived sexual victimisation suggest otherwise.

The message is clear that we need to resocialise many young men to think differently about sex, as shared experience rather than exploitation. Young women, too, need assistance in learning to express their sexual needs – whether this be for different forms of sexual activity or no sex at all – and in understanding the social forces which often place them in the role of sexual victim. There are programmes which have been effective in other areas and which could be adapted to resocialising teenagers' views of sex. These include work with families and school populations to reduce sex role stereotyping and assertion training for women and children, such as the protective behaviours programme in which children learn the difference between 'good' touching and 'bad' touching. More directly, groups which encourage men who are perpetrators of violence towards women or sexual abusers to relearn appropriate sexual relationship skills and to handle their violence more effectively are being piloted in a number of centres.

VICTIMS

The high attractiveness of youth, coupled with their low power and status (especially that of young girls) targets them as frequent victims of sexual violence and abuse. While we have seen that the prevalence rate is almost impossible to ascertain due to under-reporting and different reporting laws across different countries (and states or regions within countries), there is no doubt that sexual victimisation of youth, both by peers and adults, is a widespread social problem. Data from the American Humane Association indicate that there are about ten times more female victims than males, although it is believed that sexual assaults against men are more likely to go unreported (Garbarino 1985). Men's reluctance to report is undoubtedly related to both the stigma associated with male-to-male sexual contact and the high degree of shame for men in admitting victimisation. There is evidence that most sexual molestation is committed by someone known to the victim and, in fact, many of these cases involve incest, or rape by a known and trusted adult. Meiselman (1978) reports that cases of father–daughter sexual abuse constitute more than 70 per cent of such crimes.

Incest is often much harder to deal with than sexual abuse by a stranger outside the home. The following quote in a letter to her mother from a survivor of teenage incest poignantly illustrates the breach of trust experienced by this young woman and her feelings of self-blame.

It was in the context of a loving, trusting relationship. My father was somebody who represented right and wrong to me, which is why it was so difficult to understand what was happening to me at that age. One grows up with the idea that male sexuality, male passion, is somehow a woman's fault, something you're responsible for. As a little girl, I can remember being taught not to sit in a certain way, not to stand in certain ways – and it's very complicated to learn all those things, because you're supposed to be sexy and attractive to men; at the same time, you're not supposed to lead them on, you're supposed to know what the balance is. Of course, I now realise that men must take responsibility for their own sexual feelings. . . . One of the things I resent most is how it damaged my relationship with my mother. It put such a barrier between us.

(Payne 1983: 59)

Abuse by a stranger involves one incident; incest usually involves many incidents over a long period of time, and is shrouded in secrecy. Victims feel they have no one to turn to and fear that they may not be believed – a fear that is often justified. They believe that they will cause family break-up or be rejected by other family members. In the case of sexual abuse by a parent, victims may feel betrayed by their non-abusing parent, who may be perceived to be powerless as a protector, or even as colluding in the abuse.

> I have to remind myself that it is not I
> Who brings this pain into our lives.
> (From a poem by a teenage incest survivor, Payne 1983: 59)

While abuse by a stranger is traumatic, it is a situation with which people close to the victim are more likely to empathise and offer support than in incest cases. Stranger sexual abuse is also a situation in which the victim can readily interpret the perpetrator as evil and hated – therefore different from normal people. This interpretation is far more difficult, and may be impossible, when the perpetrator is a family member, with long-term consequences for psychological adjustment. In such cases the issue of who can be trusted in life is likely to loom large.

Research studies and case material examining the effects of sexual abuse on psychological functioning suggest that, together with violent stranger rapes, long-term incest beginning in childhood has the most damaging effects (Browne and Finkelhor 1986; Mackey *et al.* 1991). The clinical literature suggests that sexual abuse in childhood is associated with both negative short-term outcomes such as guilt and anxiety, and longer-term effects including drug and alcohol abuse, somatic problems, depression and suicide attempts (Browne and Finkelhor 1986). Sexual maladjustment in adulthood has been shown to result from sexual abuse in childhood and adolescence, with these young women more likely to begin sex at a younger age, to be promiscuous, to enter prostitution, or to suffer sexual dysfunction

(Courtois 1979; Fromuth 1986; Mackay *et al.* 1991; McCabe 1989; Polit *et al.* 1990; Runtz and Briere 1986; Silbert and Pines 1981).

Male and female victims of both family and stranger rape may experience some or all of the symptoms of post-traumatic stress disorder (Mezey and King 1989; Wolfe *et al.* 1989). These include a persistent reliving of the traumatic event, for example through intrusive thoughts or distressing dreams, symptoms of increased arousal such as sleeplessness and concentration difficulties, and the desire to avoid all stimuli associated with the traumatic event. Depression, fear, anxiety, and restlessness may also be present, or the victim may mask symptoms with a calm, controlled facade but experience distressing symptomatology at a later time (Carson *et al.* 1988). Rape crisis centres have in recent years played an important role in providing support and counselling for rape victims, helping them to work through the complex emotions which the trauma of rape elicits. Such centres also help victims to face the medical and court procedures necessary if they report the crime.

As well as its short-term effects, the experiences of rape and sexual abuse can have long-term effects on personality and coping styles. Murphy *et al.* (1988) compared the psychological profiles of rape victims with matched non-victims. Those who had experienced rape showed lower levels of self-esteem, a greater incidence of relationship problems, poorer work satisfaction and overall happiness, and less hope for the future, up to two years after the rape had occurred. Orr and Downes (1985) also found that sexually assaulted teenagers had poor self-esteem, serious problems with family relationships and sexual attitudes, and feelings of inability to master the external environment. Compared to non-sexually abused adolescent patients from a general adolescent clinic, sexually abused youths had significantly more problems with vocational/educational goals, showed evidence of greater psychopathology, and difficulty in their ability to master the environment. The authors conclude that the self-concept problems identified by these sexually abused youths are similar to those reported by women seeking psychiatric care long after their childhood sexual abuse occurred, and share some of the features reported among physically abused adolescents.

Briere (1988) points out that Freud's description of the hysterical personality overlaps with symptomatology often exhibited by incest survivors but that the explanation of hysteroid symptoms within an Oedipal conflict framework does not ring true in the light of what is now known about the incidence of child sexual molestation. Clients who display so-called hysterical symptoms such as inappropriate coquettishness and high excitability and who also report sexual abuse are likely to have their reports discounted by traditional psychoanalysts, who may view such reports as

Oedipal fantasies. Successful psychotherapy with sexual abuse survivors demands a high level of respect and support for the client's abuse disclosures, and an understanding of the defences and survival mechanisms displayed during the course of therapy. The traditional psychoanalytic notions need to be reconsidered with such clients.

Further, Briere also notes that the diagnosis of Borderline Personality Disorder is commonly attached to individuals who present with severe post-sexual abuse trauma in psychiatric settings. DSM III-R describes this disorder as a chronic disturbance in which there is 'a pervasive pattern of instability of self-image, interpersonal relationship, and mood, beginning by early adulthood and present in a variety of contexts' (American Psychiatric Association 1987: 346). Symptoms can include impulsiveness, unstable relationships, inappropriate intense anger, identity and self-image disturbance, mood instability, suicide or self-mutilation threats or behaviours, and feelings of emptiness and abandonment. Such a pattern of symptoms closely approximates the problems of adults and adolescents who have experienced severe or prolonged sexual abuse in childhood.

Psychiatry does not explain this disorder in terms of sexual abuse but, rather, as resulting from disturbed mother–child relationships in infancy due to 'inadequate' mothering and difficulties in the separation–individuation period of childhood. Briere offers the perspective that a significant proportion of borderline personality disorders arise from early and extended childhood sexual victimisation, usually accompanied by emotional maltreatment. If the treatment of incest survivors is based on inappropriate symptom interpretation, as suggested by writers such as Briere (1988) and Courtois (1979), then such survivors may find themselves further traumatised by the mental health system. As in the case of hysterical symptoms, the aetiology of borderline personality disorders (and their very classification in a terminology which implies inadequacy born of individual weakness) needs to be reconsidered in the light of what is now known about the aftermath of childhood sexual abuse.

Childhood and adolescent rape and sexual abuse are common and their effects devastating and often long-lasting. Their consequences are costly for the community in terms of the health, social adjustment, and relationship quality and stability of its members. There is both an economic and humanitarian argument for increasing the meagre resources currently being devoted to victims of sexual violence and the training of those who work with them.

10 Problems and limitations in studying adolescent sexuality

Conducting research about human behaviour is fraught with difficulties, as any social scientist will tell you. How can we tell what people are thinking? Do we know ourselves the motives for our own behaviour? Are we prepared to share with social scientists the details of our private lives? Are those of us who will divulge such information different in important ways from those who will not, so that generalisations to others are unwarranted? The whole issue of generalisation is a complex one – to what extent can we draw conclusions about the human condition from the experience of one person? Or ten? Or one million? Cohort and cultural differences need to be taken into account. Do behaviour patterns change markedly from generation to generation, or differ so much between cultures (or even between individuals) that general statements are impossible? How do we *measure* interesting human behaviours and characteristics, for example kindness, or sexiness? In human affairs, what are causes and what are effects? For example, if a relationship is found between perceived attractiveness and 'sexual success', can we conclude that better-looking people will attract more sexual partners? Alternatively, does previous sexual experience and 'success' confer on individuals a belief about their own heightened attractiveness which is communicated and responded to by others?

All of the problems inherent in the study of human behaviour are writ large in research on sexuality. The right to privacy in this area is jealously guarded and the topic is one which touches on intense emotions. Adolescents, often confused about their sexuality and trying to walk the fine line between peer group bravado and adult double standards, could be forgiven for telling researchers to mind their own business. Some do so directly through non-involvement or, occasionally, through sabotaging the research. Others exaggerate or under-represent when reporting their sexual behaviours and attitudes. Some are not really sure what they do or what they think – perhaps engaging in denial, perhaps not having the biological terminology or the conceptual skills to express what they do, think and feel.

In the case of behaviours less emotive or private than sex, social scientists can actually *watch* what people do as well as ask them, so that richer, more valid data can be collected. Such an option is usually not an ethical possibility for the direct study of teenage sexual behaviour, although studies of courting and sexual preliminaries could presumably use direct observation methods. In fact, most data about adolescent sexuality have been collected via self-report methodologies. In the following sections of this chapter we review the techniques and research designs used in studies of adolescent sexuality, their strengths, limitations and problems of implementation.

TECHNIQUES FOR STUDYING SEXUALITY

Self-report measures

In most research exploring adolescent sexual attitudes and behaviours (both in the narrow sense of intercourse-related situations and the broad sense of the social context surrounding sex), information is collected via self-reports. For certain kinds of research questions these are, by definition, the only measures we can use. Examples are the measurement of sexual and contraceptive knowledge, or sexual beliefs and attitudes. For these aspects of sexuality there are no clear objective checks on validity (such as observation of behaviours) because behaviours do not always reflect knowledge, attitudes or beliefs. Behaviours differ from attitudes in that they are objective and observable. In principle, the measurement of behaviours through self-report can be checked through appropriate observation. In practice, such independent corroboration against a 'gold standard' of behaviour is rarely, if ever, possible for studies of human sexuality, as we see in a later section. Self-reports of both beliefs and behaviours can be shown to vary in the success with which they provide 'useful' – that is, valid and reliable – data. The following problems are common to all self-reports, but may be particularly problematic in research on sexuality.

Conscious and unconscious distortion of responses

Questionnaire respondents may decline to reveal their beliefs to researchers, substituting, for example, random responses or a set of responses which fulfil social desirability criteria. In sex research such distortions are more likely to occur if the respondent feels pressured into completing the questionnaire or if strict privacy, confidentiality, and anonymity have not been guaranteed by the researcher. It is probably not just because of ethical constraints that most studies of sexuality use only volunteer respondents. The common belief that sex is private is likely to ensure a high proportion of response distortion among those who feel compelled to answer questions about their sexual beliefs in situations where their rights are not protected.

An example of the delicacy of this matter comes from a study conducted by the authors of this book. Young people from a variety of ethnic backgrounds were interviewed about their attitudes toward male–female relationships, sexual initiation, and other aspects of sexuality. Care had been taken to ensure that all participants were genuine volunteers; confidentiality and anonymity had been stressed, and trained peer interviewers were alert to their role of putting respondents at ease. Some interviews were conducted in a school situation, with a private office set aside for the purpose. One interview, proceeding as planned, was interrupted by the school principal walking in and looking for something in the room. This disruption unnerved the interviewee, who had previously indicated a permissive attitude to sex and voiced his approval of 'one-night-stands'. Though the interview continued after the principal had left, the participant's responses were now of the following nature:

What do you think about sex before marriage? Even though you might sometimes be forced into it, you shouldn't do it.

Does the experience of having a Greek background make a difference to any of the issues we have talked about? Probably yes, because as Greeks we have our culture, and I have always followed what the elders say, what they say through religion, or tradition, or whatever. We are more restricted.

We have no way of knowing whether these responses reflect the participant's true beliefs or not. It is quite possible that his trust in the guarantees given by the experimenters were shaken by the principal's interruption, leading to a set of answers which were not valid.

Unconscious distortion of responses is also possible, especially in the emotionally charged area of sex. In our desire to represent ourselves positively in our own, as well as others', eyes, we often 'forget', rationalise, or interpret our attitudes and behaviours in the best possible light. A woman who basically disapproves of casual sex may re-interpret a casual encounter in an unrealistically romantic light. A man may justify a violent rape by telling himself 'She was asking for it'.

The skill of the question-writer can reduce – though probably never eliminate – conscious and unconscious distortion through questions which do not imply value judgments or a socially desirable response. For example, responses to items such as the following question may reflect a high level of tolerance of AIDS sufferers in the community.

I think AIDS sufferers should have the same rights to medical care as those with any other life-threatening disease.

Strongly Agree   Agree   Not Sure   Disagree   Strongly Disagree

However, more sensitive items may reveal less positive attitudes, for example:

Given that each charity was equally needy, and you wished to make a donation of $1000 to one of the following charities for improvement in medical care, which would you choose?

Funds for (a) cancer sufferers (b) stroke victims (c) those severely injured in car accidents (d) AIDS sufferers

Various techniques can be built into self-report measures to reduce the effects of conscious and unconscious distortions. These include lie scales, forced-choice items to control for social desirability, ranking techniques, and the inclusion of a range of different kinds of measures of the same variable, for example, the use of both questionnaires and interviews to assess attitudes. Probably the best methods involve creating a secure environment for the research participant, so that he or she can express views, confident that they will be treated with respect. Techniques which use only volunteers, respect privacy, and if possible involve the respondents or their reference groups in the research design are most likely to fit these criteria.

Memory

Consider the following questions.
How many times have you had intercourse in the last six months?
Rate each of your last six occurrences of sexual intercourse on a five-point scale ranging from 'not at all enjoyable' to 'extremely enjoyable'.

Time 1 (most recent) 1	2	3	4	5
Time 2 1	2	3	4	5
Time 3 1	2	3	4	5
Time 4 1	2	3	4	5
Time 5 1	2	3	4	5
Time 6 1	2	3	4	5

How easy (or difficult) was that exercise? Catania *et al.* (1990) make the point as, we hope, does the previous exercise, that many studies of sexual behaviour, in asking the respondent about past sexual experiences, place great reliance on accurate memory of these events. They comment that

Although many respondents report being able to remember certain sexual milestones (e.g., their first coital experience) and negative sexual experiences (e.g., the time mother caught you making love in the living room with your prom date), much of a person's sexual experience may begin to blur with time.

(Catania *et al.* 1990: 345)

Forgetting may be less of an issue for the adolescent who has had few sexual experiences or who has developed a pattern of regular, monogamous experiences. More liable to memory distortions are the behaviours of those with many sexual partners or those who have been sexually active for a longer time. Highly charged emotional events can also be remembered incorrectly. Distortions may include the exaggeration of positive or negative affect, or the repression of disturbing or 'taboo' activities, such as incest experiences.

We cannot stand outside the bedroom door, with questionnaires poised, to ensure the vivid recall of our research participants' recent sexual experiences. In a study of sexually active young people's intentions to use condoms and their subsequent actual condom use, we tried to do the next best thing (Boldero *et al.* 1992). We asked participants to state their intentions about condom use in a first questionnaire, then complete a second questionnaire about actual use within 24 hours of their next sexual encounter. In this way we hoped to reduce the distorting effects of memory concerning reasons for using or not using condoms during the second encounter. Another technique for controlling for memory would be to ask adolescents to keep either structured or informal journals of their sexual activities. Such strategies improve recall but rely heavily on the honesty and commitment of the research participants. They also potentially change the behaviour being studied, as respondents are asked to be more introspective and deliberate about their actions.

Unreliable measures

Although attitudes and beliefs may alter over time, we expect some stability within a certain time-frame. This, then, requires the use of measures which do not fluctuate randomly. Test–retest reliability checks can assess the stability of questionnaire scales, such as those which measure approval of premarital sex or community acceptance of homosexuality. We can tap the stability of people's estimates of their own behaviour by, for example, giving two identical questionnaires, one week apart, asking them to report on the number of sexual partners they had in the six months from January to June. Surprisingly, few studies of sexual behaviour include this check

(Catania *et al.* 1990). Some that do have shown significant variability in the reporting of frequency and occurrence of particular sexual behaviours (e.g., Rodgers 1982; Saltzman *et al.* 1987).

Inadequate definition of the construct under consideration

The extent to which questionnaires can provide valid information about behaviour and the mechanisms underlying behaviour depends on the skill of the question-writer to include items which adequately sample the universe of content which make up these behaviours or constructs. For example, a test of knowledge of contraception needs to include items about a range of different kinds of contraception. Depending on the purpose of such a test, it might tap such issues as the knowledge that various techniques exist, the situations and types of people for which they are most suited, how to use them, and how they work. The delineation of what constitutes adequate coverage of content is not always easy, depending on the researchers' own insights into the construct in question. In the knowledge of contraception example, a researcher may not have considered that information about how to obtain various contraceptive devices is as important as knowing that they exist, at least in relation to probable use.

In the area of attitudes, a questionnaire designed to measure attitudes to condoms may reflect population trends toward largely negative attitudes if most items are slanted toward the hassles and disadvantages of condoms. Inclusion of items about their erotic and pleasurable potential is likely to change the picture markedly (Chapman *et al.* 1990).

Another important issue in relation to validity arises from the format of the questionnaire used. In current research, survey measures are usually framed in multichoice or true/false formats. While easy to score, these can have limitations in the kind of content assessed. Although less frequently used open-ended techniques such as 'complete the story' or 'draw your understanding of . . . ' are sometimes difficult to interpret, they can produce a richness of data which extends our knowledge of the construct being studied. Use of a wide range of data collecting techniques is important for the researcher who wishes to explore behaviour and attitudes from as many aspects as possible. Valid conclusions depend on valid measuring instruments and this means instruments which cover all relevant aspects of the construct in question.

Inappropriately worded questions

Problems in the wording of questions contribute to poor reliability and validity. Questions containing ambiguities and double negatives produce uninterpretable answers. For example, the answer 'no' to the question, 'Has sex education influenced your attitude to using condoms?' could mean that the person had not experienced sex education, that sex education had no effect because he/she was already committed to a way of thinking about condoms, or that it had no effect because of the quality of the education. 'Leading' questions (When were you last unfaithful to your partner?) also produce uninterpretable responses.

In relation to wording, an important issue in sex research is to get the terminology right. Some people will not understand the formal terminology of sodomy, fellatio, cunnilingus, and pederasty. However, while less specific terminology may not offend sensibilities, it may be interpreted differently by different individuals. For example, in the question 'How many sexual encounters have you had in the last six months?', 'sexual encounter' can imply a range of activities varying from flirtation to intercourse. Use of the sexual vernacular can mean that respondents understand the question, but it can be a tricky business for researchers to work out what the current vernacular is. Changes are rapid in the sexual domain and regional and subcultural variations frequently occur. For example, words such as 'spunk', 'cum', and 'sprog' – slang words which are used to denote semen – are not universally recognised as such, but among some groups would be understood more readily than the word 'semen' itself. Even a word like 'slut', common in Australia and Great Britain, is out of favour in the United States, according to one informant. Also, while use of sexual jargon in questionnaires may be acceptable to some teenagers, it may offend others. At a practical level, those who give permission for researchers to study adolescents (parents, school principals, ethics committees, and the adolescents themselves) are often loath to approve studies in which questions are couched in the vernacular. These groups are more likely to find formal sexual terminology acceptable despite the potential for problems of comprehension.

Differences across presentation mode

Questionnaires may be self-administered, such as occurs with mail-out surveys or group testing, or may be administered by a trained interviewer, either over the telephone or in a face-to-face situation. Self-administered questionnaires enhance privacy under appropriate conditions, are often less threatening to the respondent, and are certainly a less expensive way to collect data. They are limited in usefulness, however, by the respondent's reading ability, level of education, motivation to complete, and the researcher's skill in employing questions and terminology which suit the whole range of the population to be tested. For example, a commonly used data collection method is to administer a questionnaire to a class or lecture group of adolescents or young adults. If the researcher's interest is in sexual behaviour and condom use, very few questions are needed for the virgins or the sexually inexperienced in the sample. However it is ethically inappropriate to give out separate surveys to virgins and nonvirgins, or even to draw attention to one group by a questionnaire which takes nonvirgins a longer time to complete. While this would be less of a problem using mail-outs, the need for one set of questions for virgins and nonvirgins alike could pose problems. Virgin respondents may feel offended and alienated by the sexual detail required for questions which are 'not applicable' to them. One way of overcoming this difficulty is in the use of individual computers which are programmemed to 'lead' respondents through an appropriate set of questions, depending on their responses.

Catania *et al.* (1990) suggest that telephone interviews are a preferred mode for the collection of highly sensitive information, such as sexual data. People may be less embarrassed about revealing themselves in this relatively anonymous manner, and the interviewer has the opportunity to tailor questions to the respondent's answers, as well as give encouragement and verbal rewards for completing. Fears that the contacts will be misinterpreted as obscene phone calls can be overcome to some extent by advance letters or other mechanisms which give the respondent the opportunity to check the caller's credentials. Contrasting telephone surveys and face-to-face interviews of sexual behaviour, Czaja (1987–8) found that respondents were more likely to admit to less traditional sexual behaviours over the telephone, although there were no group differences in responses to some intimate questions, such as 'How many times per week do you have sexual intercourse?'. Locander *et al.* (1976) also concluded from their study that telephone interviewees were more likely to report socially undesirable behaviours than those interviewed face-to-face. One problem with telephone interviewing is that certain groups are under-represented by this methodology. Some of these groups, for example homeless youth, transients, and IV drug users, are very important to access when studying sexual behaviour, as they represent at-risk populations with respect to sexually transmissible diseases, unplanned pregnancies, and health care generally.

Face-to-face interviews allow for explanation of problem questions, probing, and the clarification of unclear responses. If a comfortable rapport develops between interviewer and interviewee, then respondents may be more honest and forthcoming. The potential exists for more reliable data to be accessed and, especially in the case of open-ended interviews, the possibility of a rich and detailed data set emerges. Self-presentation bias may be greater, however, as there is less sense of anonymity than in the case of a self-administered questionnaire. The personal characteristics and skills of the interviewer will be important factors here. Research suggests that perceived similarity between interviewee and interviewer increases rapport, with certain personal characteristics of the interviewer, such as age and style of dress, also influencing the degree of trust felt by the respondent. Chitwood (1988) examined the responses of IV drug users on sexual behaviour questions as a function of the gender match between interviewer and interviewee. Respondents were more likely to report some specific sexual behaviours to same-sexed than to opposite-sexed interviewers. These differences did not occur for the reporting of 'traditional' vaginal intercourse and were more frequent for anal sexual activities.

Alder and Sandor (1989) argue for the advantages of trained peer interviewers when researching adolescent behaviour and attitudes. In their study of homeless youths and violence, they found that trained peers were able to gain access to difficult-to-contact groups of young people, and experienced high levels of rapport with their interviewees. The use of peer interviewers for research in adolescent sexuality may increase respondent comfort and confidence in the interview process, thereby improving the likelihood of reliable data. But these inexperienced interviewers are less likely than professionals to have the important skills of question presentation and clarification, listening, rewording, probing, using appropriate non-verbal behaviours, and resisting the expression of value judgments. Careful training in these techniques is important if maximum value is to be obtained from peer interview methodology (Moore and Rosenthal 1992b).

Variations on self-report techniques

There are two main variations used by researchers. The first is to use a multi-informant strategy. Asking sexual partners or friends of the same sex to corroborate answers given by individuals being studied can provide added insight. For example, in many studies adolescents are asked about their peer group attitudes to sexual issues. Only rarely is the accuracy of these perceptions assessed by asking the peers themselves. Similarly, asking one marriage partner about frequency of sexual intercourse may yield different answers from a study in which both partners are asked. The differences between individuals' perceptions of the same event provide enlightening data about the meaning of that event as well as enabling reliability checks for accuracy.

In the second, projective questionnaires and exercises are employed. These are techniques which draw conclusions about individuals' experiences, emotions, beliefs and attitudes on the basis of their responses to ambiguous stimuli. These vary in their degree of 'projectiveness', so that some such techniques present only lightly disguised scenarios for the subject to interpret (for example, 'what do people your age think about sex before marriage?') to highly disguised, extremely ambiguous stimuli such as the Rorschach Ink Blot test. Can we assume that responses are true projections of the person's motives and/or future behaviours? The 'trade-off' for possible loss of validity with these techniques is that they can provide more sensitive material. They allow respondents to let down their guard about topics which may be embarrassing for them to address directly or about which they may not have conscious insights concerning their own motives.

Another interesting possibility with these methods is that they can be used in a variety of research designs. Groups of respondents can be asked to interpret hypothetical situations which vary on a detail of research interest, such as whether the protagonist is a man or a woman. For example, adolescents could be presented with a scenario which involves a sexual situation in which one of the partners insisted on condom use. In one group, teenagers could be asked to make judgments about the characters when the young woman insisted on condom use. In a second group, the scenario could be one in which a young man was the insistent partner. Differences in judgments could be assessed, to evaluate the hunch that adolescents perceive it as less appropriate for young women to take sexual initiative or responsibility.

Observations and field research

Since the dawn of time, human beings have observed each other's behaviour and tried to figure out why people behave as they do. This seems particularly true in the field of sexual mores. Watching the courting rituals of others can be a source of fascination, as anyone who goes walking in a park on a fine spring day will be aware. In social research, observations can be highly structured or open-ended (as in field research where the researcher immerses himself or herself in the situational context, trying to absorb the atmosphere). An example of the former type of research in the sexuality area would be the carefully recorded observations of intercourse behaviour by Masters and Johnson (1966), achieved through various mechanical recording devices together with the use of trained observers watching for particular behaviours. Such direct observation of actual sexual behaviour is, not surprisingly, rare. An example of field research could involve researchers attending a disco or other adolescent social meeting place, and taking notes on behaviour which may shed light on sexual mores such as conversations overheard or approaches of men to women (and women to men). Anne Campbell (1992) became a participant observer in a girls' gang in New York. From this perspective, she was able to gain inside information on female adolescent identity formation, expectations about gender roles, and beliefs and attitudes about sexuality.

Observation and field research can provide rich descriptive data which enable interesting hypotheses to be generated. An insightful, creative observer can make sense out of data which to another person may appear as a mass of unrelated happenings. Of course problems can arise from over-interpretation, so that the trained observer must be careful to distinguish between what is seen (for example, waving of hands and body), and how it is interpreted (for example, as a strange sexual ritual, or responding to an ice cube down the back, or a common adolescent style of dancing). Unless particular behaviours are targeted and carefully defined before observation begins, it may be difficult for observers to reach agreement about what has been seen. On the other hand, such careful delineation of the target behaviours may place blinkers on what is observed and limit the creative observer, who is then 'unable to see the wood for the trees'.

Other problems with observation and field research include ethical issues such as whether it is appropriate to collect data on people without telling them. If you do tell them, will it change what they do? Moreover, an observer's very presence may change the behaviour under observation, as any adult who has ever walked into a room where three or four adolescent girls are talking will verify. Ethical issues arise for participant observers, who observe 'undercover' by becoming group members. These observers may be asked to take part in activities which are dangerous, harmful to others, exploitative, or against their moral code. The potential for problems of this nature is immense in the sexuality area.

Direct observation of adolescents' intimate sexual behaviour is unlikely to be an ethical possibility but some observation of activities such as courting, dating and flirting is possible yet rarely attempted. This material could provide useful insights into adolescent sexuality over and above those obtained from self-report measures.

Physiological measures

Studies of adolescent growth, development and puberty have used these measures and researchers have attempted to link physiological variables, such as hormone levels, to behaviours such as age of initiation of coitus. Physiological measures of pubertal status are not always used because of the difficulties of obtaining these data and measures of pubertal status are often approximated by self-report indices. Few, if any, studies of adolescent sexuality have attempted to relate physiological measures of arousal to behaviours. In one study of adult sexuality, arousal was measured in a number of experimental conditions (types of fantasy and erotic films) through the use of penile plethysmographs as well as with self-report techniques (Smith and Over 1987, 1988).

Physiological measures have the potential to provide accurate and objective indicators of some aspects of sexuality. Their use raises ethical problems in that they often require the subject to be touched by the researcher, to undress, or to experience discomfort or invasion of privacy. These are particularly sensitive issues when the subject is under age and there is some question about whether participation is voluntary and involves truly informed consent. Physiological measures can also presume a reductionist approach to the topic being researched and should probably not be used without corresponding measures of the respondent's subjective experience. However, there is a great deal of potential for the creative investigator to use such measures to supplement and broaden the scope of research in adolescent sexuality. An example could be the measurement of heart-rate reactivity during the course of an assertion training programme to help young people broach difficult sexual topics, such as asking about past sexual history or asking that a condom be used during intercourse. The extent to which anxiety about such assertive behaviours is reduced by the programme could be monitored, as could the stresses associated with different types of sexual assertiveness.

TYPES OF STUDIES

Surveys and correlational studies

These studies involve collecting data from groups of individuals and describing or comparing the groups on the variables of interest. In surveys, the data are always of the self-report type; in correlational studies, self-report or other types of measures may be used. In surveys the variables of interest have not been subjected to experimental manipulation. Their variation across the population is a function of forces beyond the control of the researcher, such as genetic differences or patterns of child-rearing, or socioeconomic status. This has implications for the kinds of conclusions which can be drawn from these studies. Correlational studies enable us to describe and compare groups on particular variables (for example, comparison of early and late maturers on dating behaviour) and to measure relationships between variables (for example, between perceived attractiveness and number of sexual or dating partners). However, the documentation of relationships or group differences does not imply that the relationships are causal, or that the differences result from the characteristics selected to define the comparison groups.

In the example about perceived attractiveness and dating, as we have noted earlier, a relationship between these two variables could mean that the more attractive you think you are, the more likely you are to have dates, because of your air of self-confidence. Or it could mean that perceptions of attractiveness are relatively accurate and that more attractive people get more dates. Or attractiveness and dating success could be linked through their relationship to a third variable, such as physical maturity. Those adolescents who are more physically mature may be more interested in dating (and thus have more dates) and may also be perceived as more attractive because of their physical maturity. To establish a causal relationship between dating frequency and attractiveness would require an *experimental* design (q.v.) in which random assignment to comparison groups was possible and the experimenter could manipulate one of the variables (e.g. attractiveness via clothing or make-up), then measure the effect of the manipulated (independent) variable on the other (dependent) variable, namely dating.

In the same way, group differences established in surveys, such as differences between African-American and Caucasian-American adolescents' sexual behaviours, cannot be attributed to race *per se*. These adolescents may differ on many other variables aside from colour, such as parental and peer attitudes to sexual behaviour, social advantages or extent of non-sexual opportunities for satisfaction and achievement.

Finally, in studies of this type, if we wish to feel confident that the conclusions we reach (for example, claims about the different sexual attitudes of men and women) are typical of all men and women, we would need to sample extremely large numbers and many different groups. For the most part, generalisations must be circumspect. Sample size and composition are important factors in assessing the reliability of data collected in surveys and correlational studies.

Experiments

Unlike surveys, experimental research attempts to establish causality. This research methodology is designed to tease out the effects of experimenter-controlled variations of a particular characteristic (the independent variable) on a characteristic of interest (the dependent variable). Researchers must arrange conditions so that comparison groups are set up which do not differ in any systematic way. Of course, this is difficult to achieve. The preferred strategy is to randomly select participants and allocate them to comparison groups, and to use large groups so that the possibility of chance variations between them are minimised.

For example, we may wish to evaluate the effects of various intervention strategies on attitudes to condoms. A group of, say, 300 18-year-olds could be randomly assigned to three groups. One group could listen to a presentation on the erotic possibilities of condoms, another could be presented with material about the dangers of not using them, and a third, 'control', group could be presented with some sexual material unrelated to condom use. This last group would enable us to assess the effectiveness of both interventions. Attitudes to condoms might be assessed by a self-report inventory after the presentations. Any attitudinal differences between the groups could be attributed to the differences between the interventions, all other things being equal. Of course, 'all other things being equal' is the key phrase here. A well-controlled experiment requires that the groups are given identical treatment in every way except for the variations on the independent variable. If one group has an interesting presenter and another has a boring one, then differences in attitudes at the end of the study may be due to presenter personality, not type of intervention. Presenter personality needs to be controlled, perhaps by using the same presenter each time. The success of an experimental design in producing reliable data depends on the inclusion of control features such as this.

Another issue which must be considered in this experiment is whether the groups were originally equivalent in condom attitudes, that is, whether random sampling was successful. With large groups, this is often assumed on statistical grounds. However, it is possible to check this assumption with a pre-test of condom attitudes. Using a pre-test gives the researcher the opportunity to statistically control for pre-existing attitudinal differences. On the negative side, it may sensitise the participants to the purpose of the study, and influence how they respond to the treatment. Full discussion of the advantages and disadvantages of various types of experimental design can be found in Campbell and Stanley (1966).

The major problems with experimental designs in sexuality research are that, first, asking participants to exhibit some behaviour in a laboratory setting may change the nature of that behaviour. For example, the study of sexual arousal in a laboratory setting may produce results which do not align with what happens in real life. Second, as with surveys, people who volunteer for experimental studies of sexual behaviour may be different, in terms of the characteristics being measured, from those who do not volunteer. Third, there are ethical problems about asking or requiring individuals to participate in any research. The manipulations of participants that are part and parcel of the experimental methodology may be especially worrying in the sensitive and private area of sexuality.

Case materials and ethnographic studies

Case studies can be of individuals or groups. When they are of groups, they are usually classified as ethnographic research. The major research tool used in such studies is observation, either participant observation, in which the researcher becomes part of the group, or non-participant observation, where the researcher stands apart as a collector of information. These studies can be excellent sources of high quality descriptive data and they can generate many research questions and hypotheses as well as conceptual insights. The generalisability of data collected by these techniques is extremely limited, however. Without further research we are usually unable to generalise the conclusions and findings to other individuals or populations. As we have seen, there are other problems with these studies, centring on the reliability of the observations, and the ethical issues associated with their implementation.

A BETTER METHODOLOGY?

Surveys, experiments, observations and field-work studies can incorporate cross-sectional or longitudinal sampling in their designs. In cross-sectional studies, several groups of people or cohorts are studied at the same time. For example, we could compare the dating habits of 14-, 16-, and 18-year-old adolescents in order to draw conclusions about typical changes and developments with age. Problems arise in interpreting these studies, relating to the original equivalence of the samples chosen. If 18-year-olds date more than 16-year-olds is it because they are older or because the 18-year-old sample was dating more when they were 16 anyway? Procedures can be incorporated into the study design to maximise the possibility of equivalent samples. Participants can be chosen from similar school and socioeconomic backgrounds and they can be matched on variables thought to influence the dependent variable. However, equivalence can never be guaranteed.

Another problem arising from cross-sectional studies is the cohort effect. The year or era in which you were born and the corresponding set of shared experiences you have with your cohort can be as influential as age in affecting your behaviour, attitudes, and possibly even your personality. For example, 60-year-olds today are likely to have different attitudes to premarital sex than those of today's 20-year-olds. We do not really know if this is a function of ageing (that is, people becoming more conservative with age) or the particular social environments in which these two cohorts developed.

Longitudinal studies, which trace the same people over a period of time, can overcome some of these problems. In longitudinal studies it is possible to keep track of individual development, so we can assess whether a particular group of adolescents dated more when they were 18 years of age than at 16. The cohort issue is still a difficulty, however, as we may not be justified in generalising from one cohort of 18-year-olds, say those born in 1976, to other cohorts, such as those who will not turn 18 until the year 2000. Further, the use of longitudinal studies means that the same participants are tested repeatedly, and this repeated testing may influence their responses in ways unrelated to age. For example the experience of being asked questions might alert them to some moral or value issues to which they might not have otherwise been exposed, and they may think about those issues between one testing and the next. On the second testing the responses of participants may be different from those they would have given if pre-testing had not originally occurred.

It is possible (though expensive and difficult to organise) to combine the advantages of both longitudinal and cross-sectional methodologies through the use of time-lag designs (Baltes and Nesselroad 1973; Nesselroad and Baltes 1974). These involve selection of cross-sectional samples which are then repeatedly tested. So, for example, adolescent sexual behaviour and its initiation could be studied by comparing 13-, 15-, 17-, and 19-year-old samples in 1994, and following up each of these samples through the age groups of interest. In this way, a number of cohorts are sampled, and the longitudinal cohorts act as their own controls.

WHAT CAN WE CONCLUDE FROM STUDIES OF ADOLESCENT SEXUALITY?

The answer to the above question is 'It depends'. It depends on the sample chosen and how representative it is of the population of interest. Many studies of adolescent sexuality are about 18- to 19-year-old college students, an interesting group in themselves and certainly one that can be conveniently researched. But we are not justified in making sweeping generalisations about all adolescents from these samples. Probably most adolescent sexuality research is conducted with fully informed volunteers, a desirable situation in ethical terms, but not an optimal procedure in terms of research rigour. These volunteers are likely to have particular characteristics not shared by those who do not volunteer (Rosenthal and Rosnow 1969) and in sexuality research we do not really know what those characteristics are.

Our conclusions also depend on the type of study design, the nature of the measuring instruments chosen, and their adequacy in terms of reliability and validity of the data collected. Because our focus is adolescents and sexuality, there will be ethical and practical limitations on study designs and instrumentation. There will also be interactions between the nature of our sample, the topic, and the extent to which various research procedures work. A classroom-based questionnaire about dating presented to a group of year 8 students (aged 12 to 14 years) will initiate giggling, silly remarks, boasting, and a good deal of peer pressure not to take the exercise seriously or complete it truthfully. On the other hand, a group of 18-year-old Psychology 1 college students will probably complete such a questionnaire without a murmur. An important implication of these problems is that research findings need to be replicated, and studies developed which use a wide range of samples, research designs, and types of measuring instruments. Emphases on the qualitative as well as the quantitative is important because of the balance and human face that case material gives. A finding that can be repeated using a number of methodologies is far stronger than one that relies totally on data from self-reports of first-year college students from a single institution.

Our conclusions also depend on their context. Sexual mores and values constantly change and all societies show great variability between groups and among group members. The data on sexuality need to be continually updated because what was true for adolescents born in the 1960s may not be true for those born in the 1970s and 1980s. The spread of AIDS and other sexually transmissible diseases will influence current and future generations as will changes in the teachings and influence of world religions. We need to check our generalisations across times as well as across samples. We also need to be aware that general statements about adolescents do not tell us with any certainty about *this particular* adolescent and that, while theory and research in adolescent sexuality can be of great value in understanding the individual, it does not or cannot constrain his or her behaviours and beliefs. Theories and research must take account of individual variation. There is no law that humans must obey the theories we generate or the probabilistic statements which constitute the results of our research.

Finally, and very importantly, we need to be aware of the values framework of our research. Researchers are human and see the world through eyes that are focused through a range of unique life experiences. It is difficult, if not impossible, to see outside of our own value framework although it helps if one is attuned to other possibilities. Because sexuality is such a controversial topic it is particularly prone to distortions based on our way of looking at things. Once again, the over-reliance on particular methodologies may retard the progress of sex research into new directions and new ways of seeing things, ways which can capture the experiences of more than the narrow band within the population who think as we do.

Conclusion

Sex is something I really don't understand too hot. You never know *where* the hell you are. I keep making these sex rules for myself, and then I break them right away.

(Salinger 1951)

Salinger's teenage hero expresses the confusion that many adolescents feel about sex and issues surrounding sexuality. In the preceding chapters of this book we have dealt with some of the critical questions exercising the minds of adolescents and those adults who work and live with them. Among the wealth of research studies, models, and common-sense interpretations of sexuality which we have described, some commonalities have emerged. Four of these are discussed below.

CHANGE, VARIETY AND CONTINUITY

As far as we can tell within the limitations of the research methodology, more young people are beginning sexual activities at an earlier age than was the case in their parents' and grandparents' eras. To have experienced intercourse at least once by age 18 or 19 is the norm rather than the exception in Western society, for young men and women alike. A further change is that young people more readily admit to a range of sexual activities such as oral sex and multiple or serial partnering. The majority of teenagers, and to a lesser extent older adults, do not interpret these behaviours, in themselves, as deviant, delinquent, or irresponsible.

But . . . the more things change, the more they stay the same. Many young people still believe in love and romance, in being faithful (though probably not for life), and in the value of virginity. Along with this idealism, and sometimes existing uncomfortably alongside it, we still see evidence for the double standard in sexual matters. Experimenting is acceptable and 'natural' for boys; it is strongly sanctioned for girls. Girls have weak sex drives; young men cannot be expected to control their own overwhelming sexual urges. Girls are sexually subordinate but it is up to them to restrain boys from going too far, too fast.

Those who work with young people need to be sensitive to the wide-ranging differences between groups and individual adolescents concerning what is regarded as normal or average sexual behaviour. Tolerance of differences involves the recognition that one's children, pupils or clients may hold different value frameworks, yet to influence them it is important that the lines of communication be kept open. The permission to take control of, and be responsible for, one's sexuality, and the life-enhancing features of sexual expression are important messages adults can convey to today's adolescents, along with the usual caveats and warnings. While these have their place, they are too often the only feature of adult-to-adolescent communication about sex. Because of the realities of teenage sexual behaviour, such negative messages often have little impact, and can close off the possibilities for further communication and discussion.

There are many positive, developmentally desirable outcomes of sexual activity. Aside from being a pleasurable activity in itself, it is one of life's most important steps toward independence and can contribute to an individual's sense of self or identity. Sexual exploration can be considered as part of the training for maturity and participating in adult relationships. Sex can enable people to feel lovable, and gives the opportunity to express love, enhance closeness and sharing, and experience intimacy. These features are well recognised by adults but there is fear, for the most part unfounded, that acknowledging them in the presence of adolescents will encourage young people to experiment too soon, with negative consequences.

In dealing with change and variety in the sexual conduct of young people, the task for researchers is to monitor that conduct without imposing their own values. Researchers must also be aware of the ambiguities and paradoxes of the many sexual worlds of today's adolescents, in which sexual equality vies with the double standard, permissiveness with romantic love and faithfulness, and both liberalism and restrictiveness can be the norm. These complexities are apparent not only among different groups of adolescents, but often within the one individual.

NEW INTERPRETATIONS OF SEX

Sex is not just penetration and male orgasm. Sexual pleasure comes in many guises – some more satisfying than others, some safer, and some more conducive to developing and maintaining intimacy and loving relationships. Feminists reminded us of this in the 1960s and 1970s with the call to de-emphasise the 'phallocentrism' of sexual discourse, and in doing so move toward redressing the power differential between the sexes. Understanding of sex as more than intercourse gives validity to female experiences of pleasure without necessarily taking away from understanding male pleasure.

In the 1990s, de-emphasising intercourse has a further adaptive aspect. With AIDS and STDs in epidemic proportions, it is a dangerous time for sexual experimentation. The safest sex is no sex at all, but that is not very satisfying. Experimenting through touching, kissing, cuddling, and petting have long been the precursors to intercourse for adolescents and these are safe activities from the point of view of sexually transmissible diseases. But the lead time from petting to intercourse has shortened considerably in recent years. This is not the desired state of affairs for all adolescents and many feel pressured to move too quickly too soon. There is value in encouraging young people to savour the sexuality of touching and in giving them the confidence to say no or not yet to intercourse. Emphasising sensuality rather than penetration has two advantages. It is safer from a health-related point of view, and it also buys time. Adolescents who delay intercourse have the opportunity to develop in emotional maturity, in knowledge and understanding of themselves and of relationships, and in the confidence and skills necessary to ensure that when intercourse begins it is mutually satisfying as well as safe.

For researchers, the challenge is to find further interpretations by describing sexual cultures in ways which capture the experiences of those who live within them. This requires the skill to see beyond the obvious, to find ways of uncovering the assumptions and frameworks which can blinker data collection and analysis. Most research concerning adolescent sexuality is about intercourse-related events, and most is based on survey methodology. There is little analysis of sexuality from the adolescent's viewpoint – what it feels like, what beliefs and motives underlie experience. Qualitative research which allows respondents to provide their own, rather than a preconceived framework, enriches our understanding of the adolescent experience.

NATURE AND NURTURE

Biological changes provide an impetus to sexual behaviour, and biological make-up can influence the direction of development in terms of gender assignation, sexual preference, sexual opportunities, and the strength of sexual urges. We are learning more and more about the complex relationships between biological factors and behaviour and it is clear that these relationships are profoundly affected by social context. For example, in sexually liberated societies, individuals are given 'permission' to interpret bodily feelings as sexual urges or attraction, while in more restricted societies these feelings may be interpreted non-sexually or even repressed. Social beliefs about appropriate courtship behaviours provide the framework for sexual expression, so that biological urges may or may not be acted upon. Expectations and beliefs about the nature of men and women affect how they behave sexually and these may interact with, or even override, biological predispositions.

For adolescents there is no doubt that, while biological change plays a major role in sexual conduct, this influence always occurs in a social context. Adolescents need not be slaves to their hormones; nor need they be slaves to peer group pressure or media models of sexuality. Teaching young people about making wise choices, for example the value of sometimes delaying gratification and controlling impulses, is one way to immunise them against being pawns of fate – battered by drives on one hand and social pressures on the other.

Nevertheless it is well to be aware that these days, social influences on adolescents are far more pervasive than in earlier times. No longer are home, school, and church the only or major shaping factors. Adolescents all over the developed world now share a culture based on television, videos, music, magazines, and advertising. This media culture has the potential to offer positive models of sexuality and sometimes succeeds in doing so. All too often, though, adolescents are exposed to presentations of sexual exploitation, violence, and unhealthy relationships. The powerful models provided by the media are likely to be valued highly by young people and are therefore influential. We cannot pretend these models do not exist or successfully keep them hidden from our children. Adults have the power and potential to shape the representations of sexuality in the media. Also vital is the provision of education, caring and support for our young people as they make decisions about their sexuality.

For the researcher, there is ample scope to explore further the interactions between biology and social forces and to elucidate the effects of both nature and nurture on sexuality. How, for example, might the sexual behaviours modelled in modern films influence adolescent sexual behaviour? Who are the adolescents most vulnerable to these influences, and why? Are there critical periods in the course of puberty at which teenagers are most susceptible to these influences?

IT'S NOT ALL OVER AT TWENTY ...

Sexual development is a lifelong process, not a task that begins at 12 and finishes at 20. This is true biologically as well as psychologically. Reproductive powers peak then fall away, sexual drives wax and wane, and social expectations shape how sexuality manifests itself at different ages and stages of life. Individuals learn through successes and mistakes to incorporate sexuality into their lives. There is time for adolescents to experiment and make mistakes, yet still 'get it right' in the end. We need to be vigilant, however, to ensure that for as many young people as possible the mistakes they make are not irredeemably damaging (such as becoming HIV positive) or overly curtailing of life's possibilities (such as becoming a parent too soon). The sense of perspective gained by putting sexuality in a life-span context is valuable for parents, educators, researchers, and adolescents themselves. Yet we know little about the relationships between adolescent sexual experience and sexual outcomes in later life. Does early sexual trauma affect the potential for later fulfilment? Is the adolescent who experiments sexually during his or her teenage years likely to be more or less faithful in adult partnerships? What makes for better long-term sexual outcomes – learning earlier or later? With many partners or one?

One relevant feature of the 1990s is the world-wide trend against marrying young. There is now a chance for young people to learn more about themselves and others, to experiment sexually, and to be able to make more mature choices about whether to partner and with whom. But this opportunity also has its negative aspects. The risk of AIDS or other sexually transmissible diseases is increased if experimentation is not accompanied by safe practice. High or even unrealistic expectations about a life partner and unwillingness to compromise individual goals for couple goals are other risks. So, while sexual development was once seen as culminating at the end of adolescence with marriage and child-bearing, today young people in their twenties and even thirties may still have many sexual decisions to make before they choose a relatively stable path. Sexual conflicts are by no means over at the end of adolescence but, luckily, neither are sexual rewards.

References

Abbott, S. (1988) 'AIDS and young women', *The Bulletin of the National Clearinghouse for Youth Studies* 7: 38–41.

Abrams, D., Abraham, C., Spears, R. and Marks, D. (1990) 'AIDS invulnerability, relationships, sexual behaviour and attitudes among 16 to 19 year olds', in P. Aggleton, P. Davies and G. Hart (eds) *AIDS: Individual, Cultural and Policy Dimensions*, Lewes: Falmer Press.

Adams, G.R. (1991) 'Identity and intimacy: Some observations after a decade of investigations', *Journal of Youth and Adolescence* 10: 473–86.

Ajzen, I. and Fishbein, M. (1980) *Understanding Attitudes and Predicting Social Behaviour*, New Jersey: Prentice-Hall.

Alan Guttmacher Institute (1976) *Eleven Million Teenagers*, New York: Author.

—— (1981) *Teenage Pregnancy: The Problem That Hasn't Gone Away*, New York: Author.

Alder, C. and Sandor, D. (1989) *Homeless Youth as Victims of Violence*, Report to Criminology Research Council, Canberra, Australia.

Allen, D.M. (1980) 'Young male prostitutes: A psychosocial study', *Archives of Sexual Behaviour* 9: 399–426.

Allen, D.M. and Gorski, R.A. (1992) 'Sexual orientation and the size of the anterior commissure in the human brain', *Proceedings of the National Academy of Science* 89: 7199–202.

Allen, D.M., Hines, M., Shryne, J.E., Gorski, R.A. (1989) 'A difference in the hypothalamic structure between men and women', *Journal of Neuroscience* 9: 497.

Allen, I. (1987) *Education in Sex and Personal Relationships*, Oxford: Policy Studies Institute.

Alyson, S. (1985) *Young, Gay and Proud*, Boston, MA: Alyson.

American Psychiatric Association (1987) *Diagnostic and Statistical Manual of Mental Disorders* 3rd edn, Washington DC: American Psychiatric Association.

Ames, R. (1957) 'Physical maturing among boys as related to adult social behavior: A longitudinal study', *Californian Journal of Educational Research* 8: 69–75.

Anderson, D. (1987) 'Family and peer relations of gay adolescents', *Adolescent Psychiatry* 14: 165–78.

Antill, J. and Cunningham, J. (1980) 'The relationship of masculinity, femininity, and androgyny to self-esteem', *Australian Journal of Psychology* 32: 195–207.

Archer, J. and Lloyd, B. (1982) *Sex and Gender*, Harmondsworth: Penguin.

Archer, S.L. (1985) 'Identity and the choice of social roles' in A.S. Waterman (ed.)

Identity in Adolescence: Processes and Contents, San Francisco: Jossey-Bass.

Australian Institute of Family Studies (1981–2) *Australian Family Formation Project, Study 1: A Longitudinal Survey of Australians aged 13 to 34 years*, Canberra: Australian University Social Science Data Archives.

Bachrach, C.A. (1986) 'Adoption plans, adopted children, and adoptive mothers', *Journal of Marriage and the Family* 48: 243–53.

Baizerman, M., Thompson, J., Stafford-White, K. and 'An Old, Young Friend' (1979) 'Adolescent prostitution', *Children Today* Sept/Oct: 20–4.

Bakan, D. (1971) 'Adolescence in America: From idea to social fact', *Daedalus* 16: 979–95.

Baltes, P.B. and Nesselroade, J.R. (1973) 'The developmental analysis of individual differences on multiple measures', in J.R. Nesselroade and H.W. Reese (eds) *Life-span Developmental Psychology: Methodological Issues*, New York: Academic Press.

Bandura, A. (1982) 'Self-efficacy mechanism in human agency', *American Psychologist* 37: 122–47.

Barbeler, V. (1992) *The Young Lesbian Report*, Sydney: Report by TwentyTen, Gay and Lesbian Youth Refuge.

Bardwick, J.M. (1971) *The Psychology of Women: A Study of Biocultural Conflicts*, New York: Harper & Row.

Barlow, D., Mills, J., Agras, W. and Steinman, D. (1980) 'Comparison of sex-typed motor behavior in male-to-female transsexuals and women', *Archives of Sexual Behavior* 9: 245–53.

Barth, R.P., Schinke, S.P. and Maxwell, J.S. (1983) 'Psychological correlates of teenage motherhood', *Journal of Youth and Adolescence* 12: 471–87.

Bauman, K. and Udry, J.R. (1981) 'Subjective expected utility and adolescent sexual behavior', *Adolescence* 14: 527–538.

Bell, A.P. and Weinberg, M.S. (1978) *Homosexualities: A Study of Diversity among Men and Women*, New York: Simon & Schuster.

Bell, A.P., Weinberg, M.S., and Hammersmith, S.K. (1981a) *Sexual Preference: Its Development in Men and Women*, Bloomington, IN: Indiana University Press.

—— (1981b) *Sexual Preference: Its Development in Men and Women: Statistical Appendix*, Bloomington, IN: Indiana University Press.

Bem, S.L. (1974) 'The measurement of psychological androgyny', *Journal of Consulting and Clinical Psychology* 42: 155–62.

—— (1975) 'Sex role adaptability: One consequence of psychological androgyny', *Journal of Personality and Social Psychology* 31: 634–43.

Bene, E. (1965a) 'On the genesis of male homosexuality: An attempt to clarify the role of parents', *British Journal of Psychiatry* 111: 803–13.

—— (1965b) 'On the genesis of female homosexuality', *British Journal of Psychiatry* 111: 815–21.

Bettelheim, B. (1962) 'The problem of generation', *Daedalus*, Winter, 68–69.

Bidwell, R.J. and Deisher, R.W. (1991) 'Adolescent sexuality: Current issues', *Pediatric Annals* 6: 293–302.

Bieber, I., Dain, H.J., Dince, P.R., Drellich, M.G., Grand, H.G., Gundlach, R.H., Kremer, M.W., Rifkin, A.H., Wilbur, C.B. and Bieber, T.B. (1962) *Homosexuality: A Psychoanalytic Study*, New York: Basic Books.

Blaske, D.M., Borduin, C.M. and Henggeler, S.W. (1989) 'Individual, family, and peer characteristics of adolescent sex offenders and assaultive offenders', *Developmental Psychology* 25: 845–55.

Blos, P. (1962) *On Adolescence*, New York: Free Press.
—— (1988) 'The inner world of the adolescent', in A.E. Esman (ed.) *International Annals of Adolescent Psychiatry* 1, Chicago: University of Chicago.
Blumberg, M. and Lester, D. (1991) 'High school and college students' attitudes toward rape', *Adolescence* 26: 727–9.
Blyth, D.A., Simmons, R.G. and Zakin, D. (1985) 'Satisfaction with body image for early adolescent females: The impact of pubertal timing within different school environments', *Journal of Youth and Adolescence* 14: 207–26.
Boldero, J.M., Moore, S.M. and Rosenthal, D.A. (1992) 'Intention, context, and safe sex: Australian adolescents' responses to AIDS', *Journal of Applied Social Psychology* 22: 1375–97.
Bolton, F.J. and Belsky, J. (1986) 'The adolescent father and child maltreatment', in A.B. Elster and M. Lamb (eds) *Adolescent Fatherhood*, Hillsdale, NJ: Erlbaum.
Boocock, R.M. and Trethewie, K.J. (1981) 'Body image and weight relationships in teenage girls', *Proceedings of the Nutrition Society of Australia* 6: 166–7.
Borhek, M. (1983) *Coming Out to Parents: A Two-Way Survival Guide For Lesbians and Gay Men and Their Families*, New York: Pilgrim Press.
Boxer, A.M. and Cohler, B.J. (1989) 'The life course of gay and lesbian youth: An immodest proposal for the study of lives', in G. Herdt (ed.) *Gay and Lesbian Youth*, New York: Haworth Press.
Breakwell, G.M., Fife-Schaw, C. and Clayden, K. (1991) 'Risk-taking, control over partner choice and intended use of condoms by virgins', *Journal of Community and Applied Psychology* 1: 173–87.
Briere, J. (1988) *Therapy For Adults Molested as Children: Beyond Survival*, New York: Springer.
Brook-Taylor, G. (1970) 'Quality in recreation', in T.L. Burton (ed.) *Recreation, Research and Planning*, London: Allen & Unwin.
Brooks-Gunn, J. (1984) 'The psychological significance of different pubertal events to young girls', *Journal of Early Adolescence* 4(4): 315–27.
—— (1988) 'Antecedents and consequences of variations in girls' maturational timing', *Journal of Adolescent Health Care* 9(5): 365–73.
Brooks-Gunn, J. and Furstenberg, F.F. Jr. (1989) 'Adolescent sexual behavior', *American Psychologist* 44: 249–57.
—— (1990) 'Coming of age in the era of AIDS: Puberty, sexuality, and contraception', *The Milbank Quarterly* 68: 59–84.
Brooks-Gunn, J., Petersen, A.C. and Eichorn, D. (1985) 'The study of maturational timing effects in adolescence', *Journal of Youth and Adolescence* 14: 149–61.
Brooks-Gunn, J. and Reiter, E.O. (1990) 'The role of pubertal processes in the early adolescent transition', in S. Feldman and G. Elliott (eds) *At the Threshold: The Developing Adolescent*, Cambridge, MA: Harvard University Press.
Brooks-Gunn, J. and Ruble, D. (1979) 'The social and psychological meaning of menarche', Paper given at Biennial Meeting of the Society for Research on Child Development, San Francisco.
—— (1982) 'The development of menstrual-related beliefs and behaviors during early adolescence', *Child Development* 53: 1567–77.
Brooks-Gunn, J. and Warren, M.P. (1985) 'Measuring physical status and timing in early adolescence: A developmental perspective', *Journal of Youth and Adolescence* 14: 163–89.

—— (1989) 'Biological contributions to affective expression in young adolescent girls', *Child Development* 60: 372–85.
Brooks-Gunn, J., Warren, M.P., Samelson, M. and Fox, R. (1986) 'Physical similarity of and disclosure of menarcheal status to friends: Effects of age and pubertal status', *Journal of Early Adolescence* 6: 3–14.
Broverman, I., Broverman, D., Clarkson, F., Rosenkrantz, P. and Vogel, S. (1970) 'Sex-role stereotypes and clinical judgements of mental health', *Journal of Consulting and Clinical Psychology* 34: 1–7.
Brown, J.C. (1989) 'Lesbian sexuality in medieval and early modern Europe', in M.B. Duberman, M. Vicinus and G. Chauncey Jr. (eds) *Hidden From History: Reclaiming the Gay and Lesbian Past*, New York: Penguin.
Brown, M.E. (1979) 'Teenage prostitution' *Adolescence* 14: 665–80.
Browne, A. and Finkelhor, D. (1986) 'Impact of child sexual abuse: A review of the research', *Psychological Bulletin* 99: 66–77.
Brumberg, J.J. (1988) *Fasting Girls*, Cambridge, MA: Harvard University Press.
Buchanan, C.M., Eccles, J.S. and Becker, J.B. (1992) 'Are adolescents victims of aging hormones: Evidence for activational effects of hormones on moods and behavior at adolescence', *Pyschological Bulletin* 111: 62–107.
Burgess, A., Hazelwood, R., Rokous, F. and Hartman, C. (1988) 'Sexual rapists and their victims: Recruitment and repetition', *Annals of the New York Academy of Sciences* 528: 277–95.
Bury, J. (1984) *Teenage Pregnancy in Britain*, London: Birth Control Trust.
Buzwell, S., Rosenthal, D.A. and Moore, S.M. (1992) 'Homeless youth: Explorations of sexuality and AIDS risk', paper given at the Twenty-sixth Annual Conference of the Australian Psychological Society, Adelaide, September.
Caldwell, M. and Peplau, L. (1982) 'Sex differences in same-sex friendship', *Sex Roles* 8: 721–32.
Campbell, A.A. (1968) 'The role of family planning in the reduction of poverty', *Journal of Marriage and the Family* 30: 236–45.
Campbell, A. (1992) 'Girls at the crossroads: The construction of a social identity', Paper given at the First International Conference on Girls and Girlhood: Transitions and Dilemmas, Amsterdam.
Campbell, D.T. and Stanley, J.C. (1966) *Experimental and Quasi-experimental Designs for Research*, Chicago: Rand McNally.
Carlson, B. (1987) 'Dating violence: A research view', *Social Casework* 68: 16–23.
Carns, D. (1973) 'Notes on first coitus and the double sexual standard', *Journal of Marriage and the Family* 35: 677–88.
Carson, R.C., Butcher, J.N. and Coleman, J.C. (1988) *Abnormal Psychology and Modern Life* 8th edn, Boston: Scott, Foresman & Co.
Casper, R.C. (1989) 'Psychodynamic psychotherapy in acute anorexia nervosa and acute bulimea nervosa', in A.H. Esman (ed.) *International Annals of Adolescent Psychiatry*, Chicago: University of Chicago Press.
Cass, V. (1979) 'Homosexual identity formation: A theoretical model', *Journal of Homosexuality* 4: 219–35.
—— (1984) 'Homosexual identity: A concept in need of definition', *Journal of Homosexuality* 9: 105–26.
Cassell, C. (1984) *Swept Away: Why Women Fear Their own Sexuality*, New York: Simon & Schuster.
Catania, J.A., Gibson, D.R., Chitwood, D.D. and Coates, T.J. (1990) 'Methodological problems in AIDS behavioural research: Influences on measurement

error and participation bias in studies of sexual behaviour', *Psychological Bulletin* 108: 339–62.

Chapman, S. and Hodgson, J. (1988) 'Showers in raincoats: Attitudinal barriers to condom use in high-risk heterosexuals', *Community Health Studies* 12: 97–105.

Chapman, S., Stoker, L., Ward, M., Porritt, D. and Fahey, P. (1990) 'Discriminant attitudes and beliefs about condoms in young, multipartner heterosexuals', *International Journal of STDs and AIDS* 1: 1081–7.

Chassin, L., Presson, C.C. and Sherman, S.J. (1989) '"Constructive" vs "destructive" deviance in adolescent health-related behaviours', *Journal of Youth and Adolescence* 18: 245–62.

Chilman, C.S. (1980a) *Adolescent Sexuality in a Changing American Society*, Maryland: US Department of Health, Education and Welfare.

—— (1980b) 'Social and psychological research concerning adolescent childbearing: 1970–1980', *Journal of Marriage and the Family* 42: 793–805.

Chitwood, D. (1988) 'Effects of interviewer gender on responses to sexual questions by intravenous drug users', Unpublished data.

Clausen, J.A. (1975) 'The social meaning of differential physical and sexual maturation', in S.E. Dragastin and G.H. Elder, Jr. (eds) *Adolescence in the Life Cycle*, New York: Halsted.

Clifford, E. (1971) 'Body satisfaction in adolescence', *Perceptual and Motor Skills* 33: 113–25.

Clift, S. and Stears, D. (1991) 'AIDS education in secondary schools', *Education and Health* 9: 1–4.

Coleman, E. (1982) 'Developmental stages of the coming out process', in W. Paul, J.D. Weinrich, J.C. Gonsiorek and M.E. Hotvedt (eds) *Homosexuality: Social, Psychological and Biological Issues*, Beverly Hills, CA: Sage.

Coleman, J. (1980) 'Friendship and the peer group in adolescence', in J. Adelson (ed.) *Handbook of Adolescent Development*, New York: Wiley.

Coleman, J.C. and Hendry, L. (1990) *The Nature of Adolescence* 2nd edn, London: Routledge.

Coles, R. and Stokes, G. (1985) *Sex and the American Teenager*, New York: Harper & Row.

Collins, J.K. (1974) 'Adolescent dating intimacy: Norms and peer expectations', *Journal of Youth and Adolescence* 3: 317–28.

Collis, F. (1991) 'Parents' and teachers' beliefs about adolescent sexuality and HIV/AIDS', unpublished thesis, University of Melbourne, Melbourne, Australia.

Connell, R.W., Crawford, J., and Kippax, S. (1989) 'Facing the epidemic: Changes in the sexual lives of gay and bisexual men in Australia and their implications for AIDS prevention strategies', *Social Problems* 36: 384–402.

Coppen, A. and Kessel, N. (1963) 'Menstruation and personality', *British Journal of Psychiatry* 109: 711–21.

Courtois, C. (1979) 'The incest experience and its aftermath', *Victimology* 4: 337–47.

Crawford, J., Turtle, A.M. and Kippax, S. (1990) 'Student-favoured strategies for AIDS avoidance', *Australian Journal of Psychology* 42: 123–38.

Crofts, N. (1992) 'Patterns of infections', in E. Timewell, V. Minichiello and D. Plummer (eds) *AIDS in Australia*, Sydney: Prentice-Hall.

Cronin, D.M. (1974) 'Coming out among lesbians', in E. Goode and R.R. Troiden (eds) *Sexual Deviance and Sexual Deviants*, New York: William Morrow & Sons.

Crooks, R. and Baur, K. (1990) 'Homosexuality', in *Our Sexuality*, California: Benjamin/Cummings.

Cunningham, J. (1990) 'Becoming men and women', in P.C.L. Heaven and V.J. Callan (eds) *Adolescence: An Australian Perspective*, Sydney: Harcourt Brace Jovanovich.

Currie, C. (1990) 'Young people in independent schools, sexual behavior and AIDS', in P. Aggleton, P. Davies and G. Hart (eds) *AIDS: Individual, Cultural and Policy Dimensions*, London: Falmer Press.

Curry, J.F. and Hock, R.A. (1981) 'Sex differences in sex role ideals in early adolescence', *Adolescence* 16: 779–89.

Cvetkovich, G. and Grote, B. (1980) 'Psychological development and the social programme of teenage illegitimacy', in C. Childman (ed.) *Adolescent Pregnancy and Childbearing: Findings from Research*, Washington, D.C.: US Department of Health and Human Services.

Czaja, R. (1987–8) 'Asking sensitive behavioural questions in telephone interviews', *International Quarterly of Community Health Education* 8: 23–32.

Dank, B.M. (1971) 'Coming out in the gay world', *Psychiatry* 34: 180–97.

Darling, C.A. and Hicks, M.W. (1982) 'Parental influence on adolescent sexuality: Implications for parents as educators', *Journal of Youth and Adolescence*, 11: 231–45.

Darling, C.A., Kallen, D.J. and Van Dusen, J.E. (1984) 'Sex in transition, 1900–1980', *Journal of Youth and Adolescence* 13: 385–99.

Daugherty, L.R. and Burger, J.M. (1984) 'The influence of parents, church and peers on the sexual attitudes and behaviors of college students', *Archives of Sexual Behavior* 13: 351–9.

Davies, P., Weatherburn, A., Hickson, F., McManus, T. and Coxon, A. (1992) 'The sexual behaviour of young gay men in England and Wales', *AIDS Care* 4: 259–72.

Davis, G.E. and Leitenberg, H. (1987) 'Adolescent sex offenders', *Psychological Bulletin* 101: 417.

Davis, M.D., Kleumer, U. and Dowsett, G. (1991) *Bisexually Active Men and Beats: Theoretical and Educational Implications. The Bisexually Active Men's Outreach Project*, Sydney: AIDS Council of NSW and Macquarie University AIDS Research Unit.

Davis, S.M. and Harris, M.B. (1982) 'Sexual knowledge, sexual interests, and sources of information of rural and urban adolescents from three cultures', *Adolescence* 17: 471–92.

de Monteflores, C. and Schultz, S.J. (1978) 'Coming out: Similarities and differences for lesbians and gay men', *Journal of Social Issues* 34: 59–72.

Demos, J. and Demos, V. (1969) 'Adolescence in historical perspective', *Journal of Marriage and the Family* 31: 632–8.

Dennerstein, L., Spencer-Gardner, C., Brown, J.D., Smith, M.A. and Burrows, G.D. (1984) 'Premenstrual tension-hormonal profiles', *Journal of Psychosomatic Obstetrics and Gynecology* 3: 37–51.

Deutsch, H. (1944) *Psychology of Women* Vol. 1, New York: Grune & Stratton.

Devaney, B.L. and Hubley, K.S. (1981) *The Determinants of Adolescent Pregnancy and Childbearing*, Final report to the National Institute of Child Health and Human Development, Washington, D.C: Mathematical Policy Research.

DiClemente, R.J., Zorn, J. and Temoshok, L. (1986) 'Adolescents and AIDS: A survey of knowledge, attitudes and beliefs about AIDS in San Francisco', *American Journal of Public Health* 76: 1443–5.

DiMascolo, E. (1991) 'To have knowledge and to hold power: Adolescents negotiating safe sex', unpublished thesis, University of Melbourne, Melbourne, Australia.

Dodson, R.E., Shryne, J.E., Gorski, R.A. (1988) 'Effects of androgen on dimorphic nucleus of the preoptic area in perinatal rats', *Journal of Comparative Neurology* 275: 623.

Donovan, J.E. and Jessor, R. (1985) 'Structure of problem behaviour in adolescence and young adulthood', *Journal of Consulting and Clinical Psychology* 53: 890–904.

Dornsbusch, S.M., Carlsmith, J.M., Gross, R.T., Martin, J.A., Jennings, D., Rosenberg, A. and Duke, P. (1981) 'Sexual development, age and dating: A comparison of biological and social influences upon one set of behaviours', *Child Development* 52: 179–85.

Douvan, E. and Adelson, J. (1966) *The Adolescent Experience*, New York: Wiley.

Dummer, G. (1987) 'Pathogenic weight control behaviors of young competitive swimmers', *Physician and Sports Medicine* 15: 75–8.

Duncan, P., Ritter, P., Dornbusch, S., Gross, R. and Carlsmith, J. (1985) 'The effects of pubertal timing on body image, school behavior and deviance', *Journal of Youth and Adolescence* 14: 227–36.

Dunne M., McCamish M., Hamilton K. and Orth D. (1992) 'HIV testing by homosexual and bisexual men', Letter to *Medical Journal of Australia* 4: 157–212.

Dusek, J.B. (1987) 'Sex roles and adjustment', in D.B. Carter (ed.) *Current Conceptions of Sex Roles and Sex Typing*, New York: Praeger.

Dusek, J.B. (1991) *Adolescent Development and Behavior*, New Jersey: Prentice-Hall.

Duvall, E.M. (1960) *The Art of Dating*, New York: Permabooks.

Dwyer, J. and Mayer, J. (1968–9) 'Psychological effects of variations in physical appearance during adolescence', *Adolescence* 3: 353–80.

Eccles, J.S., Miller, C.L., Tucker, M.L., Becker, J., Schramm, W., Midgely, R., Holmes, W., Pasch, L. and Miller, M. (1988) 'Hormones and affect at early age adolescence', in J. Brooks-Gunn (chair) *Hormonal Contributions to Adolescent Behavior*, A Symposium conducted at the second biennial meeting of the Society for Research on Adolescence, Alexandria, VA.

Eckert, E.D., Bouchard, T.J, Bohlen, J. and Heston, L.L. (1990) 'Homosexuality in monozygotic twins reared apart', in G. Puterbaugh (ed.) *Twins and Homosexuality: A Casebook*, New York: Garland.

Edgar, D.E. (1974) *Adolescent Competence and Sexual Disadvantage*, Working papers in Sociology, Melbourne: La Trobe University.

Eisen, M., Zellman, G.l., Leibowitz, A., Chow, W.K. and Evans, J.R. (1983) 'Factors discriminating pregnancy resolution decisions of unmarried adolescents', *Genetic Psychology Monographs* 108: 69–95.

Ekstrand, M.L. and Coates, T.J. (1990) 'Gay men in San Francisco are maintaining low risk behaviors but young men continue to be at risk', *American Journal of Public Health* 80: 973–7.

Elkind, D. (1985) 'Egocentrism redux', *Developmental Review* 5: 218–26.

Ellis, L. and Ames, M. (1987) 'Neurohormonal functioning and sexual orientation: A theory of homosexuality-heterosexuality', *Psychological Bulletin* 101: 233–58.

Elliott, D.S. and Morse, B.J. (1989) 'Delinquency and drug use as risk factors in teenage sexual activity', *Youth and Society* 21: 32–60.

Emmons, C., Joseph, J., Kessler, R., Wortman, C., Montgomery, S. and Ostrow, D. (1986) 'Psychological predictors of reported behaviour change in homosexual men at risk for AIDS', *Health Education Quarterly* 13: 331–45.

Ensminger, M.E. (1987) 'Adolescent sexual behaviour as it related to other transition behaviors in youth', in S. Hofferth and C. Hayes (eds) *Risking the Future: Adolescent Sexuality, Pregnancy and Childbearing* Vol. 2, Working papers and statistical appendices, Washington, D.C.: National Academy of Science.

Erikson, E. (1959) 'Identity and the life cycle', *Psychological Issues* 1: 1–71.

—— (1963) *Childhood and Society* 2nd edn, New York: Norton.

—— (1968) *Identity, Youth and Crisis*, New York: Norton.

Erikson, P. and Rapkin, A. (1991) 'Unwanted sexual experiences among middle and high school youth', *Journal of Adolescent Health* 12: 319–25.

Farrell, C. (1978) *My Mother Said: The Way Young People Learned about Sex and Birth Control*, London: Routledge & Kegan Paul.

Faust, M.S. (1977) 'Somatic development of adolescent girls', *Monographs of the Society for Research in Child Development* 42 (whole).

Feather, N.T. (1985) 'Masculinity, femininity, self-esteem, and subclinical depression', *Sex Roles* 12: 491–500.

Feldman, S.S. and Brown, N. (1992) 'A mediated model of family influences on adolescent male sexuality: The role of restraint', Manuscript under review.

Feldman, S.S., Rosenthal, D.R., Brown, N.L. and Canning, R.D. (1993) 'Predicting sexual experience in adolescent boys from peer rejection and acceptance during childhood', *Journal of Research on Adolescence*, in press.

Fine, M. (1988) 'Sexuality, schooling, and adolescent females: The missing discourse of desire', *Harvard Educational Review* 58: 29–53.

Firme, T.P., Grinder, R.E. and Barreto, M.S. (1991) 'Adolescent female prostitutes on the streets of Brazil: An explanatory investigation of ontological issues', *Journal of Adolescent Research* 6: 493–504.

Fischer, J.L. (1981) 'Transitions in relationship style from adolescence to young adulthood', *Journal of Youth and Adolescence* 10: 11–24.

Fischman, S. (1977) 'Delivery or abortion in inner-city adolescents', *American Journal of Orthopsychiatry* 47: 127–33.

Fishbein, M. and Ajzen, I. (1975) *Beliefs, Attitudes, Intention, and Behaviour: An Introduction to Theory and Research*, Reading, MA: Addison-Wesley.

Fitzpatrick, P., Boulton, M., Hart, G., Dawson, J. and McLean, J. (1990) 'Variation in sexual behaviour in gay men', in P. Aggleton, P.M. Davies and G. Hart (eds) *AIDS: Individual, Cultural and Policy Dimensions*, London: Falmer Press.

Ford, N. and Morgan, K. (1989) 'Heterosexual lifestyles of young people in an English city', *Journal of Population and Social Studies* 1: 167–85.

Forrest, J. and Silverman, J. (1989) 'What public school teachers teach about preventing pregnancy, AIDS and sexually transmitted diseases', *Family Planning Perspectives* 21: 65–72.

Freeman, D. (1983) *Margaret Mead and Samoa: The Making and Unmaking of an Anthropological Myth*, Cambridge, MA: Harvard University Press.

Freud, A. (1969) 'Adolescence as a developmental disturbance', in G. Caplan and S. Lebovici (eds) *Adolescence*, New York: Basic Books.

Freud, S. (1924) 'The passing of the Oedipal complex', in *Collected Papers* Vol. 2, London: Hogarth.

—— (1935) *A General Introduction to Psychoanalysis*, New York: Liveright.

—— (1950) 'Some psychological consequences of the anatomical distinction between the sexes', in *Collected Papers* Vol. 5, London: Hogarth.

—— (1953) 'Three essays on the theory of sexuality', in *Standard Edition* VII, London: Hogarth Press.

Frisch, R. and Revelle, R. (1970) 'Height and weight at menarche and a hypothesis of critical body weights and adolescent events', *Science* 169: 397–9.

Frisk, M., Tenhunen, T., Widholm, O. and Hortling, H. (1966) 'Psychological problems in adolescents' advanced or delayed physical maturation', *Adolescence* 1: 126–40.

Fromuth, M.E. (1986) 'The relationship of childhood sexual abuse with later psychological and sexual adjustment in a sample of college women', *Child Abuse Negligence* 10: 5–15.

Fromuth, M.E., Burkhart, B.R. and Jones, C.W. (1991) 'Hidden child molestation: An investigation of adolescent perpetrators in a noncultural sample', *Journal of Interpersonal Violence* 6: 376–84.

Furstenberg, F.F. Jr. (1976) *Unplanned Parenthood: The Social Consequences of Teenage Childbearing*, New York: Free Press.

Furstenberg, F.F. Jr., Brooks-Gunn, J. and Chase-Lansdale, L. (1989) 'Teenaged pregnancy and childbearing', *American Psychologist* 44: 313–20.

Furstenberg, F.F. Jr., Brooks-Gunn, J. and Morgan, S.P. (1987) *Adolescent Mothers in Later Life*, Cambridge: Cambridge University Press.

Gabrielson, I.W., Klerman, L.V., Currie, J.B., Tyler, N.C. and Jekel, J.F. (1970) 'Suicide attempts in a population pregnant as teen-agers', *American Journal of Public Health* 60: 2289–301.

Gaddis, A. and Brooks-Gunn, J. (1985) 'The male experience of pubertal change', *Journal of Youth and Adolescence* 14: 61–9.

Gagnon, J.H. and Simon, W. (1973) *Sexual Conduct: The Social Sources of Human Sexuality*, Chicago: Aldine.

Gallatin, J.E. (1975) *Adolescence and Individuality*, New York: Harper & Row.

Gallois, C. and Callan, V.J. (1990) 'Sexuality in adolescence', in P. Heaven and V.C. Callan (eds) *Adolescence: An Australian Perspective*, Sydney: Harcourt Brace Jovanovich.

Gallois, C., McCamish, M. and Kashima, Y. (1989) 'Safe and unsafe sexual practices by heterosexual and homosexual men: Predicting intentions and behaviour', paper given at the Australian Conference on Medical and Scientific Aspects of AIDS and HIV infection, Sydney.

Garbarino, J. (ed.) (1985) *Adolescent Development: An Ecological Perspective*, Columbus, Ohio: Merrill.

Garfinkel, P.E. and Garner, D.M. (1982) *Anorexia Nervosa*, New York: Brunner/Mazel.

Gavey, N. (1991) 'Sexual victimization prevalence among New Zealand university students', *Journal of Consulting and Clinical Psychology* 59: 464–6.

Gerrard, M. (1987) 'Sex, sexual guilt and contraceptive use revisited: The 1980s', *Journal of Personality and Social Psychology* 52: 975–80.

Gerstel, C.J., Feraios, A.J. and Herdt, G. (1989) 'Widening circles: An ethnographic profile of a youth group', in G. Herdt (ed.) *Gay and Lesbian Youth*, New York: Haworth Press.

Gilligan, C. (1982) *In a Different Voice*, Cambridge, MA: Harvard University Press.

Goggin, M. (1989) 'Intimacy, sexuality, and sexual behaviour among young Australian adults', unpublished thesis, Department of Psychology, University of Melbourne.

Gold, R.S., Karmiloff-Smith, A., Skinner, M.J. and Morton, J. (1992) 'Situational factors and thought processes associated with unprotected intercourse in heterosexual students', *AIDS Care* 4: 305–23.

Gold, R.S. and Skinner, M.J. (1992) 'Situational factors and thought processes associated with unprotected intercourse in young gay men', *AIDS* 6: 1021–30.

Gold, R.S., Skinner, M.J., Grant, P. and Plummer, D. (1989) 'Situational factors associated with unprotected intercourse in gay men', *Psychology and Health* 5: 259–78.

Goldman, R.J. and Goldman, J.D.G. (1982) *Children's Sexual Thinking*, Melbourne: Routledge & Kegan Paul.

—— (1988) *Show Me Yours: Understanding Children's Sexuality*, Ringwood: Penguin.

—— (1992) *An Overview of School-based HIV/AIDS Educational Programmes in Australia*, Brisbane: National Centre for HIV Social Research.

Goodchilds, J.D. and Zellman, G.L. (1984) 'Sexual signalling and sexual aggression in adolescent relationships', in N.M. Malamuth and E.D. Donnerstein (eds) *Pornography and Sexual Aggression*, New York: Academic Press.

Gordon, S. and Gilgun, J.F. (1987) 'Adolescent sexuality', in V.B. Van Hasselt and M. Hersen (eds) *Handbook of Adolescent Psychology*, New York: Pergamon.

Green (1987) *The Sissy Boy Syndrome and the Development of Homosexuality*, New Haven, CT: Yale University Press.

Greig, R. and Raphael, B. (1989) 'AIDS prevention and adolescents', *Community Health Studies* 13: 211–7.

Grief, E. and Ulman, K. (1982) 'The psychological impact of menarche on early adolescent females: A review of the literature', *Child Development* 53: 1413–30.

Griffin, C. (1992) 'Forever young: Discourses of femininity and resistance in British youth research during the 1980s', paper given at 'Alice in Wonderland', First International Conference on Girls and Girlhood, Amsterdam, June.

Hall, G.S. (1940) *Adolescence* Vol. 2, New York: Macmillan.

Hansen, S. and Darling, C. (1985) 'Attitudes of adolescents toward division of labor in the home', *Adolescence* 77: 61–71.

Hart, R. (1986) *Straight Talk About Being Gay*, Melbourne: Penguin.

Havighurst, R.J. (1951) *Developmental Tasks and Education*, New York: Longmans.

—— (1953) *Human Development and Education*, New York: Longmans.

—— (1964) 'Youth in exploration and man emergent', in H. Barrow (ed.) *Man in a World at Work*, Boston: Houghton Mifflin.

Hayes, C.D. (1987) 'Adolescent pregnancy and childbearing: An emerging research focus', in S.L. Hofferth and C.D. Hayes (eds) *Risking the Future: Adolescent Sexuality, Pregnancy, and Childbearing* 2: Working papers and statistical appendices, Washington, D.C: National Academy Press.

Hay, R.B., Kegeles, S.M. and Coates, T.J. (1990) 'High HIV risk-taking among young gay men', *AIDS* 4: 901–7.

Hein, K. (1989a) 'Commentary on adolescent acquired immunodeficiency syndrome: The next wave of the Human Immunodeficiency Virus epidemic?', *Journal of Pediatrics* 114: 144–9.

—— (1989b) 'AIDS in adolescence: A rationale for concern', *New York State Journal of Medicine* 87: 290–5.

—— (1992) 'Adolescents at risk for HIV infection', in R.J. DiClemente (ed.) *Adolescents and AIDS: A Generation in Jeopardy*, Newbury Park, CA: Sage.

Herdt, G. (1989) 'Introduction: Gay and lesbian youth, emergent identities, and cultural scenes at home and abroad', in G. Herdt (ed.) *Gay and Lesbian Youth*, New York: Haworth Press.

Herek, G.M. and Birrell, K.T. (1992) *Hate Crimes: Confronting Violence Against Lesbians and Gay Men*, Newbury Park, CA: Sage.

Heron, A. (1983) *One Teenager in Ten: Testimony by Gay and Lesbian Youth*, Boston, MA: Warner Books.

Hersch, P. (1988) 'Coming of age on city streets', *Psychology Today* 22: 28–37.

Hill, J.P. (1987) 'Research on adolescents and their families: Past and prospect', in C.E. Irwin (ed.) *Adolescent Social Behavior and Health: New Directions for Child Development*, San Francisco: Jossey-Bass.

Hingson, R. and Strunin, L. (1992) 'Monitoring adolescents' responses to the AIDS epidemic: Changes in knowledge, attitudes, beliefs, and behaviors', in R.J. DiClemente (ed.) *Adolescents and AIDS: A Generation in Jeopardy*, Newbury Park, CA: Sage.

Hite, S. (1977) *The Hite Report: A Nationwide Study on Female Sexuality*, Sydney: Summit Books/Paul Hamlyn.

Hofferth, S.L. (1987a) 'Factors affecting initiation of sexual intercourse', in S.L. Hofferth and C.D. Hayes (eds) *Risking the Future: Adolescent Sexuality, Pregnancy and Childbearing* 2: Working papers and statistical appendices, Washington DC: National Academy of Science.

—— (1987b) 'Teenage pregnancy and its resolution', in S.L. Hofferth and C.D. Hayes (eds) *Risking the Future: Adolescent Sexuality, Pregnancy and Childbearing* 2: Working papers and statistical appendices, Washington DC: National Academy of Science.

—— (1987c) 'Social and economic consequences of teenage childbearing', in S.L. Hofferth and C.D. Hayes (eds) *Risking the Future: Adolescent Sexuality, Pregnancy and Childbearing* 2: Working papers and statistical appendices, Washington DC: National Academy of Science.

Hofferth, S.L. and Hayes, C.D. (eds) (1987a) *Risking the Future: Adolescent Sexuality, Pregnancy and Childbearing* 1, Washington DC: National Academy of Science.

—— (eds) (1987b) *Risking the Future: Adolescent Sexuality, Pregnancy, and Childbearing* 2, Washington, D.C: National Academy Press.

Holland, J., Ramazanoglu, C., Scott, S., Sharpe, S. and Thomson, R. (1990) *'Don't Die of Ignorance – I Nearly Died of Embarrassment' Condoms in Context*, The Womens Risk AIDS Project, paper no. 2. London: Tufnell Press.

—— (1991) *Pressure, Resistance, Empowerment: Young Women and the Negotiation of Safer Sex*, The Womens Risk AIDS Project, paper no. 6. London: Tufnell Press.

Hollway, W. (1984) 'Women's power in heterosexual sex', *Women's Studies International Forum* 7: 66–8.

Hornick, J.P. (1978) 'Premarital sexual attitudes and behavior', *The Sociological Quarterly* 19: 534–44.

Hudson, F. and Ineichen, B. (1991) *Taking it Lying Down: Sexuality and Teenage Motherhood*, Hong Kong: Macmillan Education Ltd.

Humpreys, L. (1972) *Out of the Closets: The Sociology of Homosexual Liberation*, Englewood Cliffs, NJ: Prentice-Hall.

Hunt, A.J., Weatherburn, P., Davies, P.M., Coxon, A.P.M. and McManus, T.J. (1991) 'Sexual partners, penetrative sexual partners and HIV risk', *AIDS* 5: 723–8.

Hyde, J. and Phillis, D. (1979) 'Androgyny across the life-span', *Developmental Psychology* 15: 334–6.

Inazu, J.K. and Fox, G.L. (1980) 'Maternal influence on the sexual behavior of teen-age daughters', *Journal of Family Issues* 1: 81–102.

Ineichen, B. (1986) 'Contraceptive experience and attitude to motherhood of teenage mothers', *Journal of Biosocial Science* 18: 387–94.

Ingham, R., Woodcock, A. and Stenner, K. (1991) 'Getting to know you . . . young people's knowledge of their partners at first intercourse', *Journal of Community and Applied Psychology* 1: 117–32.

Isay, R.A. (1987) 'Fathers and their homosexually inclined sons in childhood', *Psychoanalytic Study of the Child* 42: 275–94.

Jaquish, G.A. and Savin-Williams, R.C. (1981) 'Biological and ecological factors in expression of adolescent self-esteem', *Journal of Youth and Adolescence* 10: 473–86.

Janz, N.K. and Becker, M.H. (1984) 'The health belief model a decade later', *Health Education Quarterly* 11: 1–47.

Jeske, J.M. and Overman, K. (1984) 'Gender and the official language' *International Journal of Women's Studies* 7(4): 322–35.

Jessor, S.L. and Jessor, R. (1975) 'Transition from virginity to non-virginity among youth: A social-psychological study over time', *Developmental Psychology* 11: 473–84.

—— (1977) *Problem Behaviour and Psychosocial Development: A Longitudinal Study of Youth*, New York: Academic Press.

Jones, E.F., Forrest, J.D., Goldman, N., Henshaw, S.K., Lincoln, R., Rosoff, J.I., Westoff, C.F. and Wulf, D. (1985) 'Teenage pregnancy in developed countries: Determinants and policy implications', *Family Planning Perspectives* 17: 53–63.

—— (1986) *Teenage Pregnancy in Industrialised Countries*, London: Yale University Press.

Jones, M.C. (1965) 'Psychological correlates of somatic development', *Child Development* 36: 899–911.

Jones, W., Chernovetz, M. and Hansson, R. (1978) 'The enigma of androgyny: Differential implications for males and females?', *Journal of Consulting and Clinical Psychology* 46: 298–313.

Kallen, D.J. and Stephenson, J.J. (1982) 'Talking about sex revisited', *Journal of Youth and Adolescence* 11: 11–23.

Kandel, D.B. (1990) 'Parenting styles, drug use, and children's adjustment in families of young adults', *Journal of Marriage and the Family* 52: 183–96.

Kantner, J.F. and Zelnik, M. (1972) 'Sexual experiences of young unmarried women in the United States', *Family Planning Perspective* 4: 9–18.

Kashima, Y., Gallois, C. and McCamish, M. (1992) 'Intention, past behaviour, future behaviour: When does intention to use a condom predict actual use?', unpublished manuscript.

Kasperson, R.E., Renn, O., Slovik, P., Brown, H.S., Emel, J., Goble, R., Kasperson, X. and Ratick, S. (1988) 'The social amplifation of risk: A conceptual framework', *Risk Analysis* 8: 177–87.

Katchadourian, H. (1977) *The Biology of Adolescence*, San Francisco: Jossey-Bass.

—— (1990) 'Sexuality', in S.S. Feldman and G.R. Elliot (eds) *At the Threshold: The Developing Adolescent*, Cambridge, MA: Harvard University Press.

Kegeles, S., Adler, N. and Irwin, C. (1988) 'Sexually active adolescents and condoms: Knowledge, attitudes and changes over one year', *American Journal of Public Health* 78: 260–1.

Keller, S.E., Schleifer, S.J., Bartlett, J.A. and Johnson, R.L. (1988) 'The sexual behaviour of adolescents and risk of AIDS', *JAMA* 260: 3586.

Kellogg, T.A., Wilson, M.J., Lemp, G.F., Hernande, S.R., Reardon, J., Ruizz, J., Elcock, M., Bolan, G. and Obata, B. (1991) 'Prevalence of HIV-1 among homosexual and bisexual men in the San Francisco Bay Area: Evidence of infection among young gay men', paper given at the Seventh International Conference on AIDS, Florence, Italy, June.

Kenney, A., Guardada, S. and Brown, L. (1989) 'Sex education and AIDS education in the schools', *Family Planning Perspectives* 21: 56–64.

Kessler, J. (1966) *Psychopathology of Childhood*, Englewood Cliffs, NJ: Prentice-Hall.

Khoo, S. (1985) *Family Formation and Ethnicity: Working paper no. 9*, Melbourne: Australian Institute of Family Studies.

Kinder, P. and Rampton, L. (1992) *Finding Out: A Resource Guide for People Working with Young Gay and Bisexual Men*, Auckland: The New Zealand AIDS Foundation.

King, A.J.C., Beazley, R.P., Warren, W.K., Hankins, C.A., Robertson, A.S. and Radford, J.L. (1989) 'Highlights from the Canada youth and AIDS study', *Journal of School and Health* 59: 139–45.

Kinsey, A.C., Pomeroy, W.B. and Martin, C.E. (1948) *Sexual Behavior in the Human Male*, Philadelphia: Saunders.

Kinsey, A.C. and Gebhard, P.H. (1953) *Sexual Behavior in the Human Female*, Philadelphia: Saunders.

Kippax, S. and Crawford, J. (1991) 'Heterosexuals and HIV transmission: Where do we go from here?', *National AIDS Bulletin* July: 14–18.

Kirby, D. (1992) 'School-based prevention programmes: Design, evaluation, and effectiveness', in R.J. DiClemente (ed.) *Adolescents and AIDS: A Generation in Jeopardy*, Newbury Park, CA: Sage.

Kirby, D., Ziegler, J. and Rivelis, S. (1988) 'The utilization of school based clinics and their impact upon the receipt of health care', Paper given at the American Public Health Association meetings, Boston, November.

Klein, F., Sepekoff, B. and Wolf, T.J. (1985) 'Sexual orientation: A multi-variable dynamic process', *Journal of Homosexuality* 11: 35–49.

Klingman, L. and Vicary, J.R. (1992) 'Risk factors associated with date rape and sexual assault of adolescent girls', Poster presentation, Society for Research on Adolescence, Pennsylvania State University, March.

Klitsch, M. (1990) 'Teenagers' condom use affected by peer factors, not health concerns', *Family Planning Perspectives* 22: 95.

Koedt, A. (1973) 'Myth of the vaginal orgasm', in E. Levine, A. Rapone and A. Koedt (eds) *Radical Feminism: Notes from the Second Year*, New York: Quadrangle.

Lakoff, R. (1973) 'Language and woman's place', *Language in Society* 2: 45–80.

Lamb, M.E. (1976) *The Role of the Father in Child Development*, New York: Wiley.

Lapsley, D.K., Enright, R.D. and Serlin, R.C. (1985) 'Toward a theoretical perspective on the legislation of adolescence', *Journal of Early Adolescence* 5: 441–6.

Lapsley, D.K. and Murphy, M.N. (1985) 'Another of the theoretical assumptions of adolescent egocentrism', *Developmental Review* 5: 201–17.

Lapsley, D.K. and Rice, K.G. (1988) 'History, puberty, and the textbook consensus on adolescent development', *Contemporary Psychology* 33: 210–13.

Leary, M.R. and Snell, W.E. Jr. (1988) 'The relationship of instrumentality and expressiveness to sexual behavior in males and females', *Sex Roles* 18: 509–22.

Lee, J.A. (1977) 'Going public: A study in the sociology of homosexual liberation', *Journal of Homosexuality* 3: 49–58.

Lees, S. (1986) *Losing Out: Sexuality and Adolescent Girls*, London: Hutchinson Education.

—— (1989) 'Learning to love: Sexual reputation, morality and the social control of girls', in M. Cain (ed.) *Growing Up Good: Policing the Behaviour of Girls in Europe*, London: Sage.

Leigh, B.C. (1989) 'Reasons for having sex: Gender, sexual orientation, and relationship to sexual behavior', *Journal of Sex Research* 26: 199–209.

Leonard, D. (1980) *Sex and Generation: A Study of Courtship and Weddings*, London: Tavistock.

Lerner, R.M., Orlos, J.B. and Knapp, J.R. (1976) 'Physical attractiveness, physical effectiveness, and self-concept in late adolescence', *Adolescence* 11: 313–26.

Lerner, R.M. and Spanier, G.B. (1980) *Adolescent Development: A Life-span Perspective*, New York: McGraw Hill.

Lette, K. and Carey, G. (1979) *Puberty Blues*, Melbourne: McPhee Gribble.

Le Vay, S. (1991) 'A difference in hypothalamic structure between heterosexual and homosexual men', *Science* 253: 1034–7.

Levine, E. and Kanin, E. (1987) 'Sexual violence among dates: Trends and implications', *Journal of Family Violence* 2: 55–65.

Lewin, M. and Tragoso, L.M. (1987) 'Has the feminist movement influenced adolescent sex role attitudes? A reassessment after a quarter century', *Sex Roles* 16: 125–35.

Lewis, C.E. and Lewis, M.A. (1984) 'Peer pressure and risk-taking behaviors in children', *American Journal of Public Health* 74: 580–4.

Lewis, D.O., Shanok, S.S. and Pincus, J.H. (1981) 'Juvenile male sexual assaulters: Psychiatric, neurological, psychoeducational, and abuse factors', in D.O. Lewis (ed.) *Vulnerabilities to Delinquency*, Jamaica, NY: Spectrum.

Libby, R.W. (1976) 'Social scripts for sexual relationships', in S. Gordon and R.W. Libby (eds) *Sexuality Today and Tomorrow*, North Scitiate, MA: Duxbury Press.

Libby, R.W. and Carlson, J.E. (1973) 'A theoretical framework for premarital sexual decisions in the dyad', *Archives of Sexual Behavior* 2: 365–78.

Liestol, K. (1982) 'Social conditions and menarcheal age: The importance of the early years of life', *Annals of Human Biology* 9: 521–36.

Littlejohn, P. (1992) 'Teenage pregnancy and adolescent motherhood in Australia', Research in progress.

Locander, W., Sudman, S. and Bradburn, N. (1976) 'An investigation of interview method, threat and response distortion', *Journal of the American Statistical Association* 71: 269–75.

Luckey, E. and Nass, G.A. (1969) 'A comparison of sexual attitudes and behavior in an international sample', *Journal of Marriage and the Family* 31: 364–79.

Luker, K. (1975) *Taking Chances: Abortion and the Decision Not to Contracept*, Berkeley: University of California.

McCabe, M.P. (1984) 'Toward a theory of adolescent dating', *Adolescence* 14: 159–70.

—— (1989) 'The contribution of sexual attitudes and experiences during childhood and adolescence to adult sexual dysfunction', *Sexual and Marital Therapy* 4: 133–41.

McCabe, M.P. and Collins, J.K. (1979) 'Sex role and dating orientation', *Journal of Youth and Adolescence* 8: 407–25.

—— (1989) 'Dating desires and experiences: A new approach to an old question', *Australian Journal of Sex, Marriage and the Family* 2: 165–73.

—— (1990) *Dating, Relating and Sex*, Sydney: Horowitz Grahame.

McCamish, M., Buckham, C., O'Dell, B. and Regan, L. (1988) Letter to the Editor of *Medical Journal of Australia* 149.

McCandless, B.R. (1970) *Adolescents: Behavior and Development*, Hinsdale, IL: Dryden Press.

Maccoby, E.E. (1990) 'Gender and relationships: A developmental account', *American Psychologist* 45: 515–520.

Maccoby, E.E. and Jacklin, C.N. (1974) *The Psychology of Sex Differences*, Stanford, CA: Stanford University Press.

McCord, I., McCord, W. and Verden, P. (1962) 'Family relationships and sexual deviance in lower class adolescents', *International Journal of Social Psychiatry* 8: 165–79.

MacDonald, A. Jr. (1981) 'Bisexuality: Some comments on research and theory', *Journal of Homosexuality* 6: 21–35.

McDonald, P. (1991) 'The shift away from marriage among young Australians', *Family Matters* 50: December.

Mackay, T.F., Hacker, S.S. and Weissfeld, L.A. (1991) 'Comparative effects of sexual assault on sexual functioning of child sexual abuse survivors and others', *Issues in Mental Health Nursing* 12: 89–112.

MacKenzie, J., Goggin, M. and Rosemeyer, D. (1992) *When You Say Yes Report. Safe Sex Campaign Evaluation of the Victorian AIDS Council Youth Programme*, Melbourne: Victorian AIDS Council.

McLaughlin, S.D., Manninen, D.L. and Winges, L.D. (1988) 'Do adolescents who relinquish their children fare better or worse than those who raise them?', *Family Planning Perspectives* 20: 25–32.

McRobbie, A. (1982) '"Jackie", an ideology of adolescent femininity', in B. Waites, T. Bennett and G. Martin (eds) *Popular Culture: Past and Present*, London: Croom Helm.

—— (1991) *From Jackie to Just Seventeen*, London: Macmillan.

Marcia, J. (1966) 'Development and validation of ego-identity status', *Journal of Personality and Social Psychology* 3: 551–8.

—— (1976) 'Identity six years after: A follow-up study', *Journal of Youth and Adolescence* 5: 145–60.

Marmor, J. (ed.) (1980) *Homosexual Behaviour*, New York: Basic Books.

Marshall, D.S. and Suggs, R.C. (eds) (1971) *Human Sexual Behavior: Variations in the Ethnographic Spectrum*, New York: Basic Books.

Marshall, W.A. and Tanner, J.M. (1969) 'Variations in the pattern of pubertal changes in girls', *Archives of Diseases in Childhood* 44: 291–303.

—— (1970) 'Variations in the pattern of pubertal changes in boys', *Archives of Diseases in Childhood* 45: 13–23.

Martin, D. and Lyon, P. (1972) *Lesbian Woman*, San Francisco: Glide.

Masters, W.H. and Johnson, V.E. (1966) *Human Sexual Response*, Boston: Little, Brown & Co.

—— (1979) *Homosexuality in Perspective*, Boston: Little, Brown & Co.

Mead, M. (1939) *From the South Seas: Studies of Adolescence and Sex in Primitive Societies*, New York: William Morrow & Sons.

—— (1950) *Coming of Age in Samoa*, New York: New American Library.

Meikle, S., Peitchinis, J.A. and Pearce, K. (1985) *Teenage Sexuality*, London: Taylor & Francis.

Meiselman, K. (1978) *Incest: A Psychological Study of Causes and Effects with Treatment Recommendations*, San Francisco: Jossey-Bass.

Metzler, C.W., Noell, J. and Biglan, A. (1992) 'The validation of a construct of high-risk sexual behaviour in heterosexual adolescents', *Journal of Adolescent Research* 7: 233–49.

Meyer-Bahlburg, H. (1977) 'Sex hormones and male sexuality in comparative perspective', *Archives of Sexual Behaviour* 6: 297–325.

Mezey, G. and King, M. (1989) 'The effect of sexual assault on men: A survey of 22 victims', *Psychological Medicine* 19: 205–9.

Michael, R.T., Laumann, E.O., Gagnon, J.H. and Smith, T.W. (1988) 'Number of sex partners and potential risk of sexual exposure to human immunodeficiency virus', *MMWR* 37: 566–8.

Miller, B.C., McCoy, J.K. and Olsen, T.D. (1986) 'Dating age and stage as correlates of adolescent sexual attitudes and behaviour', *Journal of Adolescent Research* 1: 361–71.

Miller, D. (1976) 'What do high school students think of their schools?' *Phi Delta Kappa* 57: 700–2.

Miller, P.Y. and Simon, W. (1980) 'The development of sexuality in adolescence', in J. Adelson (ed.) *Handbook of Adolescent Psychology*, New York: Wiley.

Millett, K. (1972) *Sexual Politics*, London: Abacus.

Milligan, D. (1975) 'Homosexuality: Sexual needs and social problems', in R. Bailey and M. Brake (eds) *Radical Social Work*, New York: Pantheon Books.

Miner, H. (1956) 'Body ritual among the Nacirema', *American Anthropological Journal* 58: 352–69.

Minichiello, V. (1992) 'Gay men discuss social issues and concerns', in E. Timewell, V. Minichiello and D. Plummer (eds) *AIDS in Australia*, Sydney: Prentice-Hall.

Minuchin, P., Rosman, B. and Baker, L. (1978) *Psychosomatic Families: Anorexia Nervosa in Context*, Cambridge, MA: Harvard University Press.

Moir, A. and Jessel, D. (1989) *Brainsex: The Real Difference Between Men and Women*, London: Mandarin.

Money, J. (1968) *Sex Errors of the Body: Dilemmas, Education, Counselling*, Baltimore: John Hopkins University Press.

—— (1988) *Gay, Straight, and In-Between*, New York: Oxford University Press.

Money, J. and Ehrhardt, A.A. (1972) *Man and Woman: Boy and Girl*, Baltimore: John Hopkins University Press.

Money, J., Hamson, J.G. and Hamson, J.L. (1955) 'An examination of some basic sexual concepts: The evidence of human hermaphroditism', *Bulletins of John Hopkins Hospital* 97: 301–19.

Money, J. and Tucker, P. (1975) *Sexual Signatures*, Boston: Little, Brown & Co.

Moore, K.A. and Caldwell, S. (1977) 'The effect of government policies on out-of-wedlock sex and pregnancy', *Family Planning Perspectives* 9: 164–9.

Moore, K., Peterson, J. and Furstenberg, F. Jr. (1986) 'Parental attitudes and the occurrence of early sexual activity', *Journal of Marriage and the Family* 48: 777–82.

Moore, S.M. and Boldero, J. (1991) 'Psychosocial development and friendship functions in young Australian adults', *Sex Roles* 25: 521–36.

Moore, S.M. and Rosenthal, D.A. (1980) 'Sex roles: Gender, generation and self-esteem', *Australian Psychologist* 15: 467–77.

—— (1991a) 'Adolescent invulnerability and perceptions of AIDS risk', *Journal of Adolescent Research* 6: 164–80.

—— (1991b) 'Condoms and coitus: Adolescents' attitudes to AIDS and safe sex behaviour', *Journal of Adolescence* 14: 211–27.

—— (1991c) 'Adolescents' perceptions of friends' and parents' attitudes to sex and sexual risk-taking', *Journal of Community and Applied Social Psychology*, 1: 189–200.

—— (1992a) 'Australian adolescents' perceptions of five health related risks', *Journal of Adolescent Research* 7: 177–91.

—— (1992b) 'The social context of adolescent sexuality: Safe sex implications', *Journal of Adolescence*, 15: 415–35.

Moore, S.M., Rosenthal, D.A. and Buzwell, S. (1991) 'Adolescent sexuality, social context and AIDS', Report of 1991 research activities and findings. Report to Commonwealth AIDS Research Grants Committee.

Morrison, D. (1985) 'Adolescent contraceptive behaviour: A review', *Psychological Bulletin* 98: 538–68.

Moscicki, B., Millstein, S.G., Broering, J. and Irwin, C.E. (1988) *Psychosocial and Behavioral Risk Factors for AIDS in Adolescence*, Interim report submitted to University of California Taskforce on AIDS, San Francisco.

Murphy, S.M., Amick-McMullan, A. and Kilpatrick, D. (1988) 'Rape victims' self esteem: A longitudinal analysis', *Journal of Interpersonal Violence* 3: 355–70.

Mussen, P.H. and Jones, M.C. (1957) 'Self-concepts, motivations, and interpersonal attitudes of late and early maturing boys', *Child Development* 28: 243–56.

National Centre in HIV Epidemiology and Clinical Research (1992) 'Australian HIV surveillance report', University of New South Wales, Australia.

Nesselroade, J.R. and Baltes, P.B. (1974) 'Adolescent personality development and historical change: 1970–1972', *Monographs of the Society for Research in Child Development* 39: 1–80.

Newcomer, S.F., Gilbert, M. and Udry, J.R. (1980) 'Perceived and actual same sex behavior as determinants of adolescent sexual behavior', paper given at the Annual Meeting of the American Psychological Association.

Newcomer, S.F. and Udry, J.R. (1983) 'Adolescent sexual behavior and popularity', *Adolescence* 18: 515–22.

—— (1983) 'Parental marital status effects on adolescent sexual behaviour', *Journal of Marriage and the Family* 49: 235–40.

Newman, B.M. and Newman, P.R. (1986) *Adolescent Development*, Columbus, Ohio: Merrill Publishing Company.

Newton-Ruddy, L. and Handelsman, M.M. (1986) 'Jungian feminine psychology and adolescent prostitutes', *Adolescence* 21: 815–25.

Nielsen, L. (1991) *Adolescence: A Contemporary View*, Fort Worth: Holt, Rinehart & Winston.

Nix, L.M., Pasteur, A.B. and Servance, M.A. (1988) 'A focus group study of sexually active black male teenagers', *Adolescence* 23: 741–3.

Nottelmann, E.D., Susman, E.J., Inoff, G.E., Dorn, L.D., Cutler, G.B., Loriaux, D.L. and Chrousos, G.P. (1985) 'Hormone level and adjustment and behavior during early adolescence', paper given at the Annual Meeting of the American Association for the Advancement of Science, Los Angeles, CA.

Nottelmann, E.D., Susman, E.J., Blue, J.H., Inoff-Germain, G., Dorn, L.D., Loriaux, D.L. and Chroussos, G.P. (1987) 'Gonadal and adrenal hormone correlates of adjustment in early adolescence', in R.M. Lerner and T.T. Foch (eds) *Biological-Psychological Interactions in Early Adolescence*, Hillside, NJ: Erlbaum.

Offer, D., Ostrov, E. and Howard, K.I. (1981) *The Adolescent: A Psychological Self Portrait*, New York: Basic Books.

O'Keefe, N., Brockopp, K. and Chew, E. (1986) 'Teen dating violence', *Social Work* 31: 465–8.

Olson, J. (1980) 'Social and psychological correlates of pregnancy resolution among adolescent women: A review', *American Journal of Orthopsychiatry* 50: 432–45.

Olweus, D. (1986) 'Aggression and hormones: Behavioral relationships with testosterone and adrenaline', in D. Olweus, J. Block and M. Radke-Yarrow (eds) *Development of Antisocial and Prosocial Behavior: Research, Theories and Issues*, San Diego, CA: Academic Press.

Orlofsky, J.L., Marcia, J.E. and Lessor, I.M. (1973) 'Ego identity status and the intimacy versus isolation crisis of young adulthood', *Journal of Personality and Social Psychology* 27: 211–19.

Orr, D.P. and Downes, M.C. (1985) 'Self-concept of adolescent sexual abuse victims', *Journal of Youth and Adolescence* 14: 401–10.

Orr, D.P., Wilbrandt, M.L., Brack, C.J., Rauch, S.P. and Ingersoll, G.M. (1989) 'Reported sexual behaviors and self-esteem among young adolescents', *American Journal of Diseases in Children* 143: 86–90.

Oz, S. and Fine, M. (1988) 'A comparison of childhood backgrounds of teenage mothers and their non-mother peers: A new formulation', *Adolescence* 11: 251–61.

Paikoff, R.C. and Brooks-Gunn, J. (1991) 'Do parent-child relationships change during puberty?' *Psychological Bulletin* 110: 47–66.

Paikoff, R.C., Brooks-Gunn, J. and Warren, M.P. (1991) 'Effect of girls' hormonal status on depressive and aggressive symptoms over the course of one year', *Journal of Youth and Adolescence* 20: 191–215.

Parke, R.D. and Neville, B. (1987) 'Teenage fatherhood', in S.L. Hofferth and C.D. Hayes (eds) *Risking the Future: Adolescent Sexuality, Pregnancy, and Childbearing* 2: 145–73, Washington, D.C: National Academy Press.

Parlee, M.B. (1979) 'Conversational politics', *Psychology Today* May: 48–56.

Payne, K. (ed.) (1983) *Between Ourselves: Letters between Mothers and Daughters 1750–1982*, Boston: Houghton Mifflin.

Peskin, H. (1967) 'Pubertal onset and ego functioning', *Journal of Abnormal Psychology* 72: 1–15.

—— (1973) 'Influence of the developmental schedule of puberty on learning and ego development', *Journal of Youth and Adolescence* 2: 273–90.

Petersen, A.C. and Taylor, B. (1980) 'The biological approach to adolescence: Biological change and psychological adaptation', in J. Adelson (ed.) *Handbook of Adolescent Psychology*, New York: Wiley & Sons Inc.

Peterson, C. (1989) *Looking Forward Through The Life Span*, New York: Prentice-Hall.

Phoenix, A. (1991) *Young Mothers?*, Cambridge: Polity Press.

Pleck, J., Sonenstein, F. and Ku, L. (1991) 'Adolescent males' condom use:

Relationship between perceived cost-benefits and consistency', *Journal of Marriage and the Family* 53: 733–46.

Polit, D.F., White, C.M. and Morton, T.D. (1990) 'Child sexual abuse and premarital intercourse among high-risk adolescents', *Journal of Adolescent Health Care* 11: 231–4.

Ponse, B. (1978) *Identities in the Lesbian World: The Social Construction of Self*, Westport, CT: Greenwood Press.

Presser, H.B. (1974) 'Early motherhood: Ignorance or bliss?', *Family Planning Perspectives* 6: 8–14.

Pumariega, A.J. (1986) 'Acculturation and eating attitudes in adolescent girls', *Journal of the American Academy of Child Psychiatry* 25: 276–9.

Puterbaugh, G. (ed.) (1990) *Twins and Homosexuality: A Casebook*, New York: Garland.

Reinhart, R.C. (1982) *A History of Shadows*, New York: Avon Books.

Reiss, I.L. (1967) *The Social Context of Premarital Sexual Permissiveness*, New York: Holt Rinehart and Winston.

—— (1971) 'How and why American sex standards are changing', in H.D. Thornbury (ed.) *Contemporary Adolescence: Readings*, Belmont: Brooks Cole Publishing Co.

Remafedi, G. (1987) 'Homosexual youth: A challenge to contemporary society', *Journal of American Medical Association* 258: 222–5.

—— (1990) 'Fundamental issues in the care of homosexual youth', *Medical Clinics of North America* 74: 1169–79.

—— (1992) 'Predictors of unprotected anal intercourse in young gay and bisexual adolescents', manuscript under review.

Remafedi, G., Farrow J. and Deisher, R.W. (1991) 'Risk factors for attempted suicide in gay and bisexual adolescents', *Pediatrics* 87: 869–75.

Remafedi, G., Resnick, M., Blum, R. and Harris, L. (1992) 'Demography of sexual orientation in adolescents', *Pediatrics* 89: 714–21.

Resnick, M. (1984) *Adoption Decision-Making Project*, Washington, D.C: Office of Adolescent Pregnancy Prevention, US Department of Health and Human Services.

Richard, R. and van der Pligt, J. (1991) 'Factors affecting condom use among adolescents', *Journal of Community and Applied Social Psychology* 1: 105–16.

Richmond, J. (1979) 'Statement of the Surgeon General of the US and Assistant Secretary for Health. Adolescent and pre-adolescent pregnancy hearings before the select committee on population', *95th Congress, Second Session* U.S. Government Printing Office: 148–58.

Roberts, G. (1992) 'Rape OK if led on, say third of boys', *The Age*, Melbourne: 5 September, p. 6.

Robertson, G. (1972) 'Parents and child relationships and homosexuality', *British Journal of Psychiatry* 121: 525–8.

Roche, J.P. (1986) 'Premarital sex: Attitudes and behaviour by dating stage', *Adolescence* 21: 106–21.

Rodgers, J.L. and Rowe, D.C. (1990) 'Adolescent sexual activity and mildly deviant behaviour: Sibling and friendship effects', *Journal of Family Issues* 11: 274–93.

Rodgers, J. (1982) 'The rescission of behaviors: Inconsistent responses in adolescent sexuality data', *Social Science Research* 11: 280–96.

Rogers, D. (1981) *Adolescents and Youth*, New Jersey: Prentice-Hall.

Rollins, B. (1989) *Sexual Attitudes and Behaviours: A Review of the Literature*, Melbourne: Australian Institute of Family Studies.

Romer, D. and Hornik, R.C. (1992) 'Using mass media for prevention of HIV infection among adolescents', in R.J. DiClemente (ed.) *Adolescents and AIDS: A Generation in Jeopardy*, Newbury Park, CA: Sage.

Rosenthal, D.A., Hall, C. and Moore, S.M. (1992b) 'AIDS, adolescents, and sexual risk-taking: A test of the Health Belief Model', *Australian Psychologist* 27: 166–71.

Rosenthal, D.A. and Moore, S.M. (1991) 'Risky business: Adolescents and HIV/AIDS', *The Bulletin for the National Clearinghouse of Youth Studies* 10: 20–5.

Rosenthal, D.A., Moore, S.M. and Brumen, I. (1990) 'Ethnic group differences in adolescents' responses to AIDS', *Australian Journal of Social Issues* 25: 220–39.

Rosenthal, D.A., Moore, S.M. and Buzwell, S. (1992a) 'Homeless youths: Sexual and drug related behaviours, sexual beliefs, and HIV/AIDS risk', Manuscript under review.

Rosenthal, D.A., Moore, S.M. and Flynn, I. (1991) 'Adolescent self-efficacy, self-esteem and sexual risk-taking', *Journal of Community and Applied Social Psychology* 1: 77–88.

Rosenthal, D.A. and Shepherd, H. (1993) 'A six-month follow-up of adolescents' sexual risk-taking, HIV/AIDS knowledge, and attitudes to condoms, *Journal of Community and Applied Social Psychology*, in press.

Rosenthal, R. and Rosnow, R. (1969) 'The volunteer subject', in R. Rosenthal and R. Rosnow (eds) *Artifact in Behavioral Research*, San Diego, CA: Academic Press.

Ross, H. and Sawhill, I. (1975) *Time of Transition: The Growth of Families Headed by Women*, Washington, D.C: Urban Institute.

Ross, M.W. (1989) 'Gay youth in four cultures: A comparative study', in G. Herdt (ed.) *Gay and Lesbian Youth*, New York: Haworth Press.

Ross, M.W. and Arrindell, W. (1988) 'Perceived parental rearing patterns of homosexual and heterosexual men', *Journal of Sex Research* 24: 275–81.

Ruble, D. and Brooks-Gunn, J. (1982) 'The experience of menarche', *Child Development* 53: 1557–66.

Runtz, M. and Briere, J. (1986) 'Adolescent acting out and childhood history of sexual abuse', *Journal of Interpersonal Violence* 1: 326–34.

Russell, G. (1978) 'The father role and its relation to masculinity, femininity, and androgyny', *Child Development* 49: 1174–81.

Russell, D.E.H. (1982) *Rape in Marriage*, New York: Macmillan.

Rust, J.O. and Lloyd, M.W. (1982) 'Sex role attitudes and preferences of junior high school age adolescents', *Adolescence* 17: 37–43.

Sachs, J., Smith, R. and Chant, D. (1991) 'How adolescents see the media', *Bulletin of the National Clearinghouse for Youth Studies* 10: 16–20.

Saghir, M.T. and Robins, E. (1973) *Male and Female Homosexuality: A Comprehensive Investigation*, Baltimore: Williams & Wilkins.

Salinger, J.D. (1951) *The Catcher in the Rye*, London: Hamish Hamilton.

Saltzman, S., Stoddard, A., McCusker, J., Moon, M. and Mayer, K. (1987) 'Reliability of self-reported sexual behaviour risk factors for HIV infection in homosexual men', *Public Health Reports* 102: 692–7.

Santrock, J.W. (1990) *Adolescence*, Dubuque, IA: William C. Brown Publishers.

Savin-Williams, R.C. and Weisfield, G.E. (1989) 'An ethological perspective on adolescence', in G.R. Adams, R. Montemayor and T.P. Gullotta (eds) *Biology of Adolescent Behavior and Development*, Newbury Park, CA: Sage.

Schafer, K. (1976) 'Sexual and social problems among lesbians', *The Journal of Sex Research* 12: 50–69.

Schofield, M. (1968) *The Sexual Behaviour of Young People*, Harmondsworth: Penguin.

Schonfeld, W.A. (1969) 'The body and the body image in adolescents', in G. Caplan and S. Lebovici (eds) *Adolescence: Psychosocial perspectives*, New York: Basic Books.

Scottish Health Education Group (1990) *Promoting Good Health*, Edinburgh: Scottish Health Education Group.

Selverstone, R. (1989) 'Adolescent sexuality: Developing self-esteem and mastering developmental tasks', *SIECUS Report* 18: 1–3.

Shainess, N. (1961) 'A re-evaluation of some aspects of femininity through a study of menstruation: A preliminary report', *Comprehensive Psychiatry* 2: 20–6.

Sharpe, S. (1987) *Falling for Love: Teenage Mothers Talk*, London: Virago Press.

Shipman, G. (1968) 'The psychodynamics of sex education', *The Family Co-ordinator* 17: 3–12.

—— (1971) 'The psychodynamics of sex education', in R.E. Muuss (ed.) *Adolescent Behavior and Society*, New York: Random House.

Shively, M.G. and De Cecco, J.P. (1977) 'Components of sexual identity', *Journal of Homosexuality* 3: 41–8.

Siedlecky, S. (1984) 'Defusing a new teenage baby boom', *Education News* 18: 20–3.

—— (1985) 'Trends in teenage births – dispelling some myths', *New Doctor* 38: 14–19.

Silbereisen, R.K., Eyferth, K. and Rudinger, G. (eds) (1987) *Development as Action in Context: Problem Behaviour and Normal Youth Development*, New York: Springer-Verlag.

Silbereisen, R.K. and Noack, P. (1988) 'On the constructive role of problem behaviour in adolescence/childhood', in N. Bolger, A. Caspi, G. Downey and M. Moorehouse (eds) *Person and Context: Developmental process*, Cambridge: Cambridge University Press.

Silbert, M. and Pines, A. (1981) 'Sexual abuse as an antecedent to prostitution', *Child Abuse and Negligence* 5: 407–11.

Simmons, R.G. and Blyth, D.A. (1987) *Moving into Adolescence: The Impact of Pubertal Change and School Context*, New York: Adline De Gruyter.

Simmons, R.G., Blyth, D.A., and McKinney, K.L. (1983) 'The social and psychological effects of puberty on white females', in J. Brooks-Gunn and A.C. Petersen (eds) *Girls at Puberty*, New York: Plenum.

Simms, M. and Smith, C. (1986) *Teenage Mothers and Their Partners*, London: HMSO.

Slattery, M. (1991) 'Adolescents' knowledge and understanding of AIDS related concepts', paper given at the International Conference on Health Education, Helsinki.

Smith, D. and Over, R. (1987) 'Correlates of fantasy-induced and film-induced male sexual arousal', *Archives of Sexual Behavior* 16: 395–409.

—— (1988) 'Relationship between male sexual arousal and vividness of imagery in different sensory modalities', *Australian Journal of Psychology* 40: 303–10.

Smith, E. (1989) 'A biosocial model of adolescent sexual behavior', in G.R. Adams, R. Montemayor and T.P. Gullotta (eds) *Biology of Adolescent Behavior and Development*, Newbury Park, CA: Sage.

Smith, E.A., Udry, J.R. and Morris, N.M. (1985) 'Pubertal development and friends: A biosocial explanation of adolescent sexual behavior', *Journal of Health and Social Behavior* 26: 183–92.

Sonenstein, F., Pleck, J. and Ku, L. (1989) 'Sexual activity, condom use and AIDS awareness among adolescent males', *Family Planning Perspectives* 21: 152–8.

Sorensen, R.E. (1973) *Adolescent Sexuality in Contemporary America*, USA: World.

Spanier, G.B. (1976) 'Formal and informal sex education as determinants of premarital sexual behavior', *Archives of Sexual Behavior* 5: 39–67.

Spence, J. and Helmreich, R. (1979) 'Comparison of masculine and feminine personality attributes and sex-role attitudes across age groups', *Developmental Psychology* 15: 583–4.

Spitzer, R.L. (1981) 'The diagnostic status of homosexuality in DSM III: A reformulation of the issues', *American Journal of Psychiatry* 138: 210–15.

Sprecher, S. (1989) 'Expected impact of sex-related events on dating relationships', *Journal of Psychology and Human Sexuality* 2: 77–92.

Steinberg, L. (1985) *Adolescence*, New York: Knopf.

Strobino, D.M. (1987) 'The health and medical consequences of adolescent sexuality and pregnancy: A review of the literature', in S.L. Hofferth and C.D. Hayes (eds) *Risking the Future: Adolescent Sexuality, Pregnancy, and Childbearing* 2: 93–122, Washington, DC: National Academy Press.

Strunin, L. and Hingson, R. (1987) 'Acquired immunodeficiency syndrome and adolescents: Knowledge, beliefs, attitudes and behaviours', *Pediatrics* 79: 825–32.

Summers, A. (1975) *Damned Whores and God's Police*, Sydney: Penguin.

Susman, E.J., Nottelmann, E.D., Inoff-Germain, G.E., Dorn, L.D., Cutler, G.B., Loriaux, D.L. and Chrousos, G.P. (1985) 'The relation of relative hormone levels and physical development and socio-emotional behavior in young adolescents', *Journal of Youth and Adolescents* 14: 245–64.

Sutton, H. (1944) *Lectures on Preventive Medicine*. Sydney: Consolidated Press.

Szirom, T. (1988) *Teaching Gender?: Sex Education and Sexual Stereotypes*, Sydney: Allen & Unwin.

Tannen, D. (1990) *You Just Don't Understand: Women and Men in Conversation*, Australia: Random House.

Tanner, J.M. (1962) *Growth at Adolescence* 2nd edn, Oxford: Blackwell.

—— (1966) 'The secular trend towards earlier physical maturation', *Trans. Soc. Geneeskd* 44: 524–38.

—— (1970) 'Physical growth', in P.H. Mussen (ed.) *Carmichael's Manual of Child Psychology* Vol. 1, New York: Wiley.

Thompson, L. and Spanier, G. (1978) 'Influence of parents, peers, and partners on the contraceptive use of college men and women', *Journal of Marriage and the Family* 40: 481–92.

Thornburg, H.D. (1975) 'Adolescent sources of initial sex information', in R.E. Grinder (ed.) *Studies in Adolescence* 3rd edn, London: Collier-Macmillan.

—— (1981) 'The amount of sex information learning obtained during early adolescence', *Journal of Early Adolescence* 1: 171–83.

Thornton, A. (1990) 'The courtship process and adolescent sexuality', *Journal of Family Issues* 11: 239–73.

Thornton, A. and Camburn, D. (1987) 'The influence of the family on premarital sexual attitudes and behavior', *Demography* 24: 323–40.

Tobin-Richards, M.H., Boxer, A.M. and Petersen, A.C. (1983) 'The psychological significance of pubertal change: Sex differences in perceptions of self during early adolescence', in J. Brooks-Gunn and A.C. Petersen (eds) *Girls at Puberty*, New York: Plenum.

Tourney, G. (1980) 'Hormones and homosexuality', in J. Marmor (ed.) *Homosexual Behaviour*, New York: Basic Books.

Townsend, S. (1982) *The Secret Diary of Adrian Mole Aged 13 3/4*, London: Methuen.

Troiden, R.R. (1989) 'The formation of homosexual identities', in G. Herdt (ed.) *Gay and Lesbian Youth*, New York: Haworth Press.

Trussell, J. (1988) 'Teenage pregnancy in the United States', *Family Planning Perspectives* 20: 262–72.

Turtle, A.M., Ford, B., Habgood, R., Grant, M., Bekiaris, J., Constantinou, C., Macek, M. and Polyzoidis, H. (1989) 'AIDS-related beliefs and behaviours of Australian university students', *Medical Journal of Australia* 150: 371–6.

Udry, J.R. (1979) 'Age at first menarche, at first intercourse and at first pregnancy', *Journal of Biosocial Science* 11: 433–41.

—— (1988) 'Biological predispositions and social control in adolescent sexual behavior', *American Sociological Review* 53: 709–22.

Udry, J.R., Billy, J.O.G., Morris, N.M., Groff, T.R. and Raj, M.J. (1985) 'Serum androgenic hormones motivate sexual behavior in adolescent boys', *Fertility and Sterility* 43: 90–4.

Udry, J.R., Talbert, L.M. and Morris, N.M. (1986) 'Biosocial foundations for adolescent female sexuality', *Demography* 23(2): 217–30.

Urberg, K.A. (1982) 'A theoretical framework for studying adolescent contraceptive use', *Adolescence* 17: 527–40.

Valdiserri, R.O., Lyter, L.D., Leviton, C.M., Callahan, C.L., Kingsley, C.L. and Rinaldo, C.R. (1988) 'Variables influencing condom use in a cohort of gay and bisexual men', *American Journal of Public Health* 78: 801–5.

Van Ness, S.R. (1984) 'Rape as instrumental violence: A study of youth offenders', *Journal of Offender Counseling, Services, and Rehabilitation* 9: 161–70.

Van Wyk, P. (1984) 'Psychosocial development of heterosexual, bisexual and homosexual behaviour', *Archives of Sexual Behaviour* 13: 505–44.

Walkerdine, V. (1984) 'Some day my prince will come: young girls and the preparation for adolescent sexuality', in A. McRobbie and M. Nava (eds) *Gender and Generation*, Basingstoke, UK: Macmillan.

Wallis, Y. (1992) *The Victorian Community's Attitudes to Child Sexual Abuse*, Victoria: Protective Services for Children and Young People, Community Services, Victoria.

Walsh, M. and Bibace, R. (1991) 'Children's conceptions of AIDS: A developmental analysis', *Journal of Pediatric Psychology* 16: 273–85.

Warren, C.A.B. (1974) *Identity and Community in the Gay World*, New York: Wiley.

Warshaw, R. (1990) *I Never Called it Rape*, New York: Basic Books.

Warwick, I. and Aggleton, P. (1990) 'Adolescents, young people and AIDS research', in P. Aggleton, P. Davies and G. Hart (eds) *AIDS: Individual, Cultural and Policy Dimensions*, Lewes: Falmer Press.

Waters, L. (1992) 'The nature and development of preadolescents' and adolescents' understanding of HIV/AIDS', unpublished thesis, Department of Psychology, University of Melbourne.

Watney, S. (1992) 'The killing fields of Europe', *National AIDS Bulletin* 6: 27–8.
Weber, F.T., Elfenbein, D.S., Richards, N.L., Davis, A.B. and Thomas, J.T. (1989) 'Early sexual activity of delinquent adolescents', *Journal of Adolescent Health Care* 10: 398–403.
Weeks, J. (1977) *Coming Out: Homosexual Politics in Britain from the Nineteenth Century to the Present*, London: Quartet.
Weideger, P. (1976) *Menstruation and Menopause*, New York: Knopf.
Werner, B. (1988) 'Fertility trends in the UK and in thirteen other developed countries, 1966–86', *Population Trends* 51: 18–24.
Westney, O.E., Jenkins, R.R. and Benjamin, C. (1983) 'Sociosexual development in preadolescents', in J. Brooks-Gunn and J. Peterson (eds) *Girls at Puberty*, New York: Plenum.
Weston, C. (1988) *Girltalk about Guys: Real Questions and Real Answers*, New York: Harper & Row.
Wheeler, L. and Nezlek, L. (1977) 'Sex differences in social participation', *Journal of Personality and Social Psychology* 35: 742–54.
Whitam, F. (1980) 'The prehomosexual male child in three societies: The United States', *Archives of Sexual Behaviour* 9: 87–99.
Whitely, B.E. (1983) 'Sex role orientation and self esteem: a critical meta-analytical review', *Journal of Personality and Social Psychology* 44: 765–78.
Whitley, B.E. Jr. (1988a) 'Masculinity, femininity and self esteem: A multitrait-multimethod analysis', *Sex Roles* 18: 419–31.
—— (1988b) 'The relation of gender-role orientation to sexual experience among college students', *Sex Roles* 19: 619–38.
Wielandt, H., Boldsen, J. and Jeune, B. (1989) 'Age of partners at first intercourse among Danish males and females', *Archives of Sexual Behaviour* 18: 449–54.
Williams, J. and Best, D. (1982) *Measuring Sex Stereotypes: A 30 Nation Study*, Beverley Hills, CA: Sage.
Wilson, P. and Arnold, J. (1986) *Street Kids: Australia's Alienated Young*, Blackburn: Collins Dove.
Wolf, N. (1991) *The Beauty Myth*, London: Vintage.
Wolfe, V.V., Gentile, C. and Wolfe, D. (1989) 'The impact of sexual abuse on children: A PTSD formulation', *Behavior Therapy* 20: 215–28.
Wood, J. (1984) 'Groping towards sexism: boys' sex talk', in A. McRobbie and M. Nava (eds) *Gender and Generation*, Basingstoke, UK: Macmillan.
Worth, D. (1989) 'Sexual decision-making and AIDS: Why condom promotion among vulnerable women is likely to fail', *Studies in Family Planning* 20: 297–307.
Wyn, J. and Stewart, F. (1991) *Young Women and Sexually Transmitted Diseases*, Working Paper no. 7, Melbourne: Youth Research Centre.
Yankelovich, D. (1974) *The New Morality: A Profile of American Youth in the 1970s*, New York: McGraw-Hill.
Zelnik, M. and Kantner, J. (1977) 'Sexual and contraceptive experience of young unmarried women in the United States, 1976, 1971' *Family Planning Perspectives* 9: 55–71.
—— (1980) 'Sexual activity, contraceptive use, and pregnancy among metro-area teenagers', *Family Planning Perspectives* 12: 30–6.
Zelnik, M., Kantner, J. and Ford, K. (1981) *Sex and Pregnancy in Adolescence*, Beverly Hills, CA: Sage.
Zelnik, M. and Shah, K.F. (1983) 'First intercourse among young Americans', *Family Planning Perspectives* 15: 64–70.

Ziegler, C., Dusek, J. and Carter, D. (1984) 'Self concept and sex-role orientation: An investigation of multidimensional aspects of a personality development in adolescence', *Journal of Early Adolescence* 4: 25–39.

Zilbergeld, B. and Evans, M. (1980) 'The inadequacy of Masters and Johnson', *Psychology Today* August: 29–43.

Zuger, B. (1989) 'Homosexuality in families of boys with early effeminate behavior: An epidemiology study', *Archives of Sexual Behaviour* 18: 155–65.

Name index

Abbott, S. 127, 134
Abrams, D. 126, 129, 130, 142, 143
Adams, G. 32
Adelson, J. 22, 31
Aggleton, P. 126
Ajzen, I. 68, 137–8
Alan Guttmacher Institute 145, 152
Alder, C. 193
Allen, D. 110, 174
Allen, I. 74
Alyson, S. 114
American Psychiatric Association 181, 184
Ames, M. 110
Ames, R. 55
Anderson, D. 118
Antill, J. 36
Archer, J. 26
Archer, S. 31
Arindell, W. 113
Arnold, J. 171, 172–3, 174–5

Bachrach, C. 154
Baizerman, M. 172
Bakan, D. 23
Baltes, P. 200
Bandura, A. 136
Barbeler, V. 109, 116, 121
Bardwick, J. 45, 57
Barlow, D. 113
Barth, R. 157, 164
Bauman, K. 60
Baur, K. 107, 112, 113, 114
Becker, M. 138
Bell, A. 102, 103, 109, 111, 113, 115, 116, 119–20

Belsky, J. 163
Bem, S. 35, 82
Bene, E. 113
Best, D. 82
Bettelheim, B. 10
Bibace, R. 133
Bidwell, R. 102
Bieber, I. 113
Birrell, K. 114
Blaske, D. 176
Blos, P. 28, 29
Blumberg, M. 178
Blyth, D. 55, 57, 82
Boldero, J. 95, 99, 135, 136, 138, 139, 189
Bolton, F. 163
Borhek, M. 114
Boxer, A. 103, 113, 120
Breakwell, G. 130, 136
Briere, J. 183, 184
Brook-Taylor, G. 70
Brooks-Gunn, J. xi, 1, 47, 54, 55, 56, 58, 59, 78, 79
Broverman, I. 35
Brown, J. 103
Brown, M. 170, 171, 172
Brown, N. 66
Browne, A. 182
Brumberg, J. 54
Buchanan, C. 49
Burger, J. 68
Burgess, A. 176
Bury, J. 146–7, 151
Buzwell, S. 135

Caldwell, M. 95

Subject index